ROOTS AND BRANCHES

ROOTS AND BRANCHES

CONTEMPORARY ESSAYS BY WEST COAST WRITERS

COLLECTED
FROM

ZYZZYVA

A QUARTERLY OF WEST COAST WRITERS & ARTISTS

EDITED BY HOWARD JUNKER

MERCURY HOUSE, INCORPORATED
SAN FRANCISCO

To subscribe to *ZYZZYVA,* a quarterly of West Cost writers and artists, send
$20 to: *ZYZZYVA,* 41 Sutter Street, Suite 1400, San Francisco, CA 94104.

Published in the United States by
Mercury House
San Francisco, California

Text designed by Zipporah W. Collins
Printed on acid-free paper
Manufactured in the United States of America

Library of Congress Cataloging-in-Publication Data

Roots and branches : contemporary essays by west coast writers / edited by
Howard Junker.
   p.   cm.
   ISBN 1–56279–014–5 : $10.95
   1. American essays — West Coast (U.S.)   2. West Coast (U.S.) — Intellectual life.   3. West Coast (U.S.) — Social life and customs.   I. Junker,
Howard.
PS569.R66   1991
814'.54080979 — dc20   91–9961
                                                                             CIP

All things have roots and branches.
All affairs have beginnings and ends.
To know what is first and what is last
will lead one near the way.

from the TA HSUEH ("GREAT LEARNING"),
a classic text of Confucianism

PĚN-MÒ

◊

a compound: roots and branches;
the beginning and the end;
the whole story

◇ CONTENTS ◇

◇ DEEDS

Acknowledgments

tracing out of air unseen roots and branches of sense
  I share in thought,
filaments woven and broken where the world might light
  casual certainties of me

  Robert Duncan, "ROOTS AND BRANCHES"

Many thanks to Thomas Christensen, executive editor of Mercury House, for his vision, good faith, and due diligence. To assistant editor Alison Macondray. To publisher William Brinton and his noble associates, Po Bronson, Zipporah Collins, Anne Dickerson, Sharon Smith, Barbara Stevenson, Ellen Towell, Genevieve Anderson, Margaret Muirhead, and Chet Shaw. To all the writers — of fiction, poetry, and nonfiction — who have cast their lot with us. To all their agents and publishers. To my *ZYZZYVA* co-editors, Heather Hendrickson and Adam Beyda. To Blair Fuller and my Board of Directors. To the Friends of *ZYZZYVA*. To the California Arts Council, California Tamarack Foundation, Wallace Alexander Gerbode Foundation, James Irvine Foundation, LEF Foundation, National Endowment for the Arts, Bernard Osher Foundation, San Francisco Foundation, and Zellerbach Family Fund for their sustained support. To *ZYZZYVA*'s loyal and generous advertisers. To Richard Diebenkorn and Gemini G.E.L., who donated the lithograph on the cover, to be sold for the benefit of *ZYZZYVA*. And, of course, most of all, to Rozanne and Madison.

◇ INTRODUCTION ◇

Like a Diebenkorn lithograph, the concept "West Coast" is fragile, neither as monolithic nor as exotic as journalists often pretend. Its bravura surface speaks of surprise and thrill; its sense of structure insists on order and precedent. It is both diffident and defiant. One moment, it glows with familiar, sunny pleasures; the next, it veers toward abstract, complex anguish.

The image changes, depending on where you're at. Back East the West Coast takes shape as a shimmering, far-off, but still reasonably precise, region of the mind. Out Here it disappears, like the air we breathe, invisible except in smoggy L.A. or foggy, summertime San Francisco.

I never feel that Easterners are called on to assert their Coastness, as I am. They are like "whites," who, as Shelby Steele (author of *The Content of Our Character* and professor of English at San Jose State) has observed, "do not have to spend precious time fashioning an identity out of simply being white. They do not have to self-consciously imbue whiteness with an ideology, look to whiteness for some special essence, or divide up into factions and wrestle over what it means to be white."

We West Coasters do have to spend precious time fashioning, imbuing, dividing up, and wrestling. I feel no special affinity with Oregonians, for example, apart from an opposition — to the dominant culture of the East, that dimly perceived Other, that original (and much too formal for my taste) Garden (now irretrievably sullied), from which so many of us are glad to have emigrated.

Escapism, then, is built into the West Coast character. We constantly need to create new selves. (It is no accident that Hollywood is *the Coast.*) We are always troubled about where we came from and where we fit in now. These urgencies constitute both opportunity and threat. Luckily, the power structure in our neighborhood has never seemed terribly powerful; there have always been ways to evade its strictures. So, too, the powerful have never been able to get a lock on all the good things; the West Coast has always offered too much ready access—originally to gold and land and climate and now to fresh food, nature, new beginnings, cultural diversity, the Pacific Rim. . . .

We take it for granted that great possibilities still lie before us, although the obverse is also true: We have reached the end of the road, have exhausted every chance America had to offer. It is no simple irony that that site-of-choice for suicide, the Golden Gate Bridge, is one of our greatest tourist attractions.

Because the West Coast has remained so loosely organized, so unhomogeneous and even unmapped, those emblematic utopias called cults have flourished. A litmag is a cult: tiny (the print run of ZYZZYVA, from whose pages these essays are drawn, is 3,500); of fierce, cosmic significance to its devotees; surprisingly commercial (we have more ads than any other litmag in the country); and yet dedicated to the transcendence of beauty (we run more art images than any other litmag). In the margins of the riches of our region—beyond the pale of (New York) Publishing—we are allowed to live out our dementia and even, in our tiny way, to prosper.

When we started ZYZZYVA, our theory was that none of the West Coast litmags then on the stands were in the same league as the giants of the East. Or the South. Or even the Midwest. And that writers who lived here suffered accordingly, being deprived of access to editors (like ourselves), and being underrepresented, down the line, in terms of contacts and contracts, grants and awards, and even inclusion in anthologies such as this one. Armed with these prideful assumptions, we felt there was a niche: to serve as a flagship journal for West Coast writers only. Our protectionist policy, given our vulnerability to the flood of goods from the East Coast, could, we hoped, be forgiven.

We had no desire to try to define a regional sensibility, and still don't. All we hoped to do—and felt we had to do—was provide a vehicle for the many, various voices. . . . We resolved to publish the full spectrum of writing, both mainstream and experimental, including many genres. This nonsectarian approach, this openness to all beings — the reverse of cultism — is, of course, very West Coast.

Most litmags specialize in "creative writing," the stuff that consumer magazines don't want much of anymore, but that writers continue to produce unrelentingly. We've always included this standard fare, as well as a good measure of nonfiction, because we like the quirkiness of it all, the off-the-wall character of hard, lucid facts set against the ambiguities of difficult poetry, the obvious vulnerability of memoir set against the intricate maskings of fiction. An essay, in our book, is *everything else* that can be used to grapple with the world. As John Gross said in his introduction to *The Oxford Book of Essays,* the great essays share only two qualities, "informality and independence." That's West Coasty enough, isn't it?

In fact, we have cast a wide net: from inscriptions carved in a set of slate panels (about a slave freed in Los Angeles in 1856) to transcriptions of the working sessions of venture capitalists. From the conversations of Armenian grandmothers to the confessions of (several different) dope-fiends. From the nostalgia of a bamboo gardener to the reveries of a Death Valley tourist. From the business plan of the importer of Mao's Little Red Book to a recipe for violet candies from Chez Panisse's pastry chef. From tales of drinking with Brendan Behan to an account of hassles with a hip plumber. From a poet's complaint about no money to an anthropologist's study of jokes about AIDS.

So this volume is a supply of particulars to help refute generalities, clichés, and misconceptions. It is not a coherent argument about the West Coast. It's a random walk, part of a continuing search. Not so much a mixed bag, more a cornucopia. Not a business suit, a coat of many colors.

H.J.

◇ ROOTS ◇

PĚN

◇

root; source; origin;
foundation; a native; a book

◊ WARREN L. D'AZEVEDO ◊

Feathers

One of the finest things in the world is feathers. Sometimes they is so pretty you can't believe they just grew that way out of a bird. You want to look at them all the time. When you put them all together in a fine fan, each one bound with buckskin on a handle with fancy beadwork, you think you are looking at all the sunrises in the world at the same time.

But you got to be careful with feathers. Each one got its own special ways and its own kind of power. Each one belongs to that bird it came from and you can't forget that. You can't play around with feathers like they was nothing. You have to know how to handle them. A man has to know what is best for him and what he can deal with. If he tries to take on too much or go too fast he can get hurt.

Like Eagle. You got to take it easy with eagle feathers. Some guys act like eagle feathers is for anybody. But that ain't right. You got to be ready for them. Even if a guy is a Roadchief it don't mean he should use them. You got to be clear about that. If you been in this Church a long time, the Medicine lets you know about that. Once we had a Roadchief here who got some eagle feathers and wanted to make himself a real Chief fan. He put two of them feathers between his teeth while he was binding them. But he turned them the wrong way and they knocked out his two front teeth. You got to turn them clockwise, but he turned them the other way. He wasn't ready for them. So he put them away until he learns all that. But even then he may not be ready. Not everyone can use them.

◊ *This is one of the narratives collected in the fifties by Warren L. d'Azevedo, now retired professor of anthropology, University of Nevada, Reno. It appeared in* Straight with the Medicines: Narratives of Washoe Followers of the Tipi Way, *copyright © 1985 Warren L. d'Azevedo, published by Heyday Books, Berkeley, California.*

Maybe there was something wrong the way them feathers was got. You can't just go kill an eagle. That kind will work against you. You have to get them in some way that eagle don't mind. Maybe that eagle will drop one sometime, and you can just pick it up. You thank the eagle for that. Sometimes you find one dead. You can take them feathers as long as you pray to the eagle and let him know you didn't have nothing to do with him dying. In the old days some Indians around here knew where eagles made their nest way up on the rocks. Well, if they was careful and knew their business they could go up there and find feathers all around. But if you didn't know how to talk to them eagles maybe you didn't come down from there. I heard there was certain guys in the old days that could go up and catch eagles and pull out a couple of their feathers. But they had to be pretty strong guys with special ways. Maybe they was war guys or some kind of doctors. I never heard of nobody doing that these days.

I don't mess around with eagle feathers. One time somebody gave me a bunch of different kind. There was two big long black ones he said came from some kind of eagle in Mexico. There was some brown ones with sort of red and white edges. And there was some of the yellow and brown kind like the eagles around here. But I didn't want to touch any of them. They was all real shiny and strong looking. I told that guy to take them back, because I didn't know where they come from and they might be from some kind of buzzard or something. He said he didn't know too much about them either. I don't know what he did with them, but I never seen him with any of them in his fans. I don't know why he was trying to give them to me.

I don't like to mess with loon or owl or hawk either. They don't seem right for me. But some guys try them. I like to get all kind of different color feathers from other birds. I use pheasant, sagehen, parrot. Sometimes I get them little hummingbird feathers. I like my fan to have bright colors. I been trying to get some of them peacock feathers, but I never found how to get them yet. Sometimes when I go down to San Francisco I go out to that place they keep all them animals. There is a place there with nothing but birds from all over the world. They got some real pretty ones. Sometimes feathers drop down to the ground and you can reach in and pick them up. But they don't like you to do that around there, and I got run off one time. There was a guy who worked there one time, though, and he used to save the feathers for me when he cleaned the cages. I got a lot from him. But then he stopped working there and I ain't had much luck since.

I tried to get some feathers off of them peacocks they got running around there. But them birds is pretty smart, and you can't get close enough to grab one. I don't think they would even feel it if you pulled out just one. I used to follow them around to see if they ever dropped any. I talked to them a little. But it didn't do no good. I never got any.

Some guys like to use only one kind of feathers in their fans. They say you got to use just one kind in the fan so when you spread it out or point it you can sight along that fan and see clear and fly like that bird them feathers come from. They say if you use too many different kinds the fan is going to look like a bunch of chicken feathers and your mind is going to start running around and clucking like a chicken when you use the fan. Well, that's their way, I guess. That's all right, too. But I got one good fan with all kinds of bright colored feathers and different sizes. When I spread it out or point it I feel like I am pulling all good things in the world together . . . all them fine bright things birds see when they are flying or away in other places. But I'm careful about which feathers I use. I don't just take one just because I found it. I think about them for a while, and I take some Medicine and look at them. Sometimes there's one feather that don't look right. It was pretty when I found it, but when I start looking at it strong it turns some bad way and I don't want to touch it again. Maybe that feather come from some kind of bird I can't deal with, or maybe that bird it come from got some bad idea in it for some reason. You got to be careful about that or you going to have some kind of trouble with your fan. If you don't know what you are doing you are always in danger. But that is why you have to depend on the Medicine. It can show you.

The feathers I like best is magpie. I got one special fan made from just magpie tailfeathers. Everybody sees it and knows it is my own fan and them feathers are for me some way. They are shiny black like the sky when there ain't no moon, and you can see little stars in them. I only use that fan sometimes when I am feeling just right. It took me a long time to get all them feathers. I keep a lookout for them all the time when I'm walking around. Them old Washoe Indians around here say the people liked to use magpie in the old days. Them fighting guys put one feather sticking up out of their hair when they went to war. They was tough guys and that was their way.

Them magpies is tough. Even big birds and animals don't bother them. I seen them chasing dogs and hawks away from their food. They are plenty smart, too. When you ain't trying to hunt them they come around like chickens. But when you are after their feathers, they know it, and you can't get close to them. When I been eating the Medicine they come so close to me sometimes I have to shoo them away. They know I'm not supposed to kill or bother anything when I am with the Medicine.

But one time I was sitting under that tree outside my place. Four big magpies was hopping around close to me and looking at me kind of sly. If I moved they made a racket and flew away a little bit. So I didn't move. I just sat there looking at them and keeping friendly ideas in my head. They come real close acting like they didn't know I was there. Then the biggest one started poking around and cleaning himself like they do. The other ones start doing the same. Then each one pulled out a big tail feather and dropped it right there on the ground. I saw them do that. The feathers just didn't drop off. They was pulled out. Then they made a big racket like they was laughing at me and flew up in the tree. Well, I didn't make one move. I just look up and watch them like I am in no hurry about nothing. They kept making a big racket waiting for me to make my move. But when they saw I wasn't no plain dumb Indian ready to play their game, they flew away after a while. If I look too interested and grab them feathers right away they would still be laughing at me. They are mean guys in some ways, and like to make you look dumb.

But I just sat there quiet for a long time. I took a little Medicine and prayed a little to them feathers. They looked good, the finest ones I ever seen. I sang a song in my head until I felt pretty good. Then I picked up the feathers and spread them out like a fan. I sang a little more and then took them into the house. Them same birds came back later and sat in the tree for a couple of hours. They didn't make no noise . . . just sat there keeping an eye on things. I never saw them four birds again after that day, but it seems like I can find good magpie feathers laying on the ground wherever I go. When someone wants that kind of feather they come to me for them.

Another thing I noticed since that time. Magpies don't make a racket when they come around me. If I come around, they get quiet. Everyone notices that.

◇ BARBARA A. DAVIS ◇

The Shadow Catcher

The summer of 1900, photographer Edward S. Curtis had made a trip to Montana at the invitation of George Bird Grinnell. He went by train to Browning, Montana, not far from the Canadian border, and from there with Grinnell on horseback across a windswept plateau to a high cliff, where the two men sat looking over a great encampment of Blood, Blackfeet, and Algonquin gathering for the annual sun dance. The camp formed an enormous circle, which sometimes took two days to set up and might reach a mile in diameter. Everywhere were men and women on horses, in wagons, hauling babies, puppies, and camp equipment, sometimes by travois, a simple but effective raised sled of lashed poles.

> Neither house nor fence marred the landscape, and the broad, undulating prairie stretching away toward the Little Rockies, miles away to the west, was carpeted with tipis . . . It was at the start of my concerted effort to learn about the plains and to photograph their lives and I was intensely affected.

The sun dance Curtis observed on this trip was the last held for many years; it was outlawed on the grounds of its "barbarous cruelty." Though elements of the dance varied from tribe to tribe, its central feature was sun worship and the formal self-torture of ambitious young braves offering themselves in fulfillment of a vow or in proof of their courage. Curtis described it as "wild, terrifying, and elaborately mystifying."

Curtis returned to Seattle and ten days later left for Arizona to

◇ *Barbara A. Davis lives in Seattle. This excerpt appeared in* Edward S. Curtis, The Life and Times of a Shadow Catcher, © *1985 Barbara A. Davis, published by Chronicle Books, San Francisco.*

◇ *Edward S. Curtis, 1906*

photograph on the Hopi Reservation, an abrupt schedule which suggests impatience to be about his work. But any impression of single-minded interest in Indians is counter-balanced by the publication within weeks of his exotic "Egyptian" and "Desert Queen" pictures and by his columns on composition and lighting for amateur photographers in Seattle's new publication, *The Western Trail.* Although showing that he was abreast of the current arguments surrounding art photography, Curtis's pronouncements were few and reserved:

> Many photographers claim that a photograph cannot be a work of art. However, I do not think that even the most radical of them can deny that a photograph can show artistic handling and feeling. After all, it is the finished product which hangs on our wall and not the implements with which it is made.

◇

The first few years of the twentieth century in America are popularly regarded as a tranquil period, and compared to what lay ahead for the country, it was a good time for most people. But an extraordinary rise of jingoistic ideas belies the lack of open conflict in those years: Americans were under strain and grasping at a sense of order. President Theodore Roosevelt was raising the powerful rallying cry of Americanism, which he summed up as "the union of strong, virile qualities with steadfast devotion to a high ideal." Americanism became the hallmark of "a new type, a new race," hammered out by the stern land from "the best racial characteristics of Europe." In this highly charged atmosphere of altruism and self-interest, every facet of national history was reexamined to lend strength to the new patriotism. Seizing Texas from the Mexicans was eulogized as "an adventure like that of Norse sea-rovers," and the Texans themselves were praised as "warlike, resolute, and enterprising: [having] all the marks of a young and hardy race, flushed with the pride of strength." The Cuban chapter of the Spanish-American War was recast as a brilliant campaign against the weak Spanish infidels.

After close scrutiny, Western expansion was seen as hinging on the "subduing, displacement, and removal [of] the most formidable, savage foes ever encountered by colonists of European stock." The dimensions of this struggle for the North American continent grew in the public mind until Roosevelt's regular references to it as "the most impressive triumph of the English-speaking race" were regarded as fact. Promoting the valor and ferocity of Indians as opponents, and the "new breed of rugged, individualistic Westerners" who subdued them when the French and Spanish could not, glorified the myth of the winning of the West and the "race accomplishment" it signified.

This backhanded admiration of Indians because of their fighting abilities and fierce loyalty to their "primitive" way of life was fed by a fascination with legends of conquest and loss, and with the contrast between civilized and primitive peoples. During the first decade of this century the demand for images and information about Indians seemed insatiable. An intricate white subculture sprang up around the reservations, particularly in the Southwest, the center of activity for American archeologists and ethnologists. One group worked to supplant old ideas with modern ones about hygiene, jobs, and property so that the Indians might become merged in the American whole as quickly as possible; the other group—ethnologists, writers, and artists—worked to compile records of classical Indian cultures before they disintegrated. This decade represented not only the apex of racial explanations of history and social organization but of public curiosity about Native Americans as well.

The final heightening of interest in the West set the stage for Edward Curtis's emergence as a nationally known photographer. The record of his activities in 1903 is sparse, but in July—less than two months after Seattle had welcomed Roosevelt as a war hero and "true Westerner"—Curtis gave his first formal show of Indian photographs. He displayed his prints in the studio gallery and announced them as "the latest images of the Mohave, Zuni, Havasupai, and Apache," presumably from his second trip to the Southwest made the previous year. A *Seattle Times* article published that November provides a glimpse of public reaction to Curtis's images and to Native Americans in general:

> Instead of the painted features, the feathers, the arrows, and the bow, we find him in [the] bluejeans and cowboy hat of semi-civilization. Enshrined though he may be in the weird habits and mysterious rites of his forefathers, the mystery has vanished and the romance has gone in the actuality of the present day.
>
> And so Edward S. Curtis, of Seattle, found him. For the time being, Curtis became an "Indian." He lived "Indian," he talked it, he became "heap white brother." . . . He dug up tribal customs, he unearthed the fantastic costumes of a bygone era. He won confidences, dispelling distrust. He took the present lowness of today and enshrined it in the romance of the past . . . he changed the degenerated Indian of today into the fancy-free king of yesterday that has long since been forgotten in the calendar of time.

Curtis's pictures were clearly intended to evoke the past. Yet evidence abounds that those "weird habits" were still very much a part of Native Americans' lives. Although many Indians wore blue jeans or manufactured dresses, they still dressed in traditional costume for many ceremonial occasions; and on reservations far from population centers, white ways had made few inroads. For many tribes, real assimilation had scarcely begun.

Early ethnologists chose not to study acculturation and preferred to isolate habits and languages believed to be disappearing in order to

◊ *A burial platform — Apsaroke, 1908*

record them in as pure a form as possible for future enlightenment about cultural evolution. For this reason, Curtis photographed Indians not on the streets of Seattle in their obvious poverty and mixture of white and traditional clothing, but on the reservations. His work deemphasized whatever acculturation had taken place, usually by highlighting traditional elements of his subjects' dress or habits. He began asking tribes to reenact famous battles or to conduct portions of ceremonies for the benefit of his camera, and he would sometimes remove white goods or tools from his set-ups, though inconsistently; many of his pictures show a large admixture of white culture. In 1905 photography was not a prominent element in ethnological research; suppressing detail in photographs was not the issue it is today. In photographing the Kwakiutl in British Columbia, the fastidiously correct Franz Boas sometimes used blankets to hide settings and even removed distracting figures from some images by retouching — though he, like Curtis, was inconsistent.

It was not Curtis's occasional editing of white influences that set him apart from other photographers of Indians early in the century, but his romanticism. Even when Curtis photographed tribes whose lives were still aboriginal, where no reconstruction or staging was needed, his work was distinctly idealized, portraying the Indians as living relics, the embodiment of the vanishing frontier. As the country realized it had a "glorious" past in the West, it would come to remember the magnificence through Frederick Remington's cowboys, Owen Wister's Virginian hero, and Curtis's splendid Indians.

A few weeks after the newspaper article that contrasted Curtis's pictures with the "'degenerated' types of today," a reporter for the *Post-Intelligencer* wrote up Curtis's now-famous portrait of Chief Joseph, made when the Nez Percé chief visited Seattle. Then probably the best-known surviving great chief, Joseph had worked for years to gain permission for his people to leave the reservation in northeastern Washington and return to their traditional home on the Wallowa River in northeastern Oregon; he had even traveled to Washington, D.C., to enlist aid for his cause. In Seattle he had the support of two friends of Curtis: the powerful Sam Hill, president of the Northern Pacific Railroad and son-in-law to the "empire builder" himself, James J. Hill; and Edmond Meany, an ambitious University of Washington history professor. Joseph came west over the Cascade Mountains to deliver an evening speech on behalf of his people, and the following day he and his nephew, Red Thunder, went to the Curtis Studio to have their portraits made.

The *Post-Intelligencer* published two accounts of Joseph's visit to Seattle, expressing a typical air of racial contempt. The first piece appeared under the headline "Old Chief Likes City, Meets a Famous Indian Artist, Then Takes a Bath." Joseph was described as looking like a "turkey cock on dress parade," Curtis as a "professional Indian tamer"; Curtis was quoted as saying, "I do not consider that Chief Joseph's head is a good type of the Indian, nor is he the best to be found among the Nez Percés." Whatever Curtis said or thought of his model, the two surviving 1903 portraits of Joseph are moving studies, and Curtis would later select one of them for prominence in publication.

In contrast to the fragmented record of Curtis's activities in the previous few years, his career work in 1904 is well documented and clearly pivotal. At the beginning of the year he hired Adolph Muhr to manage his darkroom. Muhr had worked for Frank A. Rinehart, then one of the most famous photographers of Indians, and arrived with impressive credentials in the darkroom and as a photographer in his own right. As Rinehart's assistant, he had been assigned to photograph the 1898 Trans-Mississippi Omaha Exposition, a major Indian congress with delegates from thirty-six tribes; and Muhr's platinum prints and accompanying descriptions had become well known under Rinehart's name. Although Muhr never took any photographs credited to Curtis, Curtis referred to him with singular deference as "the genius in the darkroom" and turned over all his personal printing to him. Between the aid of his new manager and his wife's family, Curtis was now free of most of his responsibilities in Seattle, and he worked away from home most of each year after 1904.

By this time, Curtis hoped that his Indian photographs of the previous few years could form the basis of a vast work; he planned to photograph all of the Indian tribes who "still retained to a considerable degree their primitive customs and traditions." The most enlightened scholarly opinion expected Native American cultures eventually to be absorbed into white society and entirely disappear. In wanting to catalogue their ceremonies, beliefs, and habits, Curtis was in keeping with the scientific drive of the day and was especially influenced by his experiences with the Harriman Expedition. From the outset, though, Curtis wanted his work to be both scientific and artistic, to provide new data for professional ethnologists and a beautiful record of pictures and descriptions for the general public, so that the Indian could not "by future generations be forgotten, misconstrued, too much idealized or too greatly underestimated." While his overall conception of his efforts was still taking shape, Curtis set out to make his great project and publication a reality.

Early in 1904, Curtis traveled to the East Coast to discuss his work with Frederick Webb Hodge, then a respected figure at the Smithsonian Institution's Bureau of American Ethnology, and also with William Henry Holmes, chief of the Bureau of American Ethnology. On the same trip he had an appointment in New York with Walter Page at Doubleday and Company to discuss the possibility of publishing his photographs. Page at first told him there was no point in even attempting to publish his Indian photographs, saying, "The market's full of 'em. Couldn't give 'em away." But according to a newspaper report, Curtis went ahead and showed him several prints — "a nervy thing to do, but Edward S. Curtis was from Seattle." After seeing his work, Page was said to have been interested in printing some of the images in lots of 5,000. The results of Curtis's trip to Washington and his subsequent field work among the Navajo were reported in the *Seattle Times* on May 22:

> When Mr. Curtis was in Washington, D.C., recently, government scientists who have devoted a lifetime to the study of Indians chanced to mention the great Yabachai dance. It seems this dance is hidden among the most sacred rites of the Navajos. It is a ceremony that lasts nine days, all told. . . . Smithsonian Institution men told Mr. Curtis that pictures of the dance . . . would be priceless from the standpoint of the Indian historian. But they also told him that the government had been working to get the views for twenty years without result, and [had] reached the conclusion that it was beyond the pale of the possible . . . Curtis started for the land of the Navajo. This trip he took with him a moving picture machine, something he had never carried before. To all questions he answered: "I am going to Arizona. I don't know how long I will be gone." And he went to Arizona, and he stayed just long enough to accomplish that which Uncle Sam, with all his power and authority, had tried for two decades to do and failed . . . In addition to individual pictures of the masked dancers and the "fool," Curtis brought back a "moving picture" of the dance itself, . . . something that thrown upon the screen will convey to the onlooker the exact and lifelike picture of a dance that, in its reality, had never been seen by light of day, or had been looked upon by the eyes of a white man.

Years later, the suggestion that a movie camera had been carried in Indian country as early as 1906 was dismissed on the grounds that the process had not then been sufficiently developed, a difficulty of which Curtis was evidently not informed. It is not known how Curtis came to use a motion picture camera at such an early date — only one year after one of the first "story films," *The Great Train Robbery,* had been shown to mystified audiences in New York — but that he did is an indication of his wide-ranging curiosity and eagerness to experiment.

◇ DOLORES HAYDEN ◇
◇ CHRISTOPHER STINEHOUR ◇

Biddy Mason, Time & Place

Forty-four settlers
from Mexico
establish the pueblo
of Los Angeles—
twenty-six have
African ancestors,
1781.

The Plaza Church is dedicated in Los Angeles, now part of the newly independent Mexican nation, 1821

◇ *Dolores Hayden is the author of* Seven American Utopias, The Grand Domestic Revolution, *and* Redesigning the American Dream. *She is a professor of urban planning at UCLA, an architect, and founder of The Power of Place. Her text was carved in slate panels by Christopher Stinehour — these are his graphite rubbings of the panels — and installed as "Biddy Mason, Time & Place," a memorial wall in the Broadway-Spring Center (between Third and Fourth Streets, downtown Los Angeles), designed by Sheila Levrant de Bretteville.*

Eighteen year old Biddy
and her sister Hannah
become the property
of Robert Smith,
a plantation owner
in Logtown, Mississippi,
1836.

The United States
sends Lieutenant Ord
to survey Los Angeles
and he names this street
Calle Primavera
after his sweetheart,
1849.

Smith transports
slaves to California,
a free state, where
Judge Hayes declares
Biddy Mason's family
entitled to freedom
and free forever,
1856.

From ten years' wages
Biddy saves $250
to buy this homestead
Lots 3 and 8, Block 7
of the Ord survey,
a bit out of town, amid
gardens and groves
1866.

Biddy calls a meeting
here in her home
to organize
the Los Angeles
First African Methodist
Episcopal Church
1872.

Biddy nurses the sick,
comforts prisoners,
and pays a grocery
at Fourth and Spring
to feed all the families
made homeless
by seasonal floods,
1880–1890.

Robert & Henry Owens,
Biddy's grandsons,
start a livery stable
here on part of
her homestead when
Los Angeles is booming,
1885.

Spring Street between
Fourth and Seventh
is the financial center
of Los Angeles,
a city of over 50,000,
including 1,258 blacks,
1890.

The Chinese around Monterey Bay

◊ Mustard

The Chinese provided more than just muscle to the fledgling agricultural revolution against wheat. With their wide experience of more intensive farming in a crowded land, the Chinese brought a wider vision to California than did the Yankee farmers. If you had asked a Yankee farmer how many uses he could name for the land and plants in the Pajaro Valley, he might be able to list six; had you asked a Chinese the same question, he would have been able to cite dozens. Without question, raw Chinese labor was extremely valuable to the development of California agriculture, but the gift of vision and inspiration was priceless. It was the Chinese who transformed the mustard weeds which grew wild throughout the Monterey Bay Region into agricultural gold.

The mustard was probably introduced during the Spanish era. One legend has it that the Franciscan friars scattered mustard seeds along the trails which linked the missions so they would be tied together with a network of yellow blossoms in the spring. Whether planted intentionally or by accident, the mustard proved to be an aggressive guest, quickly crowding out the native grasses. By the mid-1850s the region was covered with the plant:

> . . . the most sublime scene I ever saw was one June following a wet winter, and the entire Salinas Valley from the Pacific Ocean to Paso Robles was covered with mustard, some of it reaching ten feet in height. I saw this vast yellow blanket being fanned into ripples by the wind from

◊ *Sandy Lydon lives in Aptos, California. He is currently on leave from the history department of Cabrillo College. These accounts appeared in* Chinese Gold: The Chinese in the Monterey Bay Region, © *1985 Sandy Lydon, published by the Capitola Book Company.*

the foothills . . . The ground was so fertile and the mustard grew so high that it furnished wonderful protection to all kinds of game and animals that came down out of the wooded mountains to make it their home during the summer.

Ranchers and farmers considered mustard a nuisance that crowded cultivated crops and could not be eaten by livestock.

Picturesque to travelers, a nuisance to farmers, the fields of mustard were seen as an opportunity by the Chinese who entered the region in the 1860s. Mustard seed contained an oil highly valued as a seasoning both in Europe and China, and according to a local story, the first Chinese to exploit the value of the wild mustard was "Poison Jim." Jim earned his living by poisoning ground squirrels for San Juan Valley farmers; besides their voracious appetites, ground squirrels were extremely hazardous to horseback riders — a mis-step in a squirrel hole could break a horse's leg. One spring, following a wet winter when the mustard crop threatened to crowd out the entire grain crop in the San Juan Valley, Jim went to each of the farmers in the valley and offered to cut down the mustard in exchange for the mustard seeds. Since mustard is an annual, the seeds were the culprits, and if Jim cut down the plants and removed the seeds, he would break the cycle and the mustard would not reappear in the fields. The farmers eagerly agreed to Jim's offer. Jim then went to San Francisco and contracted several dozen fellow Chinese. Working as a crew, they cut the mustard, spread it out on canvas, and beat it with flails to remove the seeds. Jim was able to sell enough of his mustard seed to a San Francisco broker to pay his workers, but most of the seed was bagged and stored. That same year the mustard crop failed in both Europe and South Africa, and European mustard brokers began to scour the world for mustard seed. Eventually a French mustard buyer heard of Poison Jim's mustard cache near San Juan Bautista and sought him out. After spirited negotiations Jim sold the mustard for an astounding $35,000 in gold.

The story of the mustard-turned-into-gold spread quickly through the Monterey Bay Region, and farmers began to hire Chinese farm laborers to harvest the mustard. In 1865 Dodge and Millard of Moss's Landing employed a crew of twenty Chinese to harvest wild mustard growing nearby. By the 1870s it was not unusual for upwards of 400,000 pounds of mustard seed to be shipped from the Salinas Valley each fall. The Chinese harvesters received from two to three cents per pound for harvesting, flailing, and bagging the seeds. By 1882 wild mustard had become scarce enough to require the *intentional* planting and cultivation of mustard in the Salinas Valley; the plant had made the full evolution from a nuisance weed to a valuable crop:

> The yellow mustard fields of the Salinas Valley are very beautiful . . . It is cultivated mainly by Chinese. During the past nine months of the present year [1882] about 250,000 pounds were shipped from this city [San Francisco] . . . There is a brisk demand for mustard in Eastern [United States] markets.

An opportunity to make money was never lost on David Jacks, a wealthy Monterey landowner, and in 1887 he cultivated mustard on hundreds of acres of his Chualar Ranch under the careful attention of sharecropping Chinese farmers: "Yellow mustard on David Jacks' ranch . . . farmed by the Chinamen, is turning out 25 sacks to the acre."

In the 1890s the Monterey County Assessor often listed mustard seed on his unsecured property tax rolls. Sam Sing, the Salinas merchant, paid taxes on 17 tons of mustard seed in 1890, and in 1894 Charley Mack, the Castroville labor contractor, paid taxes on a healthy 26 tons. The year 1895 appears to be the high-water mark: Sam Sing had 34 tons of mustard on hand, while Sam So Chong had a whopping 68 tons of mustard seed. Chinese continued to grow and harvest mustard into the early twentieth century, but as the Chinese population in the Monterey Bay Region declined, so did the commercial mustard industry. Mustard is no longer commercially harvested in the Monterey Bay Region, but it is often used by farmers between crops as a ground cover because the plant's roots help break up the soil. It is also planted between rows of fruit trees in orchards for the same reason.

Poison Jim became famous in San Juan Bautista for his philanthropy. During a serious drought he bought several wagons of provisions which were distributed to the needy in San Benito County; later in his life he enjoyed treating children at Christmas:

> A prosperous San Juan Mongolian, named Jim Jack, distributed one hundred pounds of candy among the school children of San Juan on Christmas day. [The Hollister newspaper] says he is of quite a benev-

olent nature, and has expended several hundred dollars in charity during the past year.

The people of San Juan Bautista knew him as "Jim Jack," the kind old Chinese who gave candy to children, but few knew that he was also a famous alchemist who had taught an entire region how to turn weeds into gold.

◊ Impact on the Chinese

Articles and books about the anti-Chinese movement in the United States reveal much about the majority community and its politics, but they rarely say much about the Chinese people, the target of those movements. In many studies of the issue, the Chinese are viewed through the eyes of the anti-Chinese protagonists, and these works may, in a subtle way, have encouraged the continued use of stereo-types which originated in the anti-Chinese movement. An accurate picture of the Chinese cannot be gained through the window of the anti-Chinese movement. Anti-Chinese writers described the Chinese as mindless, faceless unskilled laborers who were all either railroad workers or laundrymen; they all smoked opium, gambled, visited prostitutes, and ran away at the slightest threat. Just as anti-Chinese proponents characterized the Chinese as villains, later studies characterized them as helpless victims—a fact not borne out by their responses to harassment.

The Chinese responded to the anti-Chinese movement with their feet. They did not have to take a referendum to determine the most and least comfortable places for them in the Monterey Bay Region during the nineteenth century—they showed their preference by their numbers. Monterey was the most comfortable, Santa Cruz the least, with Watsonville and Salinas varying according to the political tenor of the time. The constant racist pressure toughened the Chinese and taught them how to fight within the legal system. Chinatowns hired their own policemen (Watsonville's Chinatown had a security guard listed in the 1880 manuscript census) and their own attorneys (often the best attorneys in town). They actively pursued justice, as when they took the Portuguese whalers to court for cutting their fishing nets in Monterey. When need required, they called upon the legal and financial resources of the Chinese Six Companies and the Chinese Vice-Consul in San Francisco. (The Six Companies came into the region to investigate the murders of Tim Wong and Lou Sing.) The myth of the Chinese fleeing with their queues flying before the anti-Chinese forces does not fit the Monterey Bay Region. When push came to shove, they dug in and fought legally for rights to which they were entitled.

But the Chinese suffered greatly from legal restrictions against which they had no recourse. Immigration restrictions meant that most Chinese in California (as well as the rest of the United States) were single men who had had to leave their families and had no hope of bringing them to the United States. The family was the primary focus of traditional Chinese culture. The Chinese character for the spoken word "alone" has as one of its two symbols the character for "orphan"; to be alone was to be an orphan, adrift. The overwhelming emphasis on male children and continuation of the family line was also a hedge against old age; Chinese children supported their parents in old age. More, it was a religious necessity; the ancestor worship common to China required that the spirits of the deceased be cared for, fed, and made to feel a part of the living world. The bond between the living and the dead and the seasonal festivals which strengthened it welded the family together. Those single men who came alone to the Golden Mountain might survive in old age without the aid of the family, but their spirits could not possibly be at rest after death without the ministrations of the family.

Trapped by economic realities and immigration restrictions, most of the single Chinese who had not founded families on the Golden Mountain faced a lonely death and an even more lonely existence as hungry ghosts, wandering uncared for and unfed through the spirit world. This relentless urge to die in the security of one's family goes a long way to explain the tenacity with which elderly Chinese men worked to get back to China. Misunderstood by whites, this was taken as evidence that the Chinese were mere transients, sojourners; where Chinese immigrants established families in the Monterey Bay Region, the urge to return to China to die was tempered by the knowledge that one's spirit would be cared for by children and grandchildren already born in America.

But for those who had no families, the Chinese organized Benevolent Associations to provide at least some of the missing familial securities and comforts — caring for the indigent and sick, holding funerals, tending graves, and shipping the bones of the dead back to

China. In Chinese funerals in the region, a burial brick identifying the deceased and his village of origin was put in the coffin "for identification as later, the bones would be removed to be sent back to [China] for burial." Within a decade of burial, the body would be exhumed, placed in a box, and shipped back to the family village for final and permanent burial, to be cared for by the deceased's family — forever. The district associations took responsibility for sending the bones back to China, each of them employing two or three men solely to "travel over the State, [make] property calculations for decomposition, and gather up the relics of their late members." When a certain number of decomposed bodies had accumulated, the bone pickers would come to town and dig up the bodies:

> They [the bone pickers] . . . take the longest bone, say the leg, get a box made of that length, and 18 inches or 2 feet wide and deep, for the reception of all the bones. Each bone is then taken out of the [coffin] and dipped into a bucket of brandy and water. They are then polished with a stiff brush until they almost shine, and are then packed closely in the smaller receptacle. The polishers do not touch the bones with their hands, but handle them very dexterously with two sticks. They are very scrupulous in preserving every bone. The small box is then nailed up . . . and the bones of the Celestial, in due time, are laid in his native land as per agreement . . .

All the cemeteries in the Monterey Bay Region underwent these periodic exhumations, usually at ten-year intervals. In 1913, for example, the bone pickers, under the direction of the Six Companies, came to Watsonville's Chinese cemetery and worked for two weeks to exhume 68 bodies of Chinese who had died over an eleven-year period. In the previous exhumation, 120 bodies had been shipped, making a total of 188 Chinese returned to China between 1902 and 1913 from Watsonville alone. A local observer estimated that eventually 10,000 boxes of bones would leave the United States for shipment to China during 1913.

Few of the cultural practices of the Chinese in California received such a strong reaction as did this practice of the exhumation of the dead for shipment to China. Non-Chinese watched in horror as the Chinese cemeteries were periodically turned over by the bone pickers and expressed their horror by enacting legislation to prevent the practice. In 1878 California passed a law titled, "An Act to Protect

Public Health from Infection Caused by Exhumation and Removal of the Remains of Deceased Persons." After 1878 it was necessary for the bone pickers to get permits from county health officials before they could exhume the bones. The law at least partially reflected a belief on the part of the non-Chinese that the shipment of the dead back to China was another measure of the disdain the Chinese felt for America.

◇ *The Ring Game*

The decade spanning the turn of the century was the golden age of the Chinese community in the Monterey Bay Region. Watsonville's busy and prosperous Brooklyn Chinatown was expanding from sugar beet cultivation to apple drying. The Chinese in Santa Cruz, though split into two communities, were busy rebuilding their community after the 1894 fire. The Chinese in Salinas also were rebuilding after their 1893 fire, and the movement of sugar beet acreage into the Salinas Valley promised an economic boom. The dried squid industry on the Monterey Peninsula was securely established, strengthened by an arrangement with the Italian and Portuguese fresh fish industry. In terms of community pride and self-esteem, the period 1895-1906 marked the high point for the Chinese in the Monterey Bay Region.

This community pride focused on Chinese culture. On the one hand, the Chinese pointed with pride to things Chinese, and on the other hand, they made it clear that they had become part of the *American* scheme of things. This renaissance in Chinese culture within the Chinese community was in part due to a new appreciation and respect for Chinese culture on the part of the non-Chinese American public. With thousands of young American men journeying to Asia to help put down the Boxer Rebellion or to participate in the suppression of the Philippine revolution, Americans rediscovered Asian culture, particularly the arts of China and Japan. "Oriental" curios, interior decoration, and classical Asian art were popularized during the period, and though the Chinese immigrants in America still wore the label of "heathen Chinee," their art and culture grew in respectability. Chinese New Year celebrations became increasingly popular with the non-Chinese public. Chinese in America were often interviewed by newspapers and magazines about Chinese religion, festivals, arts, and even political events in China. The American public found that the Chinese laundryman, cook, fisherman, and gardener had a culture after all, and through their culture, the Chinese, for the first time in their experience on the Golden Mountain, gained a modicum of respectability.

The epicenter of this cultural renaissance in the Monterey Bay Region was the Point Alones village. The oldest and largest village in the region, it was also the only one which had not moved since the 1850s. The closest thing in California to China itself, the Point Alones village became a cultural lodestone for the Chinese in the Monterey Bay Region:

> [The Point Alones village] as seen in the afternoon from the bay, with [its] junks and lateen-sailed fishing craft drawn up on the beach or coming in with their freight, the widespread nets, the children in red and yellow, the curious balconies projecting over the water, the flags, and high scaffolds and acres of drying fish, all [seemed] to be thoroughly Asiatic . . . the Asia of little fishing villages, such as travelers in China describe.

The Point Alones village became not only the cultural center for Chinese in the region but the capital of a regional Chinese community, because for the first (and last) time in the history of the region, the Chinese communities became more than just a scattering of distinct and separate Chinatowns; for this brief decade they became a true regional Chinese community.

This cultural and political upwelling is all the more remarkable in light of the continuing legal harassment directed at the Chinese by the federal government. In 1892 the Chinese Exclusion Law was not only renewed but tightened by widening the definition of who was Chinese; Chinese was race, regardless of country of birth or place of origin. Further, the Chinese were required by the Geary Act to carry identification, a requirement they grudgingly met after a lengthy legal struggle.

The annual celebration held on the second day of the second lunar month best symbolizes the maturity and pride of the region's Chinese. The festival became known as the Ring Game because of the contest held at the celebration's conclusion. Beginning in 1894, and each year thereafter until 1906, Chinese, like pilgrims to Mecca, came from throughout the Monterey Bay Region to the Point Alones village to participate in the festival. Though many non-Chinese observers believed the Ring Game to be the concluding event in the

◇ *The Ring Game (photo courtesy of the Pat Hathaway Collection, Pacific Grove)*

lunar New Year celebration, it was actually a separate festival in honor of T'u Ti, the God of Wealth.

Every village in southern China had a small statue of a god seated on his throne holding a golden ingot in his upraised hand. Most often called the earth god, the image was also known as T'u Ti, the god of wealth. The southern Chinese believed that T'u Ti had the power to confer good fortune and wealth. The festival honoring T'u Ti was a day-long affair which began with ceremonies and offerings to the god. Offerings of food were placed before the statue, and the image was covered with flowers. Later in the day Chinese men gathered for the festival's concluding event, a game which would decide who would have the blessings of wealth for the coming year.

The game required a combination of skill, strength, and, most of all, luck. A large wooden cannon mounted on a platform was loaded with a small charge of gunpowder, and a large rattan ball was fired from the cannon into the air above the assembled men of the village. When the ball came down, the men scrambled and fought to get it, for the one who possessed it would receive the smile of T'u Ti and would have wealth and good fortune for the coming year. The promise of good fortune and wealth had brought the Chinese to the Golden Mountain, and any advantage an individual Chinese might get in the pursuit of his exclusive fortune was highly prized. The man who retrieved the ball after a fierce scramble exchanged it for a small gilt ornament which he took home and placed on the household altar to symbolize imminent success and wealth. In some southern Chinese cities, as many as thirty balls were fired into the air during the afternoon, each promising a degree of good luck; one of the balls (usually the first one fired) was, however, the most propitious.

The game made its first appearance in the Monterey Bay Region in 1894, and with a few minor alterations, the celebration was a faithful replica of that conducted in China. Instead of scrambling for a rattan ball, the Chinese in California fought for a ring of woven bamboo which was blasted into the air from a giant firecracker. (The firecracker gave the event its name—the Bomb Game—in Marysville, California, and Marysville still stages the game each year on the weekend closest to the second day of the second lunar month.) The men playing the Ring Game at Point Alones often organized into teams representing the various Chinese communities so that the man successful in wrestling the ring away from his competitors brought luck to himself and honor to his teammates. Thus the local press called the event the "Chinese Games," and each community's newspaper rooted for its local team.

The Ring Game was no place for the frail or the faint of heart—it was serious and rough business. In describing the first game held in 1894, an observer noted: "As soon as a ring would descend hundreds of hands would make a grab for it, and in their mad effort to get it, Chinese would pile 15 or 20 deep in a heap." In 1901 "the ring flew skyward and mad scramble for its possession ensued, the Chinese jostling, scrambling, scratching and fighting for the coveted trinket . . ."

Considering the intensity with which the Chinese participated in this celebration, it is surprising that so few were injured. In 1899 one of the bombs exploded prematurely, injuring the eye of the ordnance expert, and in 1900 one Chinese participant died from injuries suffered during the scramble.

As the depression of the mid-1890s gave way to more prosperous times, the annual Ring Game became more elaborate, and the number of Chinese attending the event grew. The contests held at Point Alones in 1899 and 1900 attracted the largest crowds, with Chinese delegations coming from San Jose, Gilroy, Salinas, Watsonville, and Santa Cruz. The expense of the celebration in 1899 was estimated in excess of five thousand dollars and the hundreds of Chinese participants were observed by over two thousand white onlookers.

The tide of cultural confidence and pride engendered by the Ring Games carried with it the surrounding Chinese communities, and though the other communities did not stage their own Ring Game festivals, the New Year festivals of the late 1890s were the most elaborate in each of the Chinatowns in the region. One institution which originated at the Point Alones Ring Game was transplanted throughout the region—the traveling culture show known as the Chinese parade.

Chinese delegations coming to the Ring Game would usually charter special railroad cars that brought all of them to Monterey on the day of the festival. A delegation of the Point Alones Chinese met the assembled delegations at the Monterey depot, and then they walked the mile to the Point Alones village. In 1898, rather than merely walk to the village, the Chinese staged their first parade:

> This procession was one of the most unique and brilliant spectacles ever seen here [Monterey]. Headed by the American flag and the great dragon flag of the Celestials, with fantastic banners, and dressed in fine silks of every color of the rainbow, the procession of about 150 Mongolians marched through the streets to the indescribable music of two Chinese bands.

Before the 1898 Ring Game, the Watsonville Chinese rented some costumes and finery for the parade. The morning of the Ring Games they suited up in their rented costumes, and before boarding the train, they marched across the bridge and into Watsonville, walking up and down Main Street. The response of the Watsonville populace to this dress rehearsal parade was very favorable, and after winning most of the rings at Point Alones that day, the Brooklyn Chinese decided to take up a collection and invest in their own parade regalia. An order for over three thousand dollars' worth of costumes was sent to China in early March 1898, and the Chinese waited expectantly for the finery which was "expected to surpass anything the Chinese societies have shown in this part of the state . . ."

◊ *Fourth of July Parade, Watsonville, 1898 (photo courtesy of the Pat Hathaway Collection, Pacific Grove)*

The costumes arrived in June 1898. Unable to wait to show off their new regalia, the Brooklyn Chinese staged a grand celebration in early July. Beginning with an open house in Brooklyn, where the street was lined with decorations and tables in stores were laden with free food, the celebration culminated in a Chinese parade. Bow Ching Chong, the wealthy Chinese fruit grower and merchant, acted as the parade's Grand Marshal, and Chinese visitors as well as Watsonville residents lined Main Street to watch the Chinese parade with the American flag at the head of the procession.

Exactly ten years after they had moved across the river, three hundred Chinese came back across the bridge and paraded down Main Street Watsonville for all to see. The Chinese walked the entire length of Main Street before turning around and marching back to Brooklyn; over a thousand spectators lined the streets to watch "the variety and richness of costumes . . . shields and banners rich in colors. The women with bound feet were on horseback, and children had seats of honor in a wagon." Two Chinese bands provided the music and rhythm for "the most notable street parade ever witnessed in this city . . ."

Determined to get full use of their new parade costumes, the

Brooklyn Chinese took to the streets again several days later, joining the Fourth of July parade, ". . . in full regalia, with their banner, bands, dragon, devil, joss house, and other features." In the span of one short week, the Watsonville Chinese had twice experienced the heady feeling of pride as they marched down Watsonville's Main Street; wrapped in the splendor of one of the world's oldest cultures, laborers, cooks, beet pullers, ditch diggers, and laundrymen celebrated their heritage.

The Ring Game parade in Monterey in March 1899 was the grandest parade of them all. Sixty Chinese from Salinas together with two hundred well-rehearsed paraders from Watsonville formed a procession replete with decorated horses, a dragon, and all the costumes imaginable. The dragon "wound its tortuous way along the streets in the wake of a sedan chair which was made to do duty as a band wagon." And, at the head of the parade, the Chinese carried the "long silken folds of our glorious Stars and Stripes sweeping gracefully in the zephyrs." Appropriately, the Watsonville delegation again won most of the rings that day. Apparently T'u Ti was impressed with all the preparations that the Watsonville Chinese had undertaken in his honor.

The Ring Game parades continued in Monterey until the fire of May 1906. In 1902 the Chinese participated in the Monterey Fourth of July parade; their "Chinese vision with beautiful silken banners, headed by a Mongolian band, with a number of splendid floats" was the highlight of the parade. All this public adulation and praise was not for the Chinese people as they lived every day in their fishing village, but for the idealization of Chinese culture that their parade finery represented. After the 1906 fire in Point Alones, the celebration moved to the McAbee Beach Chinatown, but it lost momentum, and the final Ring Game was played in the 1920s. Today, the last ring caught at McAbee Beach resides in a place of honor in the home of Jack Yee, son of the Chinese merchant and squid drier Won Yee.

◇ ALEV LYTLE CROUTIER ◇

One Big Family

I was born in a *konak* (old house), which once was the harem of a pasha. During my childhood, servants and odalisques lived there with us. I grew up in Turkey, listening to stories and songs that could easily have come from the *One Thousand and One Nights*. People around me often whispered things about harems: my own grandmother and her sister had been brought up in one. Since then, I have come to see that these were not ordinary stories. But for me, as a child, they were, for I had not yet known any others.

My paternal grandmother, Zehra, was the first person from whom I heard the word *harem* and who made allusions to harem life. She was the daughter of a wealthy gunpowder maker in Macedonia. As was the custom until the twentieth century, she and her sisters had been brought up in a "harem," or a separate part of a house where women were isolated; the only men they encountered were their blood relatives. On rare occasions they went out, always heavily veiled. Sometimes silk tunnels were stretched from the door of the house to a carriage, so that the women could leave without being seen from the street. Their marriages had already been arranged by the family. None of them saw their husbands until their wedding day. Then they moved to his house, to live together with their mother-in-law and his other women relatives.

My grandmother married my grandfather when she was 14. He was 40 and her father's best friend. She was a simple, uneducated girl. He was a respected scholar. Ten years later, she was widowed. With

◇ *Alev Lytle Croutier lives in San Francisco. She was born in Izmir, Turkey, came to America at 18, graduated from Oberlin, made independent films, wrote the screenplay for* Tell Me a Riddle, *and worked in publishing. These excerpts appeared in* Harem: The World Behind the Veil, © *1988 Alev Lytle Croutier, published by Abbeville Press.*

one of her sisters, she moved into her brother-in-law's harem, and there the two sisters brought their children up together, as one family.

Threatened by the Balkan Wars, they left everything behind in Macedonia, including their parents, and fled to Anatolia. They sought refuge and settled down in Istanbul in 1906. They were among the last women who had lived in harems; in 1909, with the fall of Abdulhamid, harems were abolished and declared unlawful.

I do not remember very much of the house in Izmir (Smyrna) where I was born. It faced the sea, was five stories high, and it had a *hamam* (bath house) where groups of women came to bathe. A giant granite rock behind the house isolated it from the world. It was said that before us, an old pasha, his two wives, and other women occupied the place. As a child, I played dress-up with embroidered clothes that the women from another era had left behind.

In 1950, with my parents and grandmother, I moved to an apartment house in Ankara that was inhabited by assorted family members. We lived as an extended family — two uncles, three aunts, my grandmother, my great aunt, many cousins, and *odalisques* (servant girls) who were gifts from my great uncle, Faik Pasha, and owned by the family. He had found them in a cave after their parents had been killed in a border dispute near Iran. The Ottoman palaces were gone, but not the need to live as one big family: clustered apartments were occupied by large families . . . .

◊

"Lips of Beauty" is the name of a sickeningly sweet dessert we loved as children. Great Aunt Meryem was the confectioner in our family, and she kept us very happy with Lips of Beauty and her yogurt dessert.

After these totally satisfying and exhausting sweets came the great coffee ritual. One attendant brought in the coffee, another carried a tray with diamond-studded accoutrements, a third actually served the coffee. Turkish coffee was not grown in Turkey but came from Yemen — and initially met a hostile reception. It was considered a source of immorality and was banned for many years. By the mid-seventeenth century, its virtues were extolled with deliberate Turkish extravagance in such works as Katib Chelebi's *The Balance of Truth* (1650), which claimed, among other things, that boiling-hot coffee miraculously causes no burns:

◊ Left: *Faik Pasha and Great Aunt Meryem with their daughters;* right: *my aunts Muazzez and Mukaddes in World War I army uniform, because, since it was usually inappropriate for women to be photographed with men, women sometimes posed with other women dressed in men's clothes.*

Coffee is indubitably cold and dry. Even when it is boiled in water and an infusion made of it, its coldness does not depart: perhaps it increases, for water too is cold. That is why coffee quenches thirst, and does not burn if poured on a limb, for its heat is a strange heat, with no effect.

To those of moist temperament, and especially to women, it is highly suited. They should drink a great deal of strong coffee.

Excess of it will do them no harm, so long as they are not melancholic.

What distinguishes Turkish coffee is its texture of very finely ground grains, almost pulverized, and its idiosyncratic method of preparation.

◊ TURKISH COFFEE ◊

1/2 cup water   2 tsp pulverized coffee
2 tbsp sugar

Pour cold water in a *jezve* (a small cylindrical pot with a long handle). Add sugar and coffee. Stir well. Place over low flame and heat until small bubbles barely begin to form. Remove from the flame and pour off froth into demitasse cups. Bring to boil, but do not allow it to boil over. Remove from flame. Pour coffee over the froth to fill cups and serve.

It seems like a very simple operation, but making it perfectly is one of the most difficult things in the world. It has to have just the right amount of froth, and this is a function of timing.

Coffee-making was a crucially important part of a young woman's life, since her merits as a wife were initially and continually evaluated on the basis of how her coffee tasted. She painstakingly practiced to get it just right, in order to win the heart of her beloved's mother.

I myself went through an intensive training when I was about nine years old and assumed somehow that this custom of one generation of women teaching a younger generation would survive forever. But this, too, is a vanishing tradition. Indeed, Turkish coffee was nearly obsolete when I recently returned. Everyone now favored "Nescafé," which meant *any* kind of instant coffee; to ask for Turkish coffee was old-fashioned and gauche.

When I asked my grandmother what food it was the women of the harem really loved the best, I expected to hear something like a very exotic form of baklava. "Eggplant, of course," she said. "It's the most enchanted food. We believed in those days that if a woman dreamed of eggplant, she would be pregnant. We drank its bitter juice to flush down the *ifrits*. We scrubbed our faces with it. But mostly we had to know a thousand ways to cook it in order to win a man's heart. You have to know at least 50," she told me. "Otherwise, you will be an old maid."

◊

When I was a small child living in Izmir during the late forties, I knew a eunuch. His name was Suleyman Aga, a gingerbread-colored man without hair on his face, so that he looked much younger than he was.

Suleyman Aga always seemed to have a special gift just for me. I don't remember anymore what these gifts were, except one. Once, when I was sitting on his lap, he pinched my pinkie between his own pudgy dark fingers and put on it a ring with a bright red stone. He put another ring on my ring finger, a dazzling one with a colorless stone. Next, my middle finger received another ring, this time with a green stone. He continued placing rings on all my fingers: on the index finger, one with a blue stone and on my thumb, a ring with a purple one. He brought each ring out of his pocket slowly, very slowly, each time showing his amusement, his eyes fixed on my face, observing my expressions. No one has since spoiled me to that degree.

Later, in the fifties, when we moved to Ankara, he continued to visit us now and then, always bringing a large box of cream-filled chocolates. My favorite was banana cream. (I hated the crème-de-menthe.) Although he came unannounced, often just as the family was sitting down to dinner, I was delighted to see him each time. I felt a leaping in my heart as I answered the door and saw his flaccid figure standing before me. My eyes immediately traveled to his hands, which held the most seductive chocolate box.

"Open sesame, open," he would say, his golden front teeth flashing at me, his voice pitched high—although I did not really know what that signified. But I did know that he seemed more like a woman than a man, in the way he slouched forward and caved in right around his belly, and in the softness of his face. He had an hourglass figure, and to me he felt like an old aunt.

In his absence, my parents referred to him as the *hadim,* or "eunuch." The word, my mother told me, meant "beardless"; some men were just that way. Another time I overheard my father saying that there weren't many of "them" left anymore, and when these die, the species will completely disappear from the country, and it will be the close of an embarrassing era.

◊

Since men and women did not associate socially, marriages were arranged by *gorucu* (go-betweens), "agents" who visited harems, studied the merits of a certain girl, and passed their judgment on to the man's family. Sometimes, these arrangements were orchestrated between relatives to strengthen the bonds of kinship. The betrothal of

◇ *Aunt Ayhan with baby Genghiz. Ayhan was the beauty in the family, admired even by Kemal Ataturk.*

first cousins was and still is prevalent in most of the Islamic countries.

Gorucu were still operating during the sixties. Most of these women were busybodies who prided themselves on their talent for matchmaking. They sought out pubescent girls for widowed, middle-aged, or unmarried men who seemed incapable of finding wives for themselves. Unannounced, the *gorucu* appeared at a girl's house. Islamic custom not allowing one to turn away a guest, the girl's relatives would welcome the *gorucu* — because that was their obligation. They served her coffee and sweets, acted polite, and made small talk. Meanwhile, the young girl would be hiding in the kitchen or in another room, until her mother or aunts invited her in. She would be required to make and serve Turkish coffee, since great importance was attached to her ability to brew this concoction. Her eyes cast down, she served the coffee to the *gorucu* and her entourage, either leaving the room immediately after they had had a chance to scrutinize her, or sitting silently on the edge of her seat, listening to other women carry on.

My friends and I used to make fun of this primitive custom, but since we were living in a country still caught in uneasy change, it was inevitable that we, too, would encounter the *gorucu.* I recall several occasions, peeking behind the door and watching these women come for older girls in the family. I became very familiar with the ritual and antics. Barely after I had reached puberty, it was my turn. I was incensed at their gall and resisted coming out to meet them, but the older women in my family, steeped in the tradition, insisted that I present myself. In my rebellion, I did what I could to make myself unattractive, undesirable, and unwomanly—at least according to the prescribed standards. I dressed inappropriately, made bad coffee, and talked too much. It was a great relief when they left, but often a source of quarrel, since my women relatives felt I had misbehaved and I myself was humiliated by having been subjected to this archaic ritual. Although they sympathized with me—and it was always understood that I would find and choose my own husband—they felt hurt to see the age-old tradition crumble and realize that they were its last relics.

One of the most quaint and enjoyable aspects of the wedding preparations were the henna nights, which occurred on the evening before the wedding. Women spent the day at the *hamam,* bathing, grooming, luxuriating. At night, they gathered together in the same house and ceremoniously decorated the bride's hands, feet, and face with henna, then took turns applying it to one another. At the time of my childhood, henna nights had come to be considered a rural custom and were never practiced in the cities. But I do remember visiting relatives in the country and, for the first time, having both my hands covered with a gray-green paste that smelled like horse manure and that kept getting colder as the evening wore on. My hands next were wrapped up in cloth like twin mummies. I spent a restless night, incapacitated by my wrapped hands, yet so curious of the outcome that I did not dream of taking the bandage off. The next morning, one of the women carefully unwrapped my hands and washed off the hardened mud. Underneath, my fingers were orange. When I returned to the city, other children made fun of me. The henna did not come off for weeks, no matter how well I washed my hands.

◇

European merchants sometimes married local Christian women so that they could infiltrate the harems with their merchandise. Marianne Alireza describes such an encounter: "I guessed that she was some poor soul who had come for a handout and that the bundles contained our contribution. But she was a lady peddler and the bundles contained her wares. She was Circassian and had come many years before to perform the pilgrimage and like so many others decided to stay. Her goods were mostly notions and cheap toys, some bangles and trinkets, and a *buksha* with cheap gaudy fabrics and some lace. From a sheer need for some kind of excitement, women of the harem purchased almost everything."

Bundle women often appeared at our doorstep, and I cannot forget my excitement and wonder as I watched their wares slip out of the bundles. They were strange things, bedspreads of garish colors and tasteless baroque designs from Damascus, diaphanous nightgowns made of Shile fabric, and a profusion of lace and ribbons. My grandmother and my mother always bought something for my hope chest, which, I must have known deep down, represented not my needs but an excuse for my mother and grandmother to enjoy buying odd things. Over the years, the hope chest dwindled, the bedspreads and those ethereal nightgowns given away as gifts to women relatives who got married or servants who had been good to the family.

"Alev's hope chest" was still in my parents' house when I last visited them. Inside, there were just a very few things: some doilies, scarves, and the Damascus bedspread I remembered buying from the bundle woman. My mother insisted that I take it back with me, and I was caught between wanting to please her and being appalled by the wild bright orange, yellow, and green florals. It would never do. But I took it with me anyway, slightly embarrassed when Turkish customs searched my suitcase and this particular artifact was questioned. Was it an antique? Did I have special permission from the government to export it? I told them it was a gift from the family, and that it had been in my family ever since I could remember. Why was I going through such an ordeal for something I was embarrassed by and would give to the Goodwill as soon as I returned home? (It turned out that a friend who happened by while I was unpacking fell in love with this ungodly piece of "art," and it now adorns her bedroom in San Francisco.)

Again, during the same visit, I was sitting in a café in the Prince Islands, surrounded by a bevy of Arab harem women, waiting for the ferry, when a Circassian woman came through the crowd, carrying two suitcases, which in today's world had replaced the old "bundle." She spilled open her suitcases for the women and could not escape my own curious eyes as she held up her wares for them to see. I was disappointed that the exotics I remember were gone; no more strange kaftans, Damask silks, Jerusalem cottons. Now the bundle woman was selling mainly crochet and knit items made from synthetic yarns, which are ever so popular today in the Middle East, and there were some cheap Turkish towels and *bornozes* (bathrobes) from the tourist loom. The romance of the real bundle ladies was over.

◊ IRMA WALLEM ◊

Made of Lace

I lay in my curtained-off bunk and listened to Mama make her getting-up sounds. I could hear the lid rattle as it came off the iron stove and then the crackle of the fire as it caught. I heard her pouring water from the enamel bucket into the coffee pot. Then there was the rustle of bed springs as Daddy sat on the edge of the bed to put on his shoes and socks.

At last it was Sunday, October 13, the day we went every year to help my cousin Thomas eat his birthday cake. It was also the day Mama got her winter supply of winesap apples. She wrapped each apple in a leaf from the Sears Roebuck catalogue to store away in the cellar. Aunt Kate and Uncle Ted and their only child, Thomas, lived seven miles over in Arkansas. We lived across the line into Oklahoma.

I had learned never to pull aside the curtain around my bunk bed until Mama called to me. She only called after Daddy was dressed and out to the barn. A family could be modest and careful, she always said, even in a one-room cabin.

For me, it was a world of sounds. Sometimes from the direction of my parents' bed I heard squeaking or Mama sigh or giggle softly. Sometimes I heard the sharp sound of peeing in the chamber pot.

This morning there were only the sounds of hurry. Then Mama called, "You can get up now, Irma."

This morning there were no biscuits for breakfast, only a large bowl of oatmeal and a glass of warm, freshly strained milk. Then we were in our wagon, the one with the springs. Mama and Daddy sat in the seat, I sat on two pillows in the back. The air was so chilly Mama

◊ *Irma Wallem, who grew up in the Ozarks, now lives in Reedley, California. Her most recent book is* I Have a Place: Life with a Younger Man, *published by Mercury House.*

had wrapped a quilt around my shoulders. I was surrounded by bushel baskets for the winesaps. Old Dan and the gray mare were taking us off to Arkansas.

As we forded the river, a little of the water crept up into the wagon bed and wet the edge of my quilt. Mama turned and gripped my shoulder as we hit the deepest part. Daddy stood up and reined the horses harder and then, suddenly, we were on the other side of the river and out of the water. Mama was always terrified of crossing the river, but for Daddy it was a big adventure.

It was three miles until we reached the turn-off into the bad road. Daddy named it The Road Over Which No Car Will Ever Go. The stumps were so high in the middle that it would have torn up the insides of a car.

When we got to the Arkansas Line, which was just a turn in the road, Daddy sang out, "Good-bye Oklahoma, hello Arkansas!" Mama kept turning and smiling at me and patting my shoulder. I was excited too, but not about winesaps. I was going to play with somebody my own age, even if it was just a boy cousin.

As we pulled into the yard, Thomas and his speckled hound dog came tearing to meet us. Aunt Kate hurried after him with her white apron over a black and white polka-dot dress. She hugged and kissed Mama and me, then she began scolding Thomas for not wearing his Sunday shirt. We could smell fresh pork cooking. Mama asked, "Did you butcher yesterday?"

Aunt Kate beamed at us. "Yes, and you can take some home with you."

I knew what that meant, sausage and hogshead cheese and maybe even pork chops. Mama looked so happy she could hardly speak.

Thomas and I went out back of the barn to play horseshoes. After awhile I sat down on a pile of straw and Thomas got out his pocket knife and whittled on a piece of hickory twig to make me a toothbrush. I couldn't think of anything to talk about. Thomas grinned at me and looked down. "I bet you can't guess what I got in my pocket," he said.

"A dead mouse?" I asked, because there was a bump to one side of his pocket.

He laughed at me and kept grinning. "See." He unbuttoned the fly of his overalls, and there it was, but not a mouse. "You can touch it," he said. "It won't bite."

I couldn't bring myself to touch the pink skin on Thomas' thing, but I stared and shivered. "It looks like a worm, put it back."

Thomas laughed like crazy. "Don't you tell your mama," he said. "She'll tell mine and my Dad will whoop me."

Then Aunt Kate called us to come eat, and we went into the house to sit down for pork chops and mashed potatoes and gravy and biscuits and huckleberry cobbler. On the way back home I kept looking at Old Dan and remembering the thing that hung down on him, but it wasn't on the gray mare, and I didn't have one, either.

Next day I could hardly wait to get my best friend, Daisy Willis, alone, so I could talk to her. We were on our way to school and her two brothers were far ahead of us on the road.

"Did you ever see a boy—I mean, when he unbuttons his overalls?"

Daisy grinned at me. "With four brothers I cain't help it. I have to change my baby brother's diaper. Haven't you ever seen your Daddy undressed?"

"Of course not," I protested, but then I did remember once when I was five years old and I was in bed with Daddy and we were alone. Mama was up starting the fire. I'd felt something different, and I'd asked him what it was. After that he never let me get in bed when he was alone. If I had to cuddle up to get warm he would tell me to get in on Mama's side of the bed. "Do men have that thing, too?" I asked Daisy.

She looked as if she couldn't believe how dumb I was. "Of course they do. Boys use theirs to pee, but men do something else."

It was the something else that made me feel scared. I couldn't ask her what it was.

"Didn't you ever see a kitten come out of a mother cat?"

I nodded. "But I don't know how it got in the cat."

"That's what papa cats do with their thing. They put it inside and it plants a kitten." She kept shaking her head at me. "Didn't you ever hear the boys snicker when somebody says, 'Baseball Bat'?"

I guessed I had, but I hadn't noticed.

"When boys get off to themselves they say, 'Mama, Mama, what is that; hangs from Daddy like a baseball bat?' Then somebody else says, 'Hush, hush, you little brat; that's what makes your Mama fat.'"

That day at school it was hard to listen to what the teacher said. The arithmetic problems on the blackboard made my head dizzy. I tried to copy them, but I just sat there thinking about boys. Today the boys all looked different.

◇

The next Saturday Daisy came to stay all night. Mama had told Daddy she hoped I wouldn't think I had to return the visit, because she knew for sure the Willis house had bedbugs. But she also knew it got lonesome for an only child.

Mama even killed the Sunday chicken and fried it for our supper. She then explained to Daisy that even though we had company we still all had to take our Saturday night baths.

After supper we sat awhile by the fireplace and ate a popper full of popped corn that Mama dripped butter over. She told Daisy how she had grown up on an 80-acre claim over in Western Oklahoma. "You could look out the window and see for three miles on a clear day," she said.

Daddy told Daisy how in Western Oklahoma there wasn't any wood to burn in the cook stove, so people who couldn't afford to buy coal had to burn cow chips.

Then Daddy began to yawn, and Mama said it was time for our baths. Daddy carried in the round galvanized tub from the nail on the outside of the house and went after a bucket of spring water. Then, while the teakettle heated, he sat at the table and played a game of Flinch with us.

As soon as the steam started singing, Daddy got up and went outside to look at the stars, he said.

Daisy and I took off all our clothes and sat on chairs, covered with towels, with our feet in the tub of warm water. Mama handed Daisy a washcloth and the bar of store soap to pass to me when she had lathered her cloth. "You girls wash your own private parts," she said. Then she got another cloth and knelt down to get at the rust on our ankles. Mine weren't that rusty, but I squealed so Daisy wouldn't get her feelings hurt when Mama started in on her rust. Then Mama rubbed hard on the place behind our ears. I had once heard her tell Daddy how she wished she could give Daisy a Winter Bath.

Our nightgowns were warming in the oven. Before Mama put them over our clean bodies she dusted us with her own violet-smelling talcum powder. We scampered to my bunk bed and snuggled together. Mama tucked us in and then pulled the curtain so there wouldn't be a crack.

Daisy whispered to me, "Do *they* take Winter Baths, too?"

"Sure," I whispered back. "Every week."

"Do you ever peek at 'em?"

"I wouldn't dare."

"You wouldn't be so ignorant if you looked," Daisy whispered. She took the curtain in her fingers to open it a crack. I opened my eyes and looked for a second, then I closed them again. They were stark naked. I made myself look some more.

Mama was pouring water from the teakettle into the galvanized tub. Daddy sat in the chair, with his back to me, his feet in the water. "Don't scald me, woman," he said so low I could hardly hear.

Mama laughed softly, "I might just do that."

Daddy stood up and reached for the teakettle.

I closed the curtain with my fingers. "Don't look," I whispered. "They're so silly. It's awful."

"They always act silly," Daisy whispered, "just before they get on the bed."

"Your folks, too!?"

"Sure, only *they* don't take Winter Baths."

I lay there, cupped around Daisy, because the bed was so small. "I'll never do what they do," I whispered. "I'll never, never get married."

"You have to do it if you get married. You have to get married or be an old maid."

I pressed my fingers on my ear that wasn't on the pillow. I didn't want to hear the springs squeak. "I don't care," I said. "I'll *be* an old maid school teacher. I won't let a man do that to me."

"I know a boy that likes you," Daisy whispered. "Roy Brown said you are the pertiest girl in school."

"He couldn't like me. I'm bashful and I have freckles."

"He likes you anyway," Daisy whispered.

When I woke up next morning, my shoulder was stiff and my arm was asleep. I made Daisy turn over and she snuggled around me. I thought about Roy Brown. He was two years older than me. He was skinny, and he had stains on his teeth, and his hair was shaggy around his ears. But he liked me.

◇

It was October again. Daisy and I were the *big* girls now. Some days Daisy didn't make it to school, because her mother had a new baby and she had to help out at home. This morning I rode Suzie, my swayback pony, to school. When the river was low, she could ford the river with me. When the river was high, my father took me across in our small rowboat. Roy Brown came to school when he didn't have to work the crop or help his Dad chop wood for railroad ties. When he did come to school, he rode his bay mare.

This morning I heard hoof beats slowing beside me and I knew it was Roy. Suzie didn't like it when another horse got too close. She shied a little and I had to pull the reins tighter.

"Are you goin' on the possum hunt tomorrow night?" he asked, before I even turned to look at him.

"My folks won't let me go places at night," I told him.

"You could say the teacher's goin' along—you could stay all night with Daisy—you could say it's school."

Up to now I had never once lied to my folks. I looked over at Roy's hands, holding tight to his saddle horn, keeping his mare back. My eyes moved up to his face. His brown eyes were looking straight at me, waiting.

"Well, I *am* thirteen." I wanted to go on the possum hunt more than I'd ever wanted anything in my whole life. "I'm goin' on fourteen."

"My cousin over in Arkansas got married when she was fourteen," Roy said.

It was like his words went through me, making me older. All of a sudden I could talk to a boy. I talked about school. I said I hated it when the teacher was strict, but I said it was worse when the little kids got noisy. I said I liked October because I liked to pick up the pecans from the places along the river bottom where the big trees grew. But I liked it in Spring, too, when we went hunting huckleberries. Roy said how he hated chopping weeds from the corn patch, but he liked it in the woods when they chopped wood.

I knew we were almost late when I saw the teacher standing in the doorway, waiting to ring the bell until we got there.

"I'll go possum hunting tomorrow night," I said quickly. "I'll stay all night with Daisy and we can go together." As I got off Suzie, I added, "I won't tell my folks."

◇

Mama was tight-lipped about me going to stay with Daisy.

"You know they haven't got beds for all the kids," she told me. "You'll have to sleep on a pallet on the floor, and maybe in the same room with Daisy's brothers. Besides, I know good and well they have bedbugs."

"If she sleeps on the floor, they'll be floor-bugs," Daddy said, trying to make a joke.

Mama did not laugh. She packed my saddlebag with my outing nightgown, two ironed handkerchiefs, a towel and washcloth, and two apples. "No telling what they will have for breakfast," she said. "You may wake up in the morning with a bad cold."

Daddy asked, "Is she going off to war?"

Just before I reached the river I looked back. They were still standing by the gate.

Roy and Daisy both missed school that day. I rode Suzie back to Daisy's house and the boys helped me take off the saddle and turn her into their horse lot. Mrs. Willis sat in the rocker, holding the baby, while we ate supper of brown beans, cornbread, sweet potatoes, and bluish skimmed milk. I sat in Mrs. Willis' place at the table because I was company.

Daisy's brother, Larry, was going on the possum hunt, too, so Mrs. Willis didn't think twice, as Daisy said later, about girls going out at night. Larry went on ahead to walk with his girl, Mollie Lou.

When Daisy and I reached the schoolhouse, we saw the others all waiting. Roy Brown was with the three other boys. They were talking to the spotted hound dogs that Bill Thomas had brought. I saw Roy's head jerk up when he saw me, but he stayed there by the fence. Daisy and I joined Fern and Mollie Lou. They were huddled by a little fire. Mama would sure enough have been tight-lipped if she had known I was going to be with Fern. Mama said all she did was shine up to boys, trying to catch one for herself.

Mollie Lou was bent over, laughing. Daisy and I leaned over to hear what was so funny. Fern whispered in my ear, "When God made woman, he made her out of lace. He ran out of lace, so he left a little place."

Mollie Lou whispered, "When God made man, he made him out of string. He had too much string, so he left a little thing."

The boys started toward us and I hushed the girls quick. Bill and Fern set out in the lead with the dogs. Larry and Mollie Lou went next, so Daisy had to walk with bashful Buster Dees.

Roy held back and then he took hold of my arm, just above the elbow. His fingers were tight and strong. It was the very first time a boy ever took hold of my arm like that.

It was the very first time I ever walked with a boy in the dark.

Even when the path narrowed on the sidehill and we had to walk Indian style, he held on, as if I'd never walked sidehills before. When I stumbled, even just a little, he pulled me up close to his side. We kept getting behind the others. I stopped to lean against a tree and catch my breath. My heart kept jumping around.

Up ahead, the dogs barked. "It's just a squirrel," Roy said. "It's too early to tree a possum."

"It's so dark, I'm scared," I whispered.

He put his arm tight around me. "I'll take keer of you," he said. "There's nothin' can hurt you. Rattlesnakes and copperheads go in the ground at night."

We fell silent, just standing there like we were the only two folks in the world and Mama and Daddy were a hundred miles away. Roy took my hand and guided it to touch the flap of his overalls. "This won't hurt you, either," he said. "I won't let the horse outa' the barn."

I couldn't speak. I pulled my hand away, but I wasn't mad. I wasn't scared, either.

It was the first time I was ever in love.

◇ VICTOR E. VILLASEÑOR ◇

Our Dream House

I was raised the first few years of my life with my older sister and brother in the barrio of Carlsbad, California, right next door to my father's poolhall. I spoke no English until I started kindergarten, and I thought that we lived in Mexico. The *gringos,* the *Americanos,* were like foreigners from a strange land to me for the first five years of life.

But getting back to my parents' story—which is, of course, their history in the truest sense of the word, "his story"—right after they got married, my parents moved to Carlsbad. They rented a little house from Hans and Helen, and they had a wonderful first two years until my father finally admitted to my mother that he'd lied to her and he was, indeed, a bootlegger.

My mother tells me that she felt betrayed and was so ashamed that she would've left my father if she hadn't been pregnant with my older sister, Hortensia. But, also, times were hard—it was the middle of the Depression—so she could see why my father was doing it.

My father took her to see the priest, and the man of God tried to convince my mother that *la bootleggada* wasn't as bad as she might think. In fact, the priest told my mother (for a case of my father's best whiskey) that bootlegging wasn't against the laws of God and was, in some ways, actually good and made my father a better Catholic, because he made only the finest of whiskey.

But my mother wasn't about to be taken in by my father or the priest. Arriving home, she told my dad that she didn't care what the

◇ *Victor E. Villaseñor lives in Carlsbad, California. His books include* Jury: People vs. Juan Corona *and a novel,* Macho, *for which he wrote the screenplay. This excerpt appeared in* Rain of Gold, *"a history of a people—a tribal heritage," recently published by Arte Público Press, Houston.*

priest said; she was going to have a child and it would be them, not the priest, who would go to jail. So she made my father promise to get out of his illegal business as soon as he could.

My father promised, but he procrastinated. Then, a few months later, their distillery blew up in Tustin, California, almost killing my father. My mother, big with child, dragged my father's body from the burning house, put him in their truck, and drove off just as the police arrived. She was outraged and she told my father that this was, indeed, God speaking to them—a much higher authority than any priest. My father conceded to her, and this was a major turning point of their life. One, they went legal shortly after that; and two, my mother was never going to allow herself to be taken lightly again. She was 21 years old.

Then the following year, Prohibition ended, and my parents bought the poolhall in Carlsbad from Archie, who'd married my Aunt Carlota. A few months later, a man named Jerry Smith came to my father and asked him if he owned the poolhall. My father said, "Yes, I do." Jerry Smith brought out his badge, saying that he was from the Internal Revenue Service and he wanted to know why my father hadn't paid his income tax. My father insisted that he'd already paid his taxes; he'd done it when he'd bought his city business license. Jerry tried to explain to my father that one thing had nothing to do with the other. But my dad just couldn't understand what the man was saying. Finally, my father got mad and told Jerry, "Look, buddy, it sounds to me like you're telling me that the federal government is nothing but a free-loading thief! I got too much respect for this free country to believe this, so, no . . . I can't pay you any yearly taxes!"

Enjoying my dad's independent spirit, Jerry laughed and they had a few drinks together. Then, opening his briefcase and showing my dad the different income tax forms, Jerry came to realize that my father really didn't have any idea what he was talking about, nor could he read the forms. "Tell me, Sal," said the agent, "do you have anyone in your family who can read books and understand numbers?"

"My wife," said my father proudly. "She's educated and reads books easy."

That was the second big turn of events in my parents' married lives. My mother was brought into my father's business, and Jerry Smith taught her how to keep books and explained to her the responsibilities of a business person in the United States. She took over the bookkeeping of my father's poolhall with a power that surprised everyone in the barrio, especially the other women.

Then, the following year when my father couldn't buy an off-sale liquor license because he had a prison record, my mother stepped right in. "I'll buy it," she said, surprising my father and everyone else in the barrio.

In the next five years, my mother blossomed into a full-fledged businesswoman . . . even buying a second liquor store in the Anglo part of town in Carlsbad. That's when I was born. As I grew up, I'd see my mother do the banking, run the books, oversee the payroll, and do most of the hiring and firing of the ten or twelve Anglos and Mexicans alike who worked for them.

I grew up thinking that all women were the money-handlers of every marriage. And I saw that my mother had her own car, and she came and went as she pleased with bags of money and boxes of receipts. My parents became a force to be reckoned with in the area— my dad, the aggressive, imaginative leader, and my mother, the one who'd follow through and make sure that things really got done and weren't just left up in the air, as was my father's style so often. And in the evenings, I'll never forget, I'd curl up at my mother's feet while she did her bookkeeping and I'd nap as if I were in heaven itself until I was put to bed.

◊

Then, one day I remember very clearly, my older cousins came by wearing Army uniforms, and everyone was so excited, saying that the war was going so badly for us that California was now in danger of being invaded. The following week, my parents' friends, Hans and Helen— who spoke with a funny German accent—came by and told my parents that they'd been ordered to move 20 miles inland or they could have their property repossessed by the government, as was happening to the Japanese. They asked my parents to please buy their liquor store in Oceanside from them immediately. That night, my mother went over the books with Hans, and the next day we all went over to see the store. I remember that it was big and had a huge dark room in back and an attic that smelled bad. The place was booming with business. It was the first time that I recall hearing English being spoken all around me. That week, my parents bought the store and hired Hans as their manager.

Shortly after that, I'll never forget, my father came racing into the house one day all excited, telling us that the owners of the biggest, most beautiful ranch in the area were moving back to Canada before we got invaded and they were putting their place up for sale.

"This is our chance of a lifetime!" said my father.

"But what if we get invaded?" asked my mother.

"Bullshit!" screamed my father. "We're not getting invaded, and that's that! We got to keep strong in our heads, not panic like fools, and buy this ranch right now! It has orchards and pastures and cattle, horses, chickens, barns, tractors—everything! And, best of all, three hilltops—all overlooking the sea—where we can build our dream home, Lupe, and stand proud for ten generations!"

"But Salvador," said my mother, "I'm scared; we've been moving so fast."

"It's O.K. to be scared," said my father, hugging my mother close, "it keeps you alert like the chicks watching out for the hawk. Now, let's do it; pull out your magic books!"

My mother was reluctant, but that night my parents went over her books again and again, adding up all the cash they could possibly put together, hoping to see if they could come up with an offer for the ranch before anyone else got wind of it. But trying to do all she could, in the morning my mother had to tell my dad that there was just no way on earth that they could pull it off.

My father raged and raved, making references to Don Pio and how important it was for them to not back down when their dream was at hand. I couldn't figure out what was going on. All I knew was that my father and mother were yelling at each other over money once again. Finally, my father said that, well, he'd go and see Archie, but he hated to do it.

Years later, I found out that Archie turned him down again, this time saying it was just too big. My father went to the bank, over my mother's protest, and borrowed $20,000 against everything they owned. He bought the 126 acres overlooking the sea, and I'll never forget how I got to ride in the front of my father's saddle as we rode our horses through the orchards and pastures and fields of produce, going from hilltop to hilltop, trying to decide on which knoll we'd build our dream home.

Six months later, we moved to the ranch in Oceanside, two miles north of where I'd been born in the barrio of Carlsbad. The following year, my grandmother, Doña Guadalupe, died in the master bedroom of the old ranch house under the giant pepper trees. All of my mother's people came in from northern California, Arizona, and Mexico. I cried and cried and wouldn't let go of my beloved grandmother, the woman who'd given me tea and sweetbread and told me stories of the past ever since I could remember.

The following year, I started school and was truly shocked when I was told on the playground that I was Mexican and didn't belong in this country. When my little sister Linda began to talk, my parents told us that from now on, they wanted us to speak only English at home; and at school, I'd get in trouble if my friends and I were heard to say anything in Spanish. Oh, that was a terrible time. School became a scary nightmare for me.

I was seven years old when my mother finally decided on which knoll we'd build our dream home. She chose the knoll half a mile away from the sea where the wildflowers grew. "I want plenty of sunlight," she told my father, "so I can plant my mother's lilies and they can flourish; and also I want roses and night jasmine so they can fill our home with wonderful fragrance, just as I had when I grew up in La Lluvia."

My father agreed, and they hired two architects to work with my mother, who designed the house. There were carpenters, electricians—more than 20 people—who worked on my parents' dream house for the next two years. The foreman was from Detroit and he had false teeth. I'll never forget how frightened I got the first time I saw him take his teeth out and put them in his shirt pocket when he sat down to eat lunch in the shade of a tree.

Finishing the house, my parents had a *fiesta* that lasted a week. The mayor, the chief of police, and over six hundred people came to my parents' housewarming. I remember the celebration well. My mother said that she was dedicating their home to St. Joseph and Our Lady of Peace. My father said that was fine for Lupe, but he, himself, had built this huge 20-room house in revenge against Tom Mix, a man he hated from the bottom of his heart, because Mix had always knocked down five Mexicans with one punch in his no-good phony movies. "And the best revenge in all the world," my father added, "is to live well! Especially longer and better than the bastard you hate!"

The people applauded and the music began, and I remember stealing a pan of *carnitas* and going out back in the orchard and sharing them with my brother's big coyote-dog named Shep. Also, I remember my father and Archie uncovering the pit full of beef and presenting the mayor and his wife with the head of the big steer, scooping out the brains with a tortilla for the mayor's wife as a special treat. The woman shrieked and passed out, and my mother told my father off and took the poor woman into their master bedroom to lay down. The mayor got drunk on tequila and so did the chief of police. Fred Noon had to drive them both home. My father and Archie and Fred stayed up that whole first night, laughing and drinking and raising hell, remembering the good old days.

Ten days later, I was helping my older brother Jose and a couple of workers clean the place up when a short, little, sleepy-eyed Anglo cowboy came out of the orchard saying, "Where is everybody? Ain't the party still going?" My brother and I burst out laughing, telling him that the party had ended four days ago. He cursed and served himself another mug of whiskey from one of the fifty-gallon drums that was still half full and went back into the orchard to sleep some more. . . .

◇ PETE NAJARIAN ◇

Talking Is Good for Us

◇ *Almonds and the River*

–In my village we ate almonds in the spring when the nut was like milk and the green shell still soft.

–I don't remember much about where I lived.

–I remember my hometown very well. I can even tell you the names of the streets.

–They don't have those names anymore.

–The moslems live there now.

–They're supposed to be very poor.

–Let them be poor and more poor.

–Don't say that.

–Why not?

–They don't know what happened. They weren't even born then.

–So what?

–So have compassion.

–For a filthy moslem who lives in my father's house?

–You don't want that house anyway.

–You got a better house here.

–I got two houses here, so what?

–So let them live there.

–They have no right to live there. Let my own people live there.

–Who?

–Not me.

–I'd go for a visit.

◇ *Pete Najarian lives in Berkeley, California. These sections of dialogue appeared as a chorus, interspersed with drawings by the author and text, in* Daughters of Memory, © *1986 Peter Najarian, published by City Miner Books, Berkeley.*

–What for?

–She misses the almonds.

–I have an almond tree in my backyard.

–Not for the almonds. For the river.

–What river?

–The river where I played when I was a child.

–Oh you and your river.

◊ *History*

–My grandson's girlfriend came the other day to write recipes. She wants to cook for him, but she's an *odar*. I told her, "You have to live with me and cook with me to learn these foods."

–What kind of *odar* is she?

–I don't know, she says she's American.

–They all say that.

–I asked her what kind of American and she said a little of this and a little of that as if *she* were a recipe.

–There are no Americans. They just say that to make themselves feel like they're somebody.

–There won't be anymore of us either.

–Not if we marry a part of this and a part of that.

–We will be gone when we lose the language.

–Why should anyone want to keep the language?

–The language is everything.

–It gives us history.

–I don't like history.

–Let us be part of this and part of that.

–It's safer.

–What are you saying? Did my father die for nothing?

–I don't know why your father died.

–He died because he would not become a moslem.

–So they ripped his nails out and slit him open with a butcher knife, that's better than being a moslem?

–They would have done that even if he did become a moslem.

–They ripped my baby daughter from my arms and threw her in the river. Do you think I could ever be a moslem after that?

–They did something else to me.

–Christians do those things too.

–I'm not moslem and I'm not christian.

–What are you then?

–I'm a grandmother, that's what I am.

◇ *Rugs*

–Annahid's unhappy because of her breast operation.

–The television says those operations aren't needed anymore.

–Doctors like to cut breasts off.

–Only those who don't like women.

–Only those who don't like women become women doctors.

–I don't know, my doctor is a good boy and he cut both mine off.

–Annahid's depressed by it. She's still young, she's only sixty.

–She reminds me of Arpi, rest her soul. She was always worried about how she looked. Even on her deathbed she had to sugar her face. "I can't help it," she said, "I need to look good." There she was dying and she had to sugar her hair off from her face.

–My mustache is so thick I could shave it.

–Don't shave it, you'll look like a man.

–I already look like a man.

–I don't care what I look like anymore.

–No, I want to look good.

–What look good? How can we look good with these faces?

–A face is like a good rug. The more it's stepped on the better it shines.

–They don't make those kinds of rugs anymore.

–I sold my rugs.

–Those beautiful rugs?

–I'm not going to live forever. I sold them and gave the money to my children.

–They should have taken the rugs instead.

–They don't want them. They like wall-to-wall.

–Everyone has wall-to-wall.

–I'm going to have it too, it's easy to keep clean.

–How much did you sell them for?

–Five thousand. Three for the big one and two for the small ones.

–I remember when you bought them from Hightone Toomas, the importer. How much were they then, two hundred?

–That was forty years ago.

–What forty? Sixty not forty, sixty.

–Sixty, forty, what's the difference?

–They don't make them anymore. Even on the other side they make them by machines now.

–Who cares, I'm going to sell mine too.

–They're too much trouble. I was always worrying about them being stolen.

–No, I'm keeping mine. They're full of memories.

–I don't want any memories.

–I've been looking at those patterns all these years now.

–So what, get rid of them.

–My son remembers them in the apartment back east. He says he loved that apartment.

–It was his childhood.

–It was a disgusting place. You had to work like a slave to keep it clean.

–I don't miss the east.

–I miss the people.

–They're all dead.

–Not all of them.

–Let them come here, I don't want to go back there.

–I call on the phone and Maritsa says, "It's costing you too much." Her son's a millionaire and she worries about a few dollars for the phone. I tell her, "Maritsa, I can afford a few dollars to talk to you."

–You can talk all day and it's not the same.

–I don't like the telephone, there's no taste in it.

–It's better than nothing.

–I'm going to fly back. I want to see them before they die.

–I don't fly anymore. What am I going to do, ask the girl to help me to the toilet like I was a baby?

–I was going to fly back to see Charcoal Armen but she died. I talked to her husband Arsen on the phone the other day. "Arsen!" I yelled so he could hear me. "You'll be all right! The winters will be hard but in the summer you can keep busy in the garden!"

–He'll be okay. He can visit the widows because he has a good name.

–So even if he didn't have a good name, what's he going to do at his age?

–You don't know, a man his age can still be active.

–On the talk show they said that if you have a good love life it never dies.

◇ *Turkish Songs and Armenian Moslems*

–I saw Satenig last week. She just came back from Russia.

–It's not Russia. It's Armenia.

–It's still Russia.

–But we have our language there. All the street signs are in Armenian.

–They may use our language but I can hardly understand them when they speak.

–Half of their words are Russian.

–It's still our language.

–People make too much of language.

–To tell you the truth, I enjoy speaking Turkish more. It was my first tongue.

–Some of us hate it. The Dashnaks even want to change the words in the songs.

–They can't change the words. All the pleasure is in the words.

–No, they say, the words are filth.

–Listen, I know what filth is.

–I know you know.

–They lay on top of me and they left me for dead. Every one of them lay on top of me and I was only fourteen and I will never stop hating them. But when I hear their songs I love their strings and their words.

–You can say that.

–I can say it.

–Because she loves music.

–It isn't only their music. It's our music too.

–They invited my uncle to play for them. My uncle Vosdanig played the zither and my uncle Mateos sang. My uncle Mateos had the best voice in the whole city and sang for the Pasha himself, but when the massacre started his head was cut off.

–It's our music more than their music.

–It's our land too.

–It's no one's land if no one lives on it.

–No one wants to live there.

–Everyone wants to live there.

–There are still some of us left back there.

–Those who are left are moslems.

–So even if they are moslems, they're still Armenians.

–How can an Armenian be a moslem?

–Nubar's sister is a moslem now, if she's still alive. After her husband was killed a moslem took her for his wife. She had four children with him. Nubar went back and wanted her to leave, but no, she said, how could she leave her children? Her children are moslems now but they're still Nubar's nieces and nephews.

–Isn't that something, Nubar who was such a passionate Dashnak?

–He hardly knows the difference anymore. All he does is sit on the porch and tell his childhood stories.

◊ DAVID RAINS WALLACE ◊

In Bulow Hammock

◊ *The Green Tunnel*

The thing that struck me most about Bulow Hammock is the hardest to describe: the smell. Hammocks are woodlands (the name refers specifically to hardwood groves that punctuate the more open marshes and pine woods of Florida, and may derive from Indian words for "shady place," "garden place," or "floating plants"), but Bulow Hammock didn't smell like any woodlands I knew. I was used to the brisk, humus-and-chlorophyll tang of New England woods with their associations of uplifting weekend hikes. The hammock was different.

I must have been about nine years old when I first encountered the hammock, so I didn't articulate any of this. Yet I clearly remember my sensations on stepping out of my parents' car into the shade of the magnolias and cabbage palmettoes. I was fascinated but daunted. The Connecticut woods I'd played in had been inviting, welcoming. The hammock was . . . seductive. It smelled sweet, a perfumy sweetness that reminded me of the hotel lobbies and cocktail lounges I'd occasionally been in with my parents.

Smells are hard to describe because we can't really remember them as we do sights and sounds, only recognize them. Smells lie deeper than our remembering, thinking forebrains, in the olfactory lobe we inherited from the early vertebrates. Yet they are related to thought in profound ways because our nocturnal ancestors, the early mammals, lived by smell. The human ability to relate present to past and future may stem from this scent-tracking of food, an activity which takes

◊ *David Rains Wallace lives in Oakland, California. His novel* The Vermilion Parrot *was recently published by Sierra Club Books. These excerpts appeared in* Bulow Hammock, © *1987 David Rains Wallace, also published by Sierra Club Books.*

place in time as well as space, unlike a hawk's immediate striking on sight, and thus implies planning. The curious resonance smell has in memory, as when Proust conjured an epoch from a teacup, suggests that we have a great deal to learn from it.

Complex smells are the hardest to describe. Bulow Hammock smelled stranger than liquor and perfume. It smelled intricately spicy, with a sweetness not so much of flowers as of aromatic bark and leaves. There also was an air of decay in the sweetness, not the rich, sleepy, somewhat bitter decay of New England woods, more of a nervous, sour atmosphere. When I scraped my foot over fallen leaves on the ground, I didn't uncover the soft brown dirt I was used to, but white sand and a network of fine, blackish roots like the hair of a buried animal. The sand was part of the smell too, a dusty, siliceous undertone to the spice and decay.

There was something dangerous about the smell, something inhibiting to my nine-year-old mind. I didn't want to rush into the hammock as I'd have wanted to rush into an unfamiliar Connecticut woodland. It wasn't that the hammock seemed ugly or repellent, on the contrary. The seductiveness was part of the inhibition. Perhaps it was just that the hammock was *so* unfamiliar. It's easy to read things into childhood memories. But the smell was powerful.

Society is suspicious of wild places because it fears a turning away from human solidarity toward a spurious, sentimental freedom. It is interesting, in this regard, to recall how *little* of freedom there was in my first perception of Bulow Hammock, how little of the unfettered feeling I got in sand dunes, hill meadows, pine woods, or other open places that promised release from streets and classrooms. I wonder if the hammock inhibited me because there was more of humanity about it than a dune, meadow, or pine forest has; not of humanity in the sense of society and civilization, which (however irrationally, given the history of civilization) we associate with safety, but of animal humanity, of the walking primate that has spent most of its evolution in warm places like Florida, spicy, moldy, sandy places. Perhaps it wasn't the strangeness of the hammock that made it seem dangerously seductive, but a certain familiarity. It is, after all, dangerous to be human.

We'd come to Florida to visit my father's mother, who had a retirement cottage in Ormond-by-the-Sea, an early geriatric enclave complete with shuffleboard court (which, three decades later, has become somebody's driveway). On the drive south, we'd passed another stretch of coastal hammock that was being burned and bulldozed during some kind of road construction involving sweaty convicts in gray twill. There'd been something very malignant-looking about that stretch of charred palmetto. Blackened fronds had thrust at the sky like fire-sharpened spears. As though to heighten the effect, someone had erected a doll's head, also charred, on a crooked stick.

I couldn't have looked at this scene for more than a few seconds, but it made a big impression. At nine, I had no very firm grasp of its rational implications, of the likelihood that the head had been stuck up there by some whimsically ghoulish convict who'd found it while grubbing in the brush. I must have been aware of that likelihood, but other things seemed possible: that it was a real head, a baby's or a monkey's; that it manifested an unknown savage world in the uncut hammock farther from the road, of which there was a lot more in Florida then. The southern landscape threw the human and wild together more than the northern. I remember a great loneliness in it, brown fields of broomsedge reaching almost to the horizon, and unpainted shacks against ragged woods over which circled vultures in numbers out of proportion to the vacancy beneath them. The black-water swamps that the road periodically passed over seemed cheerful in comparison, albeit dangerous.

Of course, my response to the road construction—fire, sticks, head, uncut green wall in the distance—was an educated one, as was my response to Bulow Hammock's smell. It would be banal to assert that the smell awakened atavistic race memories of life in the jungle. We'd been getting our first taste of human evolution in my fourth grade class, and I'd found *that* pretty spicy, all those skeletons and hairy people: Piltdown Man (we must have been the last class to get Piltdown Man, since the hoax was discovered around that year), Java Man, Peking Man. A normally bloodthirsty fourth-grader, I'd thrilled to learn that Peking Man had scooped out and probably eaten the brains of other Peking men. I'd seen the "green hell" jungle movies of the early fifties: Charlton Heston in *The Naked Jungle*, Jeff Chandler in *Green Fire*. I had a whole set of cultural preconceptions ready for Bulow Hammock.

Yet banality is a kind of fossilized reality, the bones of insights buried in the silt of intellectual fashion. I wouldn't dismiss my nine-year-old perceptions just because they were culturally conditioned. Classrooms and movie theaters teach little about smell, for one thing, and, sophisticated as they are, they still share with nine-year-olds a descent from spicy, moldy, sandy places. We don't know enough about that descent to dismiss anything. Fire, sticks, head, and green wall have been at the center of things for most of human experience, and they still are, in a sense, although the green wall may have receded.

A green wall is what Bulow Hammock seemed as my father drove down the low sand road leading into it, or rather a green arch, a tunnel. Its surfaces seemed much solider than the crumbly coquina of the nineteenth-century sugar plantation ruins we had come to the hammock to see. The mill was roofless while the hammock enclosed us completely, from its ground-hugging coonties, dog hobble, and saw palmetto to its undergrowth of feral orange, bayberry, hornbeam, and dahoon to its canopy of live oak, redbay, magnolia, and cabbage palmetto. Glimpses of the hammock interior lacked perspective: they had the wavery, spotty aspect of underwater things. The plant forms were too eccentric for geometry — palm, spike, spray, corkscrew, club, plume, lace, spiral. It was beautiful, but the intricacy was like the complexity of smell. It inhibited. Its seductiveness was also a warning because it hinted at passionate entanglement more than freedom or tranquillity.

I followed my parents around the sugar mill ruins like a good little boy. The Seminoles had burned the plantation in 1835: that was interesting. There were displays of implements found in the ruins, and a brochure about the plantation's history. There wasn't any explanation of the hammock. There may have been signs identifying birds or plants, but if there were, they did little to elucidate the fearful seductiveness of the place, a seductiveness to which the adult world seemed curiously immune. But then, children are used to being surrounded by powerful, unexplained seductions.

I never did venture into the hammock as a child, although I wandered miles through the Connecticut woods. I don't recall going more than a few yards even into the barrier island scrub that grew behind my grandmother's cottage in the fifties, before the Ormond

Mall was built. The mailman had put his hand into a pile of leaves
(trusting children, we didn't ask why) and had withdrawn it with a
coral snake attached to the skin between his fingers. Coral snakes,
grandmother told my sister and me, had to hold and chew their
victims to inject their almost invariably fatal poison.

Grandmother wasn't a snake-hater: her deepest antipathies were
for the British Royal Family (her father was Irish), J. Edgar Hoover
(her former employer), and other select humans. She was more
passionate in her opinions than most grandmothers, always applaud-
ing when Harry Truman appeared in movie newsreels, whether or
not anybody else did. Perhaps because of this, her dictums had
considerable authority, and we weren't about to put our hands in any
dead leaves, or our feet. There were poisonous copperheads in the
Connecticut woods of course, but they didn't chew on you. We
contented ourselves with watching big toads eat little toads in her
backyard.

◊ *The Softshell*

The rainy season started one night in late May. I watched the sunset at
Bulow Creek that evening. A slate blue overcast covered the western
sky, and a wind from the south drove pennants of gray cloud over the
shoreline at a speed made all the more surprising by the apparent
immobility of banks of cumulus on the eastern horizon. The creek
was gunmetal blue and chrome in the cold light. The cord grasses and
rushes swayed over it in a way that seemed autumnal.

A small alligator glided out of the marsh and swam across the creek
so smoothly it might have been on an underwater track. I wondered
how it did it in the current, which seemed pretty strong although the
water was moving upstream instead of down. The tide was pushing it,
impressive considering that the nearest ocean inlet was several dozen
miles away, south of Daytona. I never stopped being mystified by the
tidal influence on the creek. Right in the middle of the hammock, at
least a quarter mile from the creek, there was a brackish mudflat that
shorebirds picked over when it wasn't inundated. Somehow the tidal
water got into the flat, although I could see no sign of a channel
leading to it, not above ground anyway.

The advancing tidal current seemed so powerful that it gave me a
fleeting but startling illusion. I felt for a moment that there was more
than water in the creek, that something very big was moving

upstream just under the surface. I felt a moment of vertigo, as when one looks a long time at running water, then at the ground, and sees the dry sand or earth start to eddy and flow.

It started raining as I went to bed, a soothing drizzle, but a steady pounding on the roof awoke me in the small hours. It had a peremptory sound, as though the sky couldn't wait to unload its water and had come down to roof level to do it. The downpour continued for twelve hours. When it finally cleared a little, the unburdened sky boiled up into towering thunderheads. It had rained six inches: the roads looked like canals. A lighter rain fell until the next day, finally thinning to a yellowish overcast that unexpectedly produced window-rattling thunderclaps and enough extra water to flood my grandmother's yard two inches deep in 20 minutes. Her pebbles weren't as absorbent as the neighbor's crabgrass.

The thunderstorm stopped as abruptly as it had started, and I splashed my way over the flooded roads to the hammock. I didn't expect it to have changed much in a couple of days, but, once again, I hadn't understood the hammock. It hadn't changed in ways I would have expected. I'd been afraid that the sand road would be flooded, since all the paved ones were, but there wasn't a puddle in it. The sand was firmer than it had been in the dry season: the rain had cemented it down.

There wasn't any flooding in the hammock at all. Swamp rivulets that had dried during the rainless period were full again, but the ones that hadn't dried seemed no fuller than before. I'd never seen a more graphic demonstration of the sponge-like properties of wetland. It was a little eerie. What had *happened* to all that water?

Much of it seemed never to have reached the ground. It wasn't that the vegetation had a lot of water on it, in fact it was surprisingly dry for less than an hour after a thunderstorm. It did have a surprising amount of water in it that hadn't been there before. The epiphytes— the resurrection ferns and tree mosses—that had been mere blackish encrustations on branches two days before were now lush, emerald shrouds. Individual resurrection ferns had tripled in size. It was instant rain forest: just add six inches of water and stand back.

The downpour had knocked down a few rotted limbs and tattered leaves, but the hammock was remarkably undisturbed otherwise. Mosquitoes and flies were less in evidence. Birds and tree frogs called lustily and life in general seemed encouraged rather than intimidated.

A barred owl flew out of a brushy patch and landed on a branch in full view, behavior I'd seen in the middle of the Okefenokee but not in the hammock.

A large brown frog on a snag in a swamp rivulet also refused to flee at my approach. I wondered if it was the ranid species I'd heard in the night. Maybe it was a bronze frog: the distant chorus had a clacking sound characteristic of that species. On the other hand, it might be a southern leopard frog, since its snout had a characteristic pointed shape, or a pickerel frog, since its legs had characteristic yellow patches. The frog just sat there, as though daring me to come and try an identification. Even herpetologists have trouble sorting out southern frogs.

An armadillo rummaged briskly through the leaf litter, ignoring me also although the sun hadn't begun to set. It thrust its head under the leaves, pushed its whole body into a treehole, rose bearlike on its hind legs to tear at a rotten stump. The loudness of its own scratchings seemed to startle it: it suddenly jumped sideways several feet. Then it stuck its snout back in the ground as though nothing had happened.

When I got to the ditch, a songbird scolded and another barred owl flew out of a thicket and landed in full view. It landed facing away from me, but turned its head around 180° to stare. Another began calling to the south. The rain seemed to have produced instant owls as well as instant epiphytes.

I came to the place in the pine scrub where I thought I'd heard frogs the other night, and since it wasn't getting dark yet, I left the path and pushed through the saw palmetto. In a little while, I saw an opening in the underbrush and moved toward it. I wasn't expecting much, a scattering of brackish puddles and rivulets as in other swampy parts of the hammock. I was wrong again.

The brush opened out to reveal a sizable sheet of water that was translucent black, like obsidian, quite different from the brown, murky water of the brackish swamps. It stretched eastward out of sight. Around it, and in the water at the edges, grew some of the biggest trees I'd seen in the hammock, not only palmettoes and redcedars, but great, buttressed American elms, swamp hickories, Carolina ashes, and gums. Buttonbushes grew farther out in the water, tall shrubs bearing masses of spherical white flowers, and a clump of willows stood in the sunny center.

It was a sweetwater swamp, isolated from the brackish tidelands by slightly higher land, and fed by some intricacy of limestone ground-water, some vagrant but copious outlier of Bartram's "salubrious fountains." It glowed in its scrubby setting, the new hardwood leaves reflected in water that was equally festooned with duckweeds, aquatic *Salvinia* ferns, and lotus-like floating hearts. Even underwater, the swamp was full of green vegetation, bladderworts, and stoneworts.

I thought the water's apparently endless extension to the east must be an illusion, since Bulow Creek wasn't far in that direction. As I walked along the edge, I still couldn't see an end to it, however, and it was so different from anything I'd seen in the hammock before that a sense of unreality came over me. It was like the dislocation I'd felt trying to follow the path in the dark, but it was exhilarating this time.

I skirted a palmetto trunk at the water's edge and almost stumbled over a leafless spray of wiry green stems growing on its base. It was a whisk fern, a very healthy one. A few yards farther, I almost stumbled over another of the ancient plants, growing in a little moss garden of maiden cane and liverworts and redcedar seedlings on the base of another palmetto.

I glimpsed something flying and heard a furtive splash, then a wood duck drake was swimming among the buttonbushes, making peevish noises. He climbed on a log and peered at me through the foliage. The red skin around his eye gave it an intensity that was startling even at a distance. As I stood still, not wanting to frighten the duck, I noticed other creatures I hadn't distinguished from the logs they sat on—a brown frog like the one I'd seen earlier, except that it still had a tail, and a big black cooter turtle. The turtle had its head craned anxiously, watching me. When I looked away a moment, it slipped into the water so quietly I hardly believed I'd seen it at all. When I looked back at the wood duck, it had disappeared too.

A live oak had fallen in the water, forming a kind of boardwalk. I climbed out over the slippery carpet of epiphytes that covered it and sat down where the main limbs branched from the trunk. The sky was turning red, intensifying the tree's reflection. Despite its black-ness, I could see quite clearly into the water. The mosquitofish in it seemed larger and more colorful than the ones in the brackish swamps. Many of the largest had swollen bellies; gravid females, I supposed.

I glimpsed a movement at the water's surface out of the corner of my eye. When I turned to look, I could see nothing except water plants and floating twigs. The spot was about eight feet away, far enough to focus my binoculars on. I did, and saw with a start that there was an eye down there, apparently an unconnected one, like the Cheshire cat's smile.

It wasn't the black, impassive eye of a cooter turtle or frog. This eye had a sharpness about it. It was yellow like a cat's, and it kept blinking nervously. When I leaned forward to see it better, it disappeared as though the swamp itself had shut it, as though other eyes might at any moment start appearing on tree trunks or sandbars.

I waited awhile, keeping my binoculars on the spot. Then the eye was there again. This time I noticed a dot on the water in front of it. A nostril? I leaned forward again, and as the eye vanished I glimpsed a snaky motion underwater, as of a neck being withdrawn. When the eye reappeared, I knew what it belonged to. A softshell turtle was buried in the water weeds and fallen leaves, its long neck extended to the surface with only eyes and nostrils protruding. Surface reflection concealed the rest of its strangely beaked and flattened head. To disappear, it had drawn in its neck so smoothly that my eyes hadn't caught the movement.

I'd watched softshells in the Olentangy River in Columbus, Ohio, protruding their birdlike heads from the water as rush-hour traffic roared past on the freeways. In wooded areas a little farther upstream, they'd climb out to bask on the bank a few feet from me if I stayed still, but at the slightest movement they'd drop into the water faster than my eye could follow. Softshells can catch trout. They had seemed a little fabulous, little shield-bearing dragons with their sharp eyes and beaks and flat, leathery shells. Bartram evidently was fascinated with them: he described them at length and devoted two copper plates to them in the *Travels*. One of the plates is so odd-looking that it took me a long time to figure out what it was.

Softshells belie the blunt, sleepy notions we have of turtles, our assumption that the oldest of reptiles must be the dullest. Softshells are among the oldest of living turtles. Fossils from the Cretaceous Period are classed in the same genus as living ones: they're basically unchanged from the times of *Tyrannosaurus rex*. Florida softshells may be more closely related to southern Asian species than they are to

Ohio softshells, suggesting a very long and intricate history indeed, one perhaps older than the Atlantic Ocean.

It was good to meet this anomalous creature in this unexpected place, to find a turtle in a swamp inside a swamp full of turtles.

It implied an inexhaustible interpenetration to nature, as though it would continue to open into new life no matter how far into a corner anxious civilization pushes it. Of course, it was a fairly irrational implication. Beset by human purposefulness, nature seems anything but inexhaustible. Indeed, it seems curiously exhaustible, unresistant. If the purpose of evolution is success through survival, one would expect it to fight back.

I like to think that the tangled diversity that can make Bulow Hammock seem inexhaustible is a form of resistance to civilization's oversimplifying tendencies. Yet science hasn't really been able to discern a purpose to biological diversity, to having three species of shelled, aquatic reptile in a swamp instead of one. Maybe ecosystems are more stable the more different kinds of organisms they contain, but evolution doesn't necessarily demonstrate this. Many highly diverse ecosystems have collapsed completely during life's history, and many simple ones have lasted a long time.

Ecosystems seem vague in an evolutionary perspective. Fossils demonstrate no ecological imperatives forcing organisms to live to-gether. Cabbage palmettoes may live with early primates and cinna-mon trees in one epoch, with live oaks and raccoons in another. Eco-systems aren't disciplined hierarchies marching under evolutionary orders. They're mobs rather loosely comprised of whatever happens to be available, following the laws of chance as much as anything else.

This disorder seems to offer a unique opportunity for a purposeful primate to reorganize the world in any way it thinks fit. Yet ecological randomness has certain implications for other evolutionary units, such as the organism. If ecosystems, which can seem highly disci-plined in the short run, are really evolutionary mobs, then what about these bundles of highly differentiated colonial cells that are cluttering up the landscape? Can a small mob reorganize a big one?

Of course, organisms don't slouch along trading cells and organs back and forth with other organisms the way ecosystems trade species back and forth with other ecosystems. (Well, actually, they *do* trade cells and organs by eating, impregnating, and infecting one another, but I'm not going to get tangled up in that idea right now!) Still, highly evolved and complex organisms don't necessarily survive any better than complex ecosystems, suggesting that they're no more disciplined in the long run. Chance may play just as great a part, as when a hominid happens to acquire a large brain and various accidental and rather questionable peculiarities that go with it.

This may seem a highly schizoid view of life. Certainly, it doesn't sound very holistic to suggest that the brain is an evolutionary tumor partly independent of the body, but there are holisms and holisms. It was all right to view the human organism as the basic unit of integration when we believed that the universe was organized that way, that man was the measure of all things, but we know better now. The human organism isn't the template of creation: it's one of millions of forms thrown off by an unbelievably lengthy process. Attempts to reduce the world to human scale will probably be short-lived—about as long as it takes for the dams to silt up with the eroded topsoil.

In fact, the human organism is not well integrated, it's a mass of contradictions, and we should accept it as such. In this sense, it's more holistic to see the brain as a semi-independent storer of evolutionary information than as a survival computer. Instead of a weapon against nature, a semi-independent brain would be a mediator and advisor, and I think it has served this function much longer than it has served as a weapon. Of course, being semi-independent, it is not always a reliable advisor, but it is an even less reliable weapon.

Apparently unreliable advice may be worth more than we sometimes think. The brain has always told us that nature is beautiful, but we thought that was unreliable because there is cold and hunger and disease in nature. Now we are seeing that destroying nature's beauty will not destroy cold and hunger and disease. Perhaps the brain's most unreliable-sounding advice can be its most disinterested advice.

My brain seemed to be giving me unreliable advice in finding an inexhaustible interpenetration in a few thousand acres of woods surrounded by freeways, ditches, motorcycle racecourses, and housing tracts. Experience and education said that Bulow Hammock would get pushed into smaller and smaller corners, even as a state park—the fish and alligators decimated by water pollution, the vegetation degraded by air pollution, even the migratory birds reduced by destruction of their tropical wintering places. Yet when I thought about my life, not the life I'd been taught I'd live but the life I'd actually lived, the advice made a kind of sense. I'd spent a lot of my life being pushed toward various corners, but here I was, if not inexhaustible, at least interpenetrated, breathing the air and looking at the turtle.

The turtle looked back at me and seemed prepared to do so inexhaustibly. Frogs had started calling somewhere, I couldn't tell where. It might have been in the water around me, but the quality of the sound masked any sense of location. It didn't sound like tree frogs, but it didn't sound like ranid frogs either. It was so loud that it didn't sound like quite anything, as though the noise was in my head. It got even louder, to a crescendo that made my ears ring, then stopped.

It was starting to get dark, and I hadn't brought a flashlight. I got off the log and returned to the path. I felt good. Despite the humidity, the air wasn't muggy. The thunder had cleared it. It seemed vinous again, not a beaujolais this time, something lighter, a white zinfandel. The woods looked translucent, shadowless.

When I reached the marsh there was a sweet, slightly acrid fragrance that reminded me of nights on the sleeping porch of my mother's family's house in Virginia. I'd slept out there when visiting them summers as a child. I noticed drifts of tiny white four-petalled flowers on the path and smelled one of the sprays of these flowers that covered some small evergreen trees. The smell was coming from them. They were dahoon trees, which the Seminoles used as an ingredient of a sacred drink. Bartram wrote about it in the *Travels.*

Dahoon doesn't grow as far north as Virginia, and it seemed odd that a plant with such an exotic-sounding name should evoke my grandparents' sleeping porch. Then I recalled that some big English holly trees that my grandparents had brought from Oregon grew under the sleeping porch. Holly and dahoon belong to the same genus, *Ilex,* one of the rare genera that grow on every continent (except Australia) and in both tropical and temperate zones.

The familiarity of the association made me notice something. I'd stopped smelling the spicy, seductive, dangerous smell that had struck me when I'd first been to the hammock. I couldn't even remember it. Instead of one powerful smell of exotic promise, the hammock now contained hundreds of smells, some of them rather ordinary. I wondered if I'd smell the original smell again if I came back in a few years.

In the jade swamp, I once again noticed a movement in the flooded palmetto stump where I'd found nothing but mosquito and fly larvae before. This time, I found what was making it. A small toad floated calmly in the water, duckweed on its head. It didn't dive out of sight even when I touched it, as though the rains had restored a kind of edenhood to the hammock, for toads at least. Maybe it was too excited by the opening of the breeding season to pay attention to me. I met more of them farther along the path, little buffy toads with red warts — oak toads. I'd never seen one before.

The darkness didn't evoke the uneasiness it had the other night. Frog and insect calls seemed less furtive, and the fireflies had a robustness, an orange spark, that seemed new. The sky kept glowing after the last red had faded. Drops of water in fallen leaves reflected the glow in little flashes as I passed, so that the hammock seemed full of silver lights below the fireflies' golden ones.

Initiation

Back in the spring of Freshman year, when I was sure I would not return to Amherst, I had gone through the required rushing of fraternities. The way Amherst was organized in 1963, there were no social dorms for upperclassmen—no dorms in which women were allowed without strict curfews; Sophomores, Juniors, and Seniors who did not live in fraternities got spartan rooms identical to those of Freshmen. Although independent organizations, the fraternities served as necessary housing for most of the students. Construction had begun on a complex of social dorms, but in those days most kids disappeared into the fraternity system, essentially never to be seen again in daily life except in classrooms and, occasionally, the dining hall.

The 13 fraternities at Amherst were loosely ranked by status in the minds of the students (if not anywhere else). The top two or three had most of the student leaders, two were "animal houses," and one had a reputation as the "nerd house." It pledged selectively, but advertised itself as a low pressure "good guys" environment with inside access to such activities as the radio station and the yearbook.

One fraternity was totally different. Kicked out of its national for admitting a black in the fifties, Phi Alpha Psi subsequently changed its mode of rushing. There was no pledging—no selective admittance by the brotherhood—only a sign-up sheet, until the quota was reached. More by fortuity than design, Phi Psi thus became the safety valve of the system, admitting rebels, outcasts, and generally bizarre individ-

◇ *Richard Grossinger is the publisher of North Atlantic Books, Berkeley, California; his most recent book is* Waiting for the Martian Express: Cosmic Visitors, Earth Warriors, Luminous Dreams.

uals. The membership was a maelstrom of rock musicians, poets, political activists, motorcyclists, early conceptual artists, theatrical improvisers, and foreign students. During rushing, I was charmed by Phi Psi. Since they were under the quota, I expressed my support by joining, despite my plans to transfer.

◊

Realizing I was a loner, my English professor, Leo Marx, had been inviting me to dinner every few weeks at his house. I would sit at the large hardwood table with him, his wife, their son and daughter, and tell stories about Grossinger's and childhood. And he would advise me on the correct approach to a writing career. He was a true scholar and philosopher; I was like some crazy adopted son. Even as he railed against my ridiculous notions about mysticism, I experienced in his New York Jewish personality an authentic and more fully realized version of my stepfather. . . .

That spring Professor Marx took me to lunch at the Lord Jeff Inn with a friend from New York, Catherine Carver, an editor at Viking Press. He had warned me ahead of time that she was very prominent, having worked with many famous novelists, including Saul Bellow; her willingness to meet me was an honor. A slight, dignified woman with a mannered voice, she skimmed through my novel, *Salty and Sandy*, during dessert and coffee, and then took my carbon back to New York. A week later she wrote:

> This is just to say how very glad I am to have seen you, and read some of your manuscript, on Monday. As I told you then, I think what you've written is clear evidence that you are going to be a writer; and although I can't say until I read all of it how much work this book is going to require before it can be published, I am certain that there is a novel in those 600 pages. . . . Even the roughest of them has a quality of expressiveness that is very much your own; I am most hopeful about your future in this line of work—as you should be.

For the remaining weeks of the spring term I carried those words in my mind as if they were destiny. The day before I left for Grossinger's, I received her special delivery packet with section-by-section instructions for turning my book into a publishable novel. That was to be my summer occupation!

My father rejected my plans gruffly. "You're living in my house, you work for me." I had waited all my life for him, and now, who was he? Expecting me to begin my hotel training at once, he started me in what had been his own first job—dead-letter clerk. The elderly woman who held the position full-time was assigned to train me. I was to sit at a desk the entire day logging undeliverable letters in a ledger. Since the hotel was such a transient place, there were hundreds of such letters every week addressed to guests who had left; staff who had been fired or quit, or never come in the first place; transient entertainers; even celebrities who hadn't been there for 30 years.

By the second week I was no longer under supervision, and I took to throwing more and more items into the dead-letter box without even checking the file. Finally, I threw all of them into the box. By the end of the second week I had stopped entering letters into the ledger. I would finish work after an hour and go back to the house to rewrite *Salty and Sandy*. Aunt Bunny and Emma, the maid, were my lookouts, and if my father came home from work to watch television (as he did about every other day), they alerted me and created a diversion so I could leave by the fire escape.

I began a new novel I called *The Moon,* using people from Amherst and other friends as characters and writing each chapter through the mind of a different person; every fifth chapter (assigned to "The Moon") was conceived as the mind-flow of a cosmic being.

Living at Grossinger's was the fulfillment of my oldest conscious dream, and although the experience wasn't what I once imagined it would be, it was still bounteous and filled with hope and adventure. Aunt Bunny and I had plenty of time now to talk; she opened my first beers for me ("They're just grain, and they'll put on weight"), and, on her days of cooking, introduced me to exotic foods. She had her own summer salon of friends, including journalists, sociologists, movie directors, rock'n'roll singers—different adults who came and went and sometimes came back. In their midst I was the precocious child who read the tarot, quoted poetry and novels, and interpreted their dreams. During sunny weekends I would haul my typewriter, a few informal paperweights, and a stack of paper out to the cabana at the pool and write my books, taking occasional breaks to swim or eat, and talking to the other authors around me. For an entire morning I worked next to playwright Paddy Chayefsky, who had the adjacent cabana. At one point, he looked over my shoulder and pointed out false lines in my dialogue.

◇

Phi Psi held about 40 residents, so when I realized I was returning to Amherst, I wrote ahead and was fortunate to claim the last room, which I was to share with a transfer student named Greg, brother of a former member. He turned out to be a short, husky, hairy Shakespearean actor, with a booming voice. Together we bought used desks and a large faded green couch, probably in its tenth or fifteenth student room. Intense and ambitious, Greg wanted to negotiate at once for Saturday-night use of the room, because, as he put it, he needed to get his social life going. Since I wasn't dating at all, I granted him the room indefinitely, but I soon regretted that grand gesture, for he arrived as early as possible each Saturday with a different nondescript date, and locked me out for the remainder of the evening.

Down the hall from me was a somewhat frightening character — a very tall Rasputin-looking Junior with wild eyes and a long beard named Jeff Tripp. He played the guitar religiously and was very concerned with matching notes on records of Bob Dylan and Dave Van Ronk. His favorite song was "Don't Think Twice, It's All Right," which he sang so many times and with such polish that, for a long time, I thought he had written it. I tried to avoid him because he was so dogmatic and loved confronting younger students, but I had a reputation, so he wanted to know exactly what I was about and became an early visitor to our room.

First, he guffawed at my reading habits — Robert Penn Warren; *The Once and Future King; The View From Pompey's Head;* plus the other pop American novelists I had picked up through Aunt Bunny and her friends, and Leo Marx. He laughed over my stors9y of meeting Paddy Chayefsky at the hotel. "He wrote one good line," he said. Then he spoke it in perfect mime: "I don't hate your father; your father is a prince of a man!"

Within a few weeks, he had me reading Beckett, Claude Simon, and Nabokov, and he tried to teach me the difference between the melodrama of the writers I was reading and the radical modes of his own favorites. "They're advertising men you're reading, not writers;

they don't know anything about the mysteries." He loved to intone the word dramatically, "the missss-teries," but he meant different ones from mine. He was deeply into the nihilism of *Molloy* and *Malone Dies,* and he loved to burst into my room in odd moments quoting lines that turned the universe upside-down. . . . His voice shook the plaster and radiated down the halls, and I sat there transfixed.

One night a bunch of us went from the house to the dining room together, and a Senior named Dave who was short on money for the weekend talked about selling the rights to his postmortem body to a medical school for a couple of hundred dollars. Tripp challenged him, and Dave kept saying, "What's wrong with it. Just tell me what's wrong with it, Tripp." I waited anxiously for his answer, but he turned to me and said: "My student will respond."

I gulped, thought for a second, and then said, "Because it's making too big a separation between life and death."

He broke into a big smile, and, putting his arm around my back, said, "Exactly!"

◇

Across the hall from Tripp, in the big triple with the balcony, was a Senior from the Lower East Side named Paul. He was no older than I was, but he had accelerated through the public school system and gained two years. A large ungainly kid with glasses, Paul was the opposite of Tripp; he had virtually no social poise, but he became my best friend. We sat around evenings together dialing in WWVA, Wheeling, West Virginia, listening to country-and-western music. Even Tripp approved, and joined in on guitar, adding bars of "Will the circle be unbroken, bye and bye, Lord, bye and bye."

From my summer experience at Grossinger's I was ripe for social consciousness. My father had revealed himself as a prototypical capitalist—greedy, contemptuous of the rights of others, anti-union. But it wasn't just him; it was seemingly the whole generation of my parents—apologists for Hiroshima, acquisitive, thinking only of material things, blind to our exploitation of the resources of poor countries. . . .

Those first months at Phi Psi changed my sense of the world; I was no longer bounded by dream symbols and tarot cards. I saw the James Hall raiders, the Miami Beach parties, and the materialism and opulence of the teenagers at Grossinger's as the same general, unnamed conspiracy. Of course, I had been uncomfortable all my life; I had been raised in decadence and corruption (as well as in the already-identified insanity).

Paul's motto was "the greatest good for the greatest number," and I now adopted it as my credo for myself and Phi Psi. In early October I proposed that the whole fraternity transfer to Cal-Berkeley, and I argued so persuasively at the house meeting that Paul and I were put in charge of a steering committee, to draft a group letter of application. Most of the house members signed it, though mainly as a political statement against Amherst. It was uncertain that very many would go to Berkeley in the unlikely chance the scheme should work.

Paul and I were intoxicated with the plan. We imagined a big article in *Time* explaining that the artists, writers, musicians, and many of the best students were fed up with Amherst's elitist social system and consumerist education, its fraternity gang-rapes and book-burnings. . . .

Tripp was thoroughly disgusted with me. "It's bullshit . . . the wrong issue. You don't want to have to do with *any* college. Why draw the line at Amherst?"

But I was stubborn and convinced. I took the dramatic step of petitioning to make a farewell speech in chapel. The required morning chapels were not religious services, but occasions for the whole school to gather and hear speakers of different persuasions, as at a New England town meeting. When my time came, I stood behind the podium and, with startling gumption, attacked the whole system of the school—in front of the president, Calvin Plimpton, the faculty, and the students.

In retrospect, my speech reads like the liberal clichés and adolescent utopianism of my generation—a disappointment to my memory of the force I felt running through me at that time—but it was well received, and President Plimpton invited me into his office to discuss it. He said that I raised good points, ones that were being considered by the administration, and that he hoped I would stay and contribute to change. He said that he thought it would be character-building to stick it out and participate, and he offered to give me assistance if it was at all possible.

"My office is open," he said. "Just call." I thanked him, but I imagined then that I had an appointment with destiny. I never pictured what it would really be like to enter a large public university on the other side of the country; it was simply the correct and most expressive myth for my life.

Many students were enthusiastic about my ideas, and I found myself public and articulate in a way I had never been, conducting discussions at meals in Valentine and talking openly and controversially in my classes. I had broken a lifelong silence. . . .

◊

On a moonlit night in mid-October, Junior year, while I was driving back from dropping Lindy at Smith, the Scorpio within me awoke and reclaimed his dormant energies. I thought of her as Persephone, trapped in the underworld by her advertising-man/police reporter boyfriend, and me as the animus-warrior rushing to save her before she swallowed the fateful pomegranate seeds. The Scorpion identified himself as my longtime prankster and proposed a new prank, a good one, in fact, a transforming act of the archetypal trickster: I would conduct a ceremony in the Glen on Halloween, three days before my twentieth birthday. I was so convinced of the rightness of this event, everyone in the house blended with my manic energy. . . .

On Saturday morning Polachek arrived with two records of Chinese temple music. He immediately set to work painting an impeccable high priestess on an enormous piece of plywood, a juicy veil of pomegranates behind her. Later Chuck appeared, trailing not only Josey but a short flinty kid from Bard College named Harvey. He looked both like a runt and a fiend, and he spoke in an ornery self-promoting way. As far as he was concerned, Bard was the center of the universe, at least for colleges, and he thought it was a joke that he should be dragged up to Amherst for a ceremony.

The three of them together looked like classic beatniks, but Tripp laughed at my designation of Josey as a witch. "She's a sweet chubby Jewish girl from New York, that's what she is," he whispered to me, but she did paint a beautiful abstract Moon card, with vibrations of corporealization rising from a crayfish in a pool through the charged air into a vibrating lunar node. As nightfall approached I sat at my desk and wrote an introduction to the ceremony. I was still flying on Scorpion energy.

We marched together down into the Glen where Nelson had arranged our mandalas amidst ten torches on sticks, five long candles and two wide candles on an altar, and metal railroad poles towering into the heavens. Marty had hung speakers in the trees, and the soft bells and flutes made a music of the spheres. I carried the boxes of slides I had gotten from the Biology and Geology Department files, and an extension cord, and we set the projector going in a loop — galaxies, flowers, amoebas, rivers, volcanos, craters of the moon, mountains, birds against blue sky, the planet Jupiter, glaciers — one after another, enormous and rippling on the sheets Nelson had strung up among the trees. The torchlight lit our mandalas; the sky was full of constellations; and from the darkness came the sounds of the Chinese temple. "Now this is a real party, Grossinger," Tripp said, lying back comfortably on the grass.

Then I moved into the candlelight of the altar. "Why are we out here?" I asked. And I ran through archetypes, planets of science-fiction universes now abandoned, old trick-or-treat Halloweens in ghost costumes. "We have come," I said, "finally to what we are. Through this ceremony we deny the false carnival colors and adolescent rituals of America, the neon and gloss that douse our lives with fake significance and blind us to our true natures. . . ."

Having read my speech, I was silent, and we sat there watching the images while Nelson served apple cider and cookies. Harvey was visibly moved, and he asked for a copy of my words to bring back to Bard.

◊

I had received two invitations which now fit together on my twentieth birthday. Aunt Bunny was out of the mental hospital, and her friends were holding a celebration in Manhattan. Then I got a letter from Harvey's teacher at Bard, the poet Robert Kelly, who said that he would like to meet me; he included xeroxes of some of his recent poems, which were reminiscent of Olson and quite alchemical. So I presented Lindy with the idea of a trip to New York and Bard, stopping at the hotel overnight in-between, and she nodded excitedly. . . .

◊

We parked in front of my father's house, beside the (otherwise) NO PARKING sign and walked straight to the indoor-pool building. It was past midnight and the coffee shop was closed, but I scaled the wall and opened it from inside. We sat on the reverse side of the counter, and I made us Milty Stackel milk shakes: mostly ice cream, six different flavors, malt, vanilla syrup. The machine eventually beat them into liquid, and we drank straight from the frosted metal cups with straws, feeling foolish and delighted. Then I gave her a tour of the nightclub, the enormous empty kitchens and dining rooms, the lobbies. She was appropriately wide-eyed.

◇

We came back to the car, filled it up at the hotel pumps. Then Lindy drove out the gate, left on 52 to Ellenville, then over to Kingston on 209; she lit a cigarette with the window open and I read her Kelly's poems in final preparation.

There was a wonderful ordinariness to being together — eating breakfast, deciding who would drive, her snappy turns on the back-road, the chance to lie there against the cold sunny window and read aloud (despite a touch of carsickness). I could live this way forever. We crossed the Rhinecliff Bridge over the Hudson and continued along the wooded country road.

Robert Kelly lived on the Bard campus, and we were directed to a driveway through a small parking lot that ended in a cluster of barrack apartments. I knocked on the last door. Nothing could have prepared us for the people who appeared.

A stocky coarse-looking woman, short as a dwarf, opened the door and said very loud, "You must be Richard Grossinger. Come in. Robert has been waiting for you."

Already I could hear his bellowing resonant voice from the back rooms: "Joby, is it Richard Grossinger?"

We had entered a cramped study packed to the ceiling with bookshelves filled mostly with old cloth volumes that looked like bestiaries. There were esoteric volumes and black binders on all the tables and scattered all over the faded Turkish carpet. Scanning the walls and surfaces I saw occult drawings, symbolic posters, tarot cards, horoscopes on colored paper, unfinished cups of coffee, ashtrays overflowing. It was as though we had stepped through a passageway into another zone of reality. The room was ice-cold. A large mechanical heater with a pipe up through the ceiling was not turned on. Paint was peeling from the walls, and the room was stark and unadorned except for the posters. Across the archway leading to the entrance from which Robert Kelly himself appeared was a sign with the words: TOMORROW POSSIBLE BECAUSE IT IS.

He was such a giant man that he transformed scale itself. He moved with difficulty, squeezing through the opening. He was well over six feet tall, well over 300 pounds. He had wild red hair and a bushy red beard. He wore brown-rimmed glasses that gave him a wizard's look, and he seemed to survey the room by gasping between breaths. He continued to alter space as he walked through it like a giant rock coming through water.

"Yes, yes, Richard Grossinger—wonderful speech you gave—and—" He turned magnificently to Lindy, whom I introduced. Then he scurried us to chairs like a man feeding pigeons in the park. "Is there anything happening these days at Amherst and Smith? I had thought nothing. And then Harvey Bialy returns with a story of an unlikely ceremony and carrying this beautiful piece of writing." He grabbed it from one of the tabletops and shook it.

Alternating accounts and filling in each other's details, we lamented that there was so little going on at Amherst and Smith. We told him what courses we were taking and what we were reading. He listened patiently and then indicated he would supply the remedy. He went to the back room and returned with piles of mimeographed sheets he then stapled together. They made up a magazine called *matter*. I turned through pages filled with poetry and notes, diagrams and epigraphs. Right away I saw an essay on film-making by Stan Brakhage, and I told him about his visit and screening.

"He taught you an important lesson. You see, when you are young you think you can live on anything, like junk food—and you can, and seem to do all right—you two are testament to that. But in order to grow into men and women you need real things, real imagination, not just symbols, or the ideas of some professor who hasn't been out of the university in 200 years."

He took us out to lunch in his old car named Bloisius, also filled with books, back across the river into Kingston to a Chinese restaurant, and in the course of the meal he went down a list of important issues and quizzed us on them one by one: "What planets do you think are inhabited?"

I gave an obvious response, mentioning Mars and Venus.

"But I think they are all inhabited," he said, "inhabited on their own planes and by creatures indigenous to those planes. We think of life only in three dimensions, but beings might live on worlds in other dimensions while at the same time the surfaces of those worlds would appear barren."

"Even Pluto?" I asked.

"Don't be fooled by its size. It's a planet, the same as any other, and we know nothing about it, except as we have seemed to discover and name it. You ask about Pluto. I say that the sun is inhabited. I think its core is teeming with creatures, all in a spiritual state. Not necessarily higher. Souls exist on the sun in their own occasion. Souls come to this world for specific reasons too; this is the green planet, the realm of growth; here, uniquely, creatures can transform themselves by work. That is our desperate situation, the reason we cannot dawdle. Your professors don't see it, so they fulfill their etymology: they profess; they go on and on as if we had time unto eternity. We have very little time, almost no time at all, and the moon itself is waiting to swallow us, to trap us in habitual motion so that we live our lives in an instant and effect nothing, die into darkness. That is the next task for you two—to live—now that you have declared yourself apart from the monster."

Then he asked us about dreams, and we answered with interpretations from Jung and Freud. "Good training," he said, "but this is still the Western dream you are talking about, the dream that stands for something. I am talking about a pure act of dreaming that does not have to be made subservient to any system of symbols. Remember Blake: make your own system or be enslaved by another's. Unfortunately, Blake was enslaved by his own system. Dreaming is no different from 'lifing'—that's an American Indian testament. You need not think of yourselves as bearers of artifice or requiring interpretation. Dream is its own logos, not the product of some professional establishment."

After lunch we went back to his apartment, and he offered to read from his work. We were in a hurry to get back to school, and initially we resisted, but he chided us for being typical Amherst and Smith students, and virtually mesmerized us back in our seats. "What would your good professors think if you refused a reading from William Butler Yeats?"

I thought it would be boring, but he read like an incantation, closing with a long poem called "The Alchemist," with lines as good as any I had ever heard. . . .

After the reading we left him copies of our work we had brought along for that purpose, and he promised to read them and discuss them with us the next visit, which he hoped would be soon. We left Bard and found the Taconic, winding up through New York to meet the Thruway just before the Massachusetts line. "Give me a few days to get my life together," Lindy said at the door to Laura Scales, and I nodded and drove back to Phi Psi.

◇ SARAH LIU ◇

Bones of Jade, Soul of Ice

◇ *Closet*

Place of refuge. Cozy, unlike the emptiness of the large white house, domain of my father. Of course, the closet is in this house, for I leave its walls only to go to school. I decorate it with posters, the kind I don't want my father to see: pictures of rock stars, television personalities. My father strongly disapproves of "barbaric music" and any precocious interest in the opposite sex. "I know you'll grow up and leave me some day," he moans, "but not yet."

◇ *Coat Hanger*

He wrenches it apart, uncoiling the neck, creating a crude prong. I hide behind the door of the living room, watching my father with his primitive bayonet, watching my mother cover her face with her hands, watching red scratches spring to the surface of her cheek. Later, when she has left for good, he turns it towards me. But his jabs are half-hearted. It is not as much fun to play this game with a kid.

◇ *Maturity*

You frighten me, Baba, with the smell of whiskey on your breath during the day, and the smell of cognac at night, even though you do tell good stories about Monkey and Princess Iron Fan, and Mu-Lan, who went off to the wars disguised as a boy. My mother never had time to read to me like you do. I cannot remember her playing with me at any time, but she did give me books, and took me to the store to buy school supplies. I always ask for books. I never ask for toys — to do so would be to admit I am a child.

◇ *Sara Liu is a doctoral candidate in English at the University of California, Berkeley. This essay was her first appearance in print.*

◇ *Love*

If I really loved my father, I would be like the girl who got up at six to cook her parents breakfast, or like himself at the age of ten, when he sold the most valuable stamp in his collection to buy his mother a duck for New Year. His love for me, according to the Chinese women, wives of his friends, is extravagant and touching, especially since I am a girl. "Your baba loves you so much, you are spoiled," they tut to me. I also hear them hissing, in terrible whispers, "Poor man. Abandoned by his Western wife and left with a child who doesn't even speak Mandarin properly. Ai-ya. We must find a good woman to care for him." But my father tells me he finds Asian women unattractive.

◇ *Critic*

His eight books discuss questions that arise from interpreting Chinese poetry into English, in a larger sense, conflicts inherent in bi-culturality. His books are both by and about my father, for no one is as completely bi-cultural as he. He appreciates T'ang poetry and composes his own verse in classical Chinese; he wrote a dissertation on the Metaphysical Poets and another on Virginia Woolf. He loves both Peking and Western opera, Ming porcelain and Picasso, French cognac and the Chinese liquor mao-tai.

His bridge between two worlds collapses periodically. He refuses the traditional title of "Sinologist," but he is not read or accepted as a Western theoretician. He took a British Council scholarship in 1949, never thinking that events would cut him off from his family for 30 years. His command of English is flawless. He taught me how to diagram sentences when I was in seventh grade, yet his hand strikes the table loudly when I do not kowtow low enough, or the brush trembles in my hand while we practice calligraphy.

In the early afternoon my father comes to visit. He approaches hesitantly, suddenly shy in front of the "patient" who days ago was simply his daughter. But a strained, hearty smile covers his face, to reassure both himself and this child-ghost. He carries a sagging, oval-shaped paper plate covered with tin foil. He places it on my lap. The heat quickly makes a circle of moisture on the sheets. I like the warmth.

"Happy Birthday. I brought you longevity noodles." He stops. Silence. I keep my voice casual. "Oh? Good. Thank you." Of course, on every birthday I have eaten *mein*, traditional symbol of good luck and long life. But "longevity" was an abstract concept out of Chinese fairy tales, like "immortality" or "prosperity." It was something that heroes and heroines in such stories sought, and had nothing to do with ordinary, real-life people like me.

I lift the foil from the steaming plate. As always, Baba's cooking smells wonderful. He has topped the noodles with a thick, salty, black bean sauce, with green onion and fresh cucumber mixed in. I've always thought of this as "my" dish: English cucumber with Chinese sauce. I can see Baba making this meal for me cutting the vegetables with a long, thin knife; boiling water for the noodles in the old, scarred pot; stirring the jiang sauce in the blackened wok.

"Here, it's gotten cold. Let me heat it in the microwave." My father scoops up the plate and hurries from the room, restless for activity. I hear the beeps of the microwave in the day room. Baba returns, the plate now drooping more than ever. He rummages in the paper bag he has brought, and extracts a pair of chopsticks with the air of a conjurer. "Here. So you can eat them properly." He sits back to watch me.

Poking the noodles, I find they have hardened and become coarse in their journey to the hospital and the time spent in the microwave. My chopsticks scrape against the cardboard bottom of the plate, so different from the smooth, blue-glazed bowls at home. Still, my favorite dish. From home.

"Mmm, good," I tell my father. He watches me put down the chopsticks. He moves to the edge of his chair and shakes his head.

"You've hardly eaten any at all. I cooked this especially for you. Try to eat some more."

"I can't. Maybe later. Could you wrap it up and save it in the fridge?"

"No, no, it's not worth it. It won't taste good. I can always make you more, I suppose."

He eases back in the chair and clears his throat. He looks at his watch. A greasy lock of hair keeps falling over his forehead; he pushes it back impatiently. I want him to stop staring at me. I wish he wouldn't sit there gaping. Say something. Do something.

"Don't hover," I burst out irritably. "You're like a bat, hovering over me." I imagine my father sprouting large, black wings, watch him flap annoyingly over my bed, feel the weight of the round, red eyes in their gaze.

"O.K.," he says placatingly. "I brought the Scrabble set. Would you like to play a game?"

"Sure." I don't really, but what else is there to do? I can't just sit here in silence with him. I wonder how long he plans on staying. Maybe he has to teach one of his classes soon. I can't remember, which afternoons does his seminar meet?

I am ahead, thanks to the word "taxi" on a triple-letter score, when Dr. Anderson comes in. "Sorry to interrupt. The transfusion went O.K.? Good." He notices the tears welling up in my eyes. "Look, I know it's hard, but you have to get used to it. You can't cry every time someone mentions something about your leukemia." I sniff and nod. "You're scheduled for another chemo session tonight," he continues. "We're giving you a different medication this time: methotrexate. We'll watch carefully to see if you develop any reactions, but I don't anticipate any problems."

"And what does this drug do?" my father asks nervously.

I stop listening as the doctor launches into a lengthy explanation. The drugs all do the same thing: kill cancer cells. From time to time my father nods his head in vigorous agreement. I watch him listening, the professor assimilating new knowledge, and wonder how much he actually hears. This isn't information, Baba. This is me.

Dr. Anderson finally leaves. I stage a fake yawn. "I'm very tired. Do you mind if we don't finish the game? I think I'll sleep."

"Of course, of course." My father stands up quickly. "I'll leave the board here; we can play some other time. You rest. I'll call you tomorrow." He leans over to kiss me.

"Goodbye, Baba. Baba . . . you know, next time, you could bring a book or something. You don't have to watch me while you're here. It's nice just having someone around, without fussing."

"All right. Get some sleep. Don't worry."

I am alone. The room seems lighter. I flip through a magazine, turn on the television. I try to forget the look on my father's face.

The afternoon wears on. Toward dusk, one of my roommates returns from radiation therapy. Rachel, like me, is a recently diagnosed patient, and therefore a novice at IV-pole manipulation. She curses, as her feet trip over one of the coaster struts.

"These things are *difficult,*" her father laughs. "Boy, when you turn 16, you won't need driving lessons. Hey," turning to me, "I think you've got an unfair advantage. Your pole has only three legs, but Rachel's has four."

"Well, I don't know. Fewer legs could mean less stability." I get out of bed to compare poles. Rick, our third roommate, joins us to check out the situation.

"I think Rick here wins. Five legs! That takes the cake. I haven't seen one of those before." Rick ducks his head in embarrassment, but grins. We are involved in a discussion of what a five-legged pole should be called — Pentacycle? Quintaped? — when evening rounds begin.

The doctors arrive in the usual pack, armed with clipboards and notes, medical students in tow. The patients dutifully retreat to their beds to await scrutiny.

"This is Rick, age twelve, diagnosis: Ewing's sarcoma. Left leg amputated two days ago, see notes from Dr. Benson, pediatric surgeon." The doctor presenting the case abruptly switches the tone of his voice. "How are you doing, Rick?"

"O.K. When can I go home?"

"Well, we want to keep you here a while longer until your leg heals a bit, and keep an eye on your counts."

"Can't I go home sooner?"

"Let's wait and see how you're doing in a couple of days."

"Can I ask you something?"

"Sure, anything. Shoot."

"What do they do it with? A knife?"

"Partly. They used a knife for the tissue layers, and a saw for the bone."

"Wow, a saw. Cool." Rick smiles. The doctors laugh. They move to the next patient.

In the corner by the bed Rick's mother sits, silent.

◇ PAULA GUNN ALLEN ◇

My Lebanon

I am Paula, daughter of Lee, son of Narcisco, son of Elias. I am an American of Lebanese descent, cut adrift from Lebanon by the meanders of time, history, place, and the private decisions of my family and myself. Because the course of my family river has been diverse, I have no central myth or legend, no single point of view, to enclose me. I have death, grief, snatches of history, and memory of song. I have tolerance, passion, an oddly persistent memory that can't be mine of a spring graced by the healing power of a female god, a sprite, an ancient waterbeing. I know the sound of debukke and oud. I know the sound of finger cymbals. But I don't know how to do the dances, was made foolish at my lileeah, my engagement party, by that lack so many many years ago, when I married a Hanosh, my great-grandmother's great-nephew. As her name was Haula (Paula in English), her family in Lebanon was particularly excited by the match. Haula is coming home, they rejoiced. I am told that my picture occupies a place of honor in their home, or did a few years ago, even though I divorced my Hanosh cousin 25 years ago. Or maybe the house and the picture have been bombed. Maybe all her relatives are dispersed or dead.

In my mouth sometimes I carry the taste of food, on a tongue that stumbles in saying the names: kibbe, leban (or laban), hemos, duele, mamoul, mehle, butujin, risbe habeeb, hibs, cusa mitwe, baba-ganoush, eftire, kibbe naya, kibbe sinea, kibbe erst, yubra, yuhne,

◇ *Paula Gunn Allen, born in Cubero, New Mexico, is of Laguna Pueblo, Sioux, Scottish-American, and Lebanese-American descent. She teaches at UCLA. Her great-grandfather emigrated from Lebanon in 1888; his son was twice elected to the New Mexico House of Representatives; his son was twice elected Lieutenant Governor of New Mexico, the first Lebanese-American to hold high political office in the United States. Her most recent book is* Grandmothers of the Light *(Beacon Press).*

halewe. Some of them everyone knows: Halvah, for instance, my
father calls halewe. Mehle, that in America is called baklava. Duele,
dolma, grape leaves. Risbe habeeb, rice pudding, rich and sweet,
studded with fat raisins, rich with cream. Others are too strange in
America, and that's too bad. I can't spell them because they don't spell
in English. Not the way I hear them in my ear. I carry a little of my
Lebanese people's language in my ear, a few of their stories, their ways,
their history both here and in the old country, only a little, but no
more. (Poco, poquito, pero no más, Jido is saying in my memory, in
my ear. "Pero no más.")

Lebneni (lubnaani); Syrian; Arab. When I was young, I was told
that in the east, in New York and New Jersey, they had signs up in
certain places, hotels, restaurants, "No Syrians or Jews Allowed." I
was told that that meant us too, because they called all of us "Syrians."
I guess there were no Lebanese in the minds of the anti-Semitic sign
makers, just as there were no Lebanese for the hundreds-of-years-
long occupation and colonization of Lebanon by the Syrians. Indeed,
there was no Lebanon for so long that it is still difficult, almost
impossible, to find mention of it anywhere except on the news on TV.
Does that mean that there is no Lebanon, really?

My Native American grandmother, Agnes Gunn, remembers being
excluded from the group at Indian School in Albuquerque, from the
group at home in New Laguna: "They used to tell me to go away.
They wouldn't have anything to do with me. So, I did."

She went away to Cubero in geographic location. She went away
to the home of the German-Jewish immigrant she married. She
went away to whatever version of America she could manage in
that tiny Spanish-speaking village, my grandmother Gottlieb who
never learned to speak Spanish and forgot as much Indian as she
could. Who internalized the scorn and loathing directed against
her and against her full-blood mother by their Laguna community,
who turned as racist against Indians as she could, for as long as she
could. Not because the whites rejected her. But because the Indians did.

And my mother, her daughter, who was not the biological daughter of the Jewish immigrant, but who was his stepdaughter, was

stoned by the Cubereño children, her peers, after school. "They used to chase me down the hill," she remembers, "throwing rocks at me, shouting 'Judea! India!' as they chased me." Those children were Mexican-American, Spanish, as they said of themselves in those days, before the new age of militancy and radicalism came into vogue. La gente. La Raza. "Viva la Raza! Venceremos!" They have every reason to hate the child they stone. Is she not the enemy? The despised Jew? The loathed Indian?

And me. La India. La Arabe.

◊

Like my Lebanese relatives I love the mountains and the sea; like them I am drawn to the madonna, the Mother; like them I feel safest when there is a spring nearby, as there was in my childhood Cubero, a spring I can speak with and know that the sacred sprite who lives within replies. And like them I know that the tradition may change in time and place, but that in essence it remains the same, and that it is in the stories that the sacred essence survives. Perhaps, more than anything in my life, I take that love from them.

So I have much from them. Even my body, which at barely over five feet is not much taller than my grandmother's. My father says, talking about her, "She was broad," he gestures with his hands, "hefty. Like you, and Kathy." Kathy, my sister, is five feet tall and weighs over 150. I am about five foot one and weigh around 190. When he says that, I am proud, but a little dubious. Not about matching Mama Mina in size, but in face. He says, "You look like my mother." I think, "No, Kathy does, I don't." Because I have heard them saying that one of my aunts looks exactly like her mother, and I know that Kathy looks almost exactly like that aunt. I think my father says that I look like his mother because our dispositions are a lot alike.

My body. From my mother's family I inherit arthritis, sinus trouble, hay fever, and perhaps lupus. From my father's family I inherit size, low blood pressure, a tendency toward diabetes and heart trouble. And thick, thick, curly, almost kinky hair. From them I inherit my skin, a pale olive that turns a lovely brown with the summer sun. I have one far-sighted eye and my father is far-sighted; I have one near-sighted eye and my mother is near-sighted. A little of this, a little of that: a person is made up of too many pieces, a patchwork quilt. A horse designed by a committee. The single most important part of me I inherit from Lebanon: my body. My very unfashionable, unthin, uncool, un-American as it can be; my round, big-breasted body. But even that is half-breed, three-quarters breed, for while its size is of my father's people, and though my hair is thick and tightly curly, almost kinky, I am otherwise quite hairless. Is that Indian? My mother has thin hair on her head, virtually no hair on her arms. She plucked her eyebrows thin when she was in high school in the early thirties and, she says, they never grew back. They are thin. My eyebrows are thin too. I notice that my mother's grandmother had thin eyebrows, and I don't imagine she ever plucked them. So even my body is part-Lebanese. Though what it matters, I am not sure. I think it matters to me, to know about my own proclivities, inclinations, and dreams. To know whence they are, and in that way, perhaps, to know whence they will proceed. Or maybe it's just that I'd like to know which side I, American mongrel, am on, and whether that side is or isn't "right." To know how I can justify the thoughts and emotions I experience, sometimes overpowering in their intensity, when the subject of Zionism, fascism, genocide, good guys and bad guys in the Middle East comes up in conversation or on television.

I also have a Lebanese ability to talk, wildly gesticulating. I have a love of loud parties, dancing, drinking, hollering and bonding, and eatingeatingeating. I have a love of full cupboards, laden tables, plenty for all the guests and lots left over. I have an expansiveness, a sense of cunning, a love of storytelling, a love of place, a sense of history, a personal sense, a delight in mystery, a delight in ritual of the Christian kind, a weakness for children, a tendency to humor them, to indulge them, a respect for nuns and priests that comes close to patronizing them. I enjoy doing business, I love to try to get the best of someone in a business deal. I have a pride of heritage and a quick anger, a quick, biting irritability. I have a strong sense of family, of propriety, of place. I have a sense of martyrdom, of melancholia, of great age. I have a liking for difference, a love of complication, a joy in intra-familial conflict, a sense of daring, of adventure, of the folly of humankind. I love to gamble, and I love to win. And I have a huge pile of memories to go along with the pile of memoirs I have also collected and they include the best and the worst moments of my life.

◇

My father has a piece of wood that he says is a piece of the cross that Jesus died on. He says Grandpa brought it from Lebanon. Grandpa used to peddle goods from Turkey to Jerusalem. My father says we are of the House of David, descendants of the same family that gave birth to Jesus. He says that Lebanon was the first nation to convert to Christianity. Long, long ago. Lebanon's patron saint is Mar Elias. According to the story, Elias and Moses joined Our Lord on the mountain peak. And the apostles, overcome with awe, offered to erect a tent to shelter the three, but Our Lord refused their offer, bidding them to simply watch and pray.

Elias, the assumed one, was so precious to the Father God that he did not die. They say he will return to earth in the last days, because like all men he must die. But not yet, they say, not yet. I wonder if somewhere Elias is being born, if somewhere some old patriarch named Elias is declaring himself present, present to preside over the final death of the Lebanese. Of us all.

In the church in Seboyeta, where my father was born and raised, Seboyeta that is nestled in the arms of the Cebolleta mountains on the eastern spur of Mount Taylor, Seboyeta that is one of the earliest settlements of the Spanish colonization of the northern territories of New Spain, now New Mexico, in that church, one that is very very old as things in America are dated, hangs a picture of Abraham preparing to sacrifice his son, Isaac. But the picture is actually of Saint Elias. Or that's how the story goes, because my great-grandfather ordered a painting of Lebanon's patron saint to grace the church where he worshipped on Sundays and holy days.

I went back to the church because the new young priest sent word that he had some papers and other things that had been left at the old house in Seboyeta years before, the house that had been bought by the Gallup diocese and was now the priest's house. I wanted to walk around there, remembering. Go into the church and sit, and listen, and dream. Maybe talk to some ghosts.

It didn't quite work out that way, though I guess I did talk to ghosts as I listened to the young Anglo priest, bearded and "involved" in the dynamic way the new priesthood often exhibits. He then told me about the superstitious credulity of the local people, the Seboyetaños (descendants of Spanish colonial settlers of the region who were granted possession of the land by decree of the Spanish crown a couple centuries ago). His story concerned what he called a legend about the miraculous healing of an infant boy, 60 or so years before. The story, he said, was that some local child had had some mishap — something had happened that should have killed him. But the child's grandmother and his mother had taken the baby, wrapped him in a blanket, then crawled on their knees from the church to a shrine some several miles into the hills, praying the rosary all the while. They had begged the Virgin, whose shrine it is, to save the child, and had dedicated him to her for life if she would grant their petition. Well, the baby lived, or so the story goes. And saying that, the priest shook his head pityingly. He thought the story had probably been carried from Mexico, maybe from beyond Mexico, from Spain, a quaint example of folk belief in this modern age. It was, he implied, yet another illustration of the magnitude of the difficulties he faced in this remote place.

I could see that he was university-educated, and was quite taken with the sense of himself as folklore specialist stationed in the wilds of New Mexico. He evidently didn't know that the story was quite true. That the infant in the story was my father. That the women — my grandmother and my great-grandmother — had indeed crawled all the way to Portales from Seboyeta, had dedicated the baby to Mary the Madonna, and that the baby had lived. The priest didn't know that after they did their religious best to save the child, they took him back to Seboyeta, and then to the doctor in Albuquerque, who discovered that the immediate cause of his nearly lethal injury — a screw that his sister, then about three, had given him to hold and he, infant-curious, had put in his mouth and swallowed — had passed, like God in the night.

◇

I do not know where, exactly, the village of my grandparents is. Or if it exists anymore, anywhere at all.

Déjà vu? I know how my elder halfbreed Indian relatives felt. And why a fullblood uncle used to ride on the train, claiming to be Italian. I find myself obscurely humiliated, frightened, grieved, to be one who is identified as the enemy of righteousness and good. I think Uncle Charlie must have felt that way, as many Indians have testified to feeling; because Indians have been so long the enemy of the good as that good is defined by white eyes. And so I can only watch, horrified, as the mobs, the shells, the bullets erupt. I can only listen, aghast, to my professional community as its many members denounce Lebanon and claim the right of the Arab to triumph, denying the right of the ancientancientancient Lebanese to live.

Walking to classes is painful. Today small neon-orange stickers adorn the elevators, demanding the imperialist Israel and the United States get out of Lebanon. No demand was made that all foreign powers get out; that Syria, the PLO, Palestine nationals, the Soviet Union, Iran, or whoever else is in Lebanon minding its business and murdering its citizens at least as much as the so-called imperialists cease their genocidal war on the people of Lebanon, the people of the mother's breasts, her milk-giving breasts. Lebanon is a cognate of laban, milk. Because the map of Lebanon is the map of two mountain ranges that are divided by a deep valley, the psychic-culture map shows a similar topography: the Lebanese display two towering ranges of knowledge and culture, divided by history, religion, diversity and oppression. Lebanon, recorded in the Book of Numbers as a land enslaved to Egypt, who quarried stone to send to the Egyptian rulers, carried it out of the quarries through the mountain ruggedness so Pharoah could have palaces fit for Egypt's might. Lebanon, conquered by the Aryan Turks, who split the children from the Mother, who tore the son from the tree and ripped his body to pieces, and cast the pieces upon the sea; who cast the sacred dogs of the goddess into the sea where they waited long centuries to be restored by Nordic seamen during the Second World War, the war that finally resulted in the liberation of Lebanon, for however brief a time, the liberation of the mountain wild folk, the Lebanese.

◊

I think about the ride up to Los Cerrillos Judy and I took a couple summers ago. I wanted to find the house where my grandmother was raised. The store her father kept. Early that morning my father and I sat and talked over breakfast in my parents' apartment high above the plain. Mother was in her room, Judy asleep. We talk about how he feels now, 70 years old. We talk about how he loses his memory, how it bothers him.

"Are you afraid of getting old?" I ask. Wanting to know, to know something about him, as he is to himself, in himself; wanting also to know for myself, later. So I will know where I am, when I am where he is now. He doesn't answer, just looks at me quickly, in that way he has, eyes darting over to me, away. A bird, perching for a moment on the twig of a thought, then away.

"Your grandmother was raised in Cerrillos," he says.

"Where?" I say. "You mean Los Cerrillos, up in the Sandias?"

"Yes," he says. "Up there. Her father, your Jide Michael, had a store up there. That's where she was raised."

I think this came up because I asked him about his mother. Something I haven't done much because it makes him sad to talk about her. Or it always used to. But now, maybe because he's 70, he talks about her, mostly without tears.

"How old was she when she got married, do you know?" I ask.

"Maybe 15 or 16." He shakes his head, lightly. Not sure. Or sure about the age she was when she married, but not sure how I'll take that. How it sounds.

"How old was she when she died?"

"Forty. She was 40."

"And how old were you?"

"Fifteen."

"She was young," I say. "She had so many kids in such a short time." I feel depressed, troubled. I try to calculate swiftly. Seven children that lived. Nine altogether. Fifteen from 40 is . . . I give up the attempt.

"Is the house still there, in Los Cerrillos?" I ask. He doesn't know. It might be. "Wouldn't it be great to go up there?" I say. I tell my mother, "Daddy says Mama Mina was raised in Los Cerrillos. Isn't that amazing? I didn't know that! Maybe we could go up there, see if we could find the old house, the store."

"Well, why don't you go?" she asks.

"Maybe I will," I say. "Why not."

It is late August, and the mountain is a study in floral design we drive through. White and yellow, deep gold and dark green, fuchsia and orange. We drive east out of Albuquerque, through Tijeras Canyon, turn right onto Highway 10, past San Antonito. Turn to the right a few miles later, swinging with the highway toward Santa Fe to the north. Past Golden, where the country-and-western twangs out on

Sundays at the bar there, and the hip, the cool, and the alcoholics spend a long afternoon drinking and getting stoned in 2/4 time.

I take a lifetime of memories with me on the drive, 20 or more years of drives through this lovely countryside. I take curiosity, the unanswered questions of years with me. I take eyes that look and look at the passing land, trying to hold perfect every blade of grass, every golden or purple blaze of color from the wildflowers, every stone, juniper, pine, trying to find what the land knows, what it remembers, what it means. Every period of my adult life is here with me as we drive, Judy and I, through the Sandias toward Santa Fe. My life rides in my eyes, investing everything I see with a memory, a meaning, a terror, a joy, a grief.

Somewhere is the road that goes among the tall pines where I went with some boy I was dating when I was 16. The road to the wilderness, the night, in the snow. Where I was raped, though it took me over 20 years to acknowledge the event. Somewhere else is the road that goes up to the peak, that ends near a path I walked with a man to a round stone building that looks out over the 5,000-foot drop to the plain, the city below, that looks 50,000 feet up to the sky, 50 million million miles to the stars through the openings in the stone. The round stone building where we made love and conceived twin boys. Conceived two, one of whom died.

And now, so long after, I drive that highway again, counting my life at various milestones, roads that run off here and there, at stops along the way. It's a habit I picked up from my father, and my Jido — this telling my life's stories in terms of the places we drive by. I wonder if I learned to experience my feelings the same way, from those same men. I feel filled with joy because the mountain is so ever beautiful. With melancholy because the thread that holds my life in place here or anywhere is so fragile, so tenuous. So many people I knew in terms of this mountain, these roads, that I have lost. Most of them I've never seen again.

Tristesse. I first heard that word over 20 years ago, when I went to Los Cerrillos the first time. I was with the divorced man from Iowa, or Indiana, or Illinois, the one who was an engineer, who ached for his children, his wife. "Tristesse," he said. I forget why he said it. "The sweet sadness." Tristesse is what rides with me, in my eyes, in my mind. Tristesse is what invests the wildflowered land, the beclouded sky that I look at for significance. I wonder as we go where they went, those Lebneni's who lived here once, who live here no more.

Finally we get there. It's farther from Albuquerque than I'd remembered. It's almost all the way to Santa Fe, through the mountain. We can't find it at first. We pass the turnoff a couple of times before we realize that the road that runs at an angle to the highway we're on leads to Los Cerrillos. I am filled with excitement. Sentiment. *Sentimiento. De me pensamientos.* My thoughts begin to move in awkward Spanish. Primitive Spanish, to be sure. But it is something that always happens when I go home, when I return in fact or memory to my father's house, to his land.

In the village we drive slowly up and down what we take to be the main drag, a wide gravel road. It hasn't been graveled in some time. Unlike many New Mexican villages, though, it has cross streets, stop signs, and even some sidewalks. Maybe because it's so close to Santa Fe. Or maybe because so many Anglo urbanites come up here to browse in the not-quite-quaint shops before they have dinner — if the fancy restaurant that was once here is still in operation. The oldest part of the village sports wooden sidewalks. Made of planks nailed together, raised a foot or so from the ground. Keeps the mud from covering it, makes it easy to dismount.

But we don't have a horse, and neither does anyone else. Or not for riding up to the cantina or la tienda. After a couple of slow passes, we park cater-corner from the wooden sidewalk, across the street from the few businesses that line the other side of the street. We get out, lock the car. I wonder why I'm locking it. This isn't the city. I don't have much to fear. But I lock it anyway, remembering my insurance man and feeling silly.

The questions haunt me. How long has it been since she lived here? I wonder. I try to spot a building that is old enough, built of adobe and roofed with galvanized steel. Red with age. But I know it's been too long for that to mean much. They'd have reroofed it long since. But I try. There's a building with a faded ancient sign. Circa 1930, at least. There are several buildings that might be my Jido's store. Some that might be the old house. The house that in some sense I come from, but that I've never seen.

"I'll ask," I say. "I'll just go into some store here and see if anyone knows." I do. We do. We go into a second-hand store. It may be the same one I visited 21 years ago with the man from Indiana, but I can't be sure. There's a woman tending store, and I ask her if she knows the Michaels, or where they had their store. She's very pleasant, but of course she doesn't know. Maybe so-and-so up the block, or down, I forget which, might know. We leave and try the grocery store next door. They don't know either. Spanish-American, Mexican-American, Chicano, I imagine they've lived here for generations, but they don't know. It's been a long long time since the Michaels lived and traded here, I think. It's not surprising that no one remembers them anymore. I can't even find the restaurant I ate at, so long ago.

How long has it been, anyway? Over 70 years? Over 80? She must have been born in 1888, moved from here around 1903. Eighty years, then, since she lived somewhere called Los Cerrillos, though perhaps, probably, it was a different Los Cerrillos then. She was 40 when alone, and surely in despair, she died in a mental hospital in Pueblo, Colorado in 1928, four years before my parents were married. Such a long time since she felt this wind.

We leave Los Cerrillos. Drive to Santa Fe for coffee. Or not. (I get confused, trying to remember which trip is which, which journey takes me to what place.) We drive back toward Albuquerque, the car behaving strangely. I discover it's because I've had the emergency brake on all this time. Days, probably. Maybe weeks. I release it, hoping I haven't done lasting damage, and we continue toward the city. Along the way we stop and walk around, tasting the mountain with our feet, our hands, our eyes. We take some chunks of a strange stone we find. One that's white and crumbles easily. Hard dirt, caliche, most likely. But it pulls me. I want it with me. We put it in the car to take it to California with us, to the house we haven't found yet. We will have a piece of the mountain in our new life.

Back at my parents' apartment they ask about our trip. My father is in a jovial mood. He jokes around. He knows, far better than I, I suspect, how fragile is the past. How futile the attempt to recover anything from it. And how necessary. His mother lives in his memory, his feelings, his life. And in that way only does she live in mine.

◊

"This is it," a friend said. "This is Rumie." I gaze at the tiny village, almost invisible in mountain mistiness, off to the side in the photograph. There was a picture of the ruin, high atop a hill just outside the village. "That's it!" I exclaim. "That's the place they showed on TV!" I hadn't seen much on the show, though, because the camera was focused mostly on the reporter. I remember his short-sleeve khaki outfit, my frustration at the cameraman. But the magazine spread includes a view of range after range of mountain juniper and other pine trees, sandy rocks, and a small paved road. "No wonder Jido said Lebanon was like New Mexico. No wonder they settled in Seboyeta," I said. "I always wondered how Grandpa found Albuquerque and Seboyeta, in all the world he had before him. Now I know. This looks just like home," I said. Not sure which home I was referring to in that statement. "It's very lovely. In fact, it looks just like I thought it would."

My grandmother, who we called Sitte — meaning grandmother in Lebanese — well, actually, my father's grandmother, worked in a silk factory when her husband — my Grandpa Francis — came to the United States that first time. He kept sending money home for her and their son, but his uncle wouldn't give it to her so she was forced to go to work in a silk factory. (Grandpa Francis once had silk worms sent to Seboyeta from Lebanon so that his grandchildren could raise them and see where silk came from.)

My friend Albert described the work of a silk factory to me: "They have huge vats of boiling water. The women drop the cocoons into it — you know, the worm spins a cocoon around itself and it's the thread of the cocoon that is used for making silk. The women put their hands into the water and take out the worms. They have to work very fast, because you can leave the cocoons in the boiling water only a short time, just until the worm is dead. So they would have to reach their hands into the boiling water, over and over, all day long." Albert thinks that the Arab word for bordello, *karkhana,* comes from *khafanu,* the silk factory — because the women worked nearly naked in the intense heat. "Wow," I think. "My Sitte worked in a bordello!" And this thought, obscurely, relieves me of some of that lifelong sense of shame.

I understood the anger in my father's voice every time he repeated the sorry tale of Sitte's humiliation at the hands of her husband's relatives. For no daughter of a landed family worked in a silk factory like the poor were required to, yet she, his own beloved grandmother, had been forced to do so. I realized that this had happened because Sitte, born Haula Hanosh, was from a poor family in the village. I knew it because my first husband's father, her nephew, had told me of his childhood and young manhood, when they had suffered greatly at the hands of the Druse colonial armies of the Empire. "Five men work all day eb'ry day in stone quarries," he had said. "Five strong men. And for carrying rocks on our backs for 12, 16 hours," he said, emphasizing the point by counting the hours off one finger at a time, "one loaf of bread we take back to family, women, and all the little children. We died of the yellow fever, of diphtheria, of war. We were so glad when war over, and Lebanon was made free of the Turks."

I realize that my Sitte, this man's aunt, had lived like that; so poor, so without food. She married into a family that would say, two generations later, "We never carried rocks on our backs. We were merchants, traders. We never carried rocks." Except for when we, she, worked naked in the bordello, *khafanu*. Her grandchildren would tell me about her suffering, but would display no understanding of what might have caused it: that because she came from a family that did carry rocks on its back, she was made to suffer physical and social torture at the hands of her husband's relatives when her husband was in America. Were her husband's relatives keeping her in her place? I imagine so, though I can only speculate. I know that later, after her husband returned, he found himself unable to live there amidst the multiple varieties of oppression, so he decided to emigrate permanently. That time he took her and their child with him. Over the years he brought members of their respective families over, and for a long time he was the head of the circle of Lebanese-Americans in New Mexico.

After his death, Sitte became the head. She lived to see her son a member of the New Mexico State Legislature; to see her nephews settled and prospering in various villages around the state. To see herself head of the sprawling clan of Lebneni from Rumie, and no one, man or woman, made personal, business, or political decisions without receiving her advice and concurrence. I bet it did her heart good, my Sitte. Maybe she thought about the long road she had taken from desperate ignominy in *karfanu* to being the power center of a large clan of relatives in America in those long nights while I pretended to sleep so I could watch her ready herself for bed, so I could watch her sleep.

My mother says that Sitte always greeted people by saying something that sounded like "S'lem ou klem." It was probably "Salaam o khalem," peace and greetings. Salaam o khalem, Sitte. Salaam o khalem, Lebanon.

◊ L. T. JORDAN ◊

The Balls of Malta

Ireland, Sir, for good or evil is like no other place under Heaven,
and no man can touch its sod or breathe its air
without becoming better or worse.

GEORGE BERNARD SHAW

It was, as they say at home, a nice soft morning as I made my way up Grafton Street to meet my intended brother-in-law for a couple of pints and a chat.

We call it "soft" whenever the rain falls horizontally and we hope to God it will pass quickly.

So there I was, rain streaking down the back of my neck, shoes leaking, no raincoat between me and the elements. Not that I'd forgotten, you understand, I merely didn't own one. I did, however, own a heavy Crombie overcoat, and a lovely thing it was. Thrown over the end of your bed on a winter's night it was a darlin' thing. Good enough to dress out a corpse. Regrettably, it was in the pawn. Very changeable weather, as my Mother would have it, you wouldn't know what to be pawning. The fact that it had been placed in the pawn earlier that morning meant that I had a few shillings to spend, and sure, who can have everything?

Out of the downpour I ran and into the dark comfort of McDaid's pub in Harry Street there to find Lorcan, my intended brother-in-law.

"The hard man, Larry. How's the form?"

◊ *Larry Jordan was born in Dublin. He emigrated to Los Angeles in 1960 and now lives in Redwood City, California. He writes a column for* California Golf *and is a frequent lecturer on Joyce, O'Casey, and the Abbey Theater.*

"Not bad, Lorcan. Yourself?"

"Grand, thank God. Eh, Larry, this is Brendan Behan."

I should mention that this conversation, like many others that followed it, took place entirely in Irish, for Lorcan placed no value on things English, nor did Brendan who had gone on record at the age of 16 by trying, unsuccessfully, to blow up a British warship in Liverpool.

He had gone to Borstal for his trouble and while there had taken a leaf from another Irish writer who, upon reading *War and Peace,* announced, "Jaysus, but that's a grand ould story. I think I'll write one meself."

Brendan's first effort, "I Was a Borstal Boy," appeared in an Irish journal called *The Bell* in 1942. Much later he turned this material into *The Borstal Boy,* which became a bestseller and prompted Kenneth Tynan to write: "If the English hoard words like misers, the Irish spend them like sailors; and Brendan Behan, Dublin's obstreperous poet-playwright, is one of the biggest spenders in this line since the young Sean O'Casey. Behan sends language out on a swaggering spree, ribald, flushed, and spoiling for a fight."

Dublin, as someone else once said, is a city where wit is prized above riches. It is also one of the most written about and least cared for cities in the world. A city which sometimes manifests a curious and somewhat ineradicable bent for the second-rate, as though it found the first-rate rather uncomfortable to live with. Or simply boring.

On one of my rare visits to Dublin a few years back — notice I didn't say holiday, for a trip to Dublin for me is more of a pilgrimage than anything else — I spent a few quiet hours in a pub with Brendan's widow, Beatrice. Oddly enough, it was raining that evening, too. We chatted pleasantly about any number of things, including Brendan, his work, his friends, and the like.

Her own story, *My Life with Brendan,* had been published the year before. It is a sad story of a man who could quote an 18th-century Gaelic poet as readily as he could quote Joyce, Yeats, O'Casey, or Wilde. A story of the man who said of himself, "Success is damn near killing me. If I had my way, I should prescribe that success go to every man for a month; then he should be given a pension and forgotten."

She felt, she said, that she had to write it. She had been quite upset with Ulick O'Connor's recent book, *Brendan,* and its allegations about Brendan's supposed bisexuality.

When I asked her what life was like now, she answered, "It's like living in a railway station."

As we approached closing time, I asked how she thought Brendan would like best to be remembered. Her answer took me off guard, and yet, upon reflection, it was dead on the mark. "Brendan would like to have a theatre named after him. That would be nice," she said, and her eyes looked at me with the sadness of vanishing light.

But I'm getting ahead of myself.

The morning in question was in the early fifties, 1951, I think, and Brendan was still earning his living as a housepainter. His literary career, like his death in 1964 at the age of 41, was still in front of him.

My intended brother-in-law was at that time an unpublished poet who spent most of his working days balancing mathematical equations in a government section called CIE, for Coras Iompair Eireann, or the public conveyance department.

Like most government bodies CIE never seemed to make a profit, and given the irregular schedule of their buses, I'm not surprised. Listening to politicos forever justifying the economics of it all would put bloody years on a man. Seems like we used to stand at a bus stop for a lifetime waiting for a bus to come along. On one occasion I heard an old woman screech at a bus conductor, "It's not CIE at all yiz should be callin' yourselves, but the bleedin' Banana Bus Company for yiz always come in Jaysus bunches."

How McDaid's became a hangout for poets, writers, actors, painters, and a couple of defrocked priests is beyond me, but if you sat there long enough you'd be worn out shaking hands. Perhaps it was because the place was an ass's roar from the Gaiety and the Olympia Theatres, or that Trinity College was down at the end of Grafton Street, or that the College of Surgeons and the National University were around the corner.

Or maybe it was because people felt comfortable in the place. It was certainly without pretension. You'd never see a policeman in it, and the pint was very good.

The barman called everyone "Mister EH," which, I suppose, made us all feel equal. No names, no pack drill. "Ah, good mornin' Mister EH. Nice mornin' thank God. Yes it is. A pint is it? Right yeh are." What can't be cured must be endured.

"Ah Larry, ould son, Brendan here was just telling me a gas bloody story," said Lorcan, handing me a pint. May the giving hand never falter.

"Seems like some Yank came out of the Shelbourne Hotel the other morning and got into Whacker Nolan's taxi. Poor man was devastated by the incompetence of the Celt, as he put it, and asked Whacker if we Irish had a word for *mañana* like the Mexicans do. Whacker, God love him, never bats an eyelid and says to yer man, 'Yessir, matter of fact we have three of them, but they all lack the urgency of the Spanish.'"

There are worse ways of spending a rainy morning, I'll tell you.

Brendan and I shared one thing in common. We were North-siders, having the dubious distinction of being born a few short streets away from each other in the slums of the north side of Dublin. Lorcan, on the other hand, was born in Dun Laoghaire, a fashionable suburb on the south side, as the newspaper columnists would have it, although I always thought God broke the shovel when He made that place.

Brendan was about to tell another story when the door of the pub opened on an elderly and very wet postman. "Large glass of Power's, please," said the postman and dropped his cape and postbag to the floor.

"There's no such thing as a large glass of whiskey, as Oliver St. John Gogarty once remarked," said Brendan.

"Ah, yes. Yer man. How's he keepin' at all?" inquired the postman.

"The ould bollox is not well at all."

"Jaysus, all the ould crowd is droppin' like flies."

The next time I met Brendan was about a month later in a pub in Henry Street. Long since gone, it was called the Tower Bar and looked across the street at Radio Eireann, the state-run broadcasting system. We were fortunate enough in those times, I suppose, in that we didn't have to waste time choosing a particular radio station to listen to, for there was only the one, Radio Eireann.

If you had a strong aerial you could always tune in the BBC. This, however, was considered unacceptable behavior in my circle of family and friends. "God knows what class of cod's wallop those people would have you listen to," was the way my father phrased it.

The Tower was home to any number of radio types who were given to dashing across the street between broadcasts, throwing down a few quick gins, and racing back to announce the travails of mankind to anyone who might be listening. It was only strangers who lingered close to the door. Regulars knew the dangers of blocking the way of hungover announcers.

"Jaysus, Paddy, a large gin, and quick. The nerves are gone."

"Why don't yeh have them out, like the teeth?"

"Never mind the bloody chat, and give me another. Put it on the slate."

The check-cashing and bill-paying procedures in the Tower on Saturday mornings would do justice to the House of Rothschild.

Anyway, there we were on a warm Saturday morning, Brendan, Lorcan, and myself, having a few jars on the strength of Lorcan's paycheck, when we were joined by a radio actor whose name I've forgotten. He was, I recall, a large man with rabbit eyes, small soft hands, and a voice as gentle as a summer lake. He also had the reputation of being a "toucher," one who is forever borrowing money and forgetting where he got it from. But in a nice way.

"Ah, yes. The £5, of course, to be sure. Would Friday evening be time enough for you? Terribly sorry about the delay. Had it for you last Friday, but didn't see you here."

The radio actor was, as usual, in the horrors. His complexion was reminiscent of white blotting paper. "Did yeh have any breakfast at all," asked Brendan. "A few eggs and rashers would do yeh the world of good."

"Merciful Jaysus, Brendan, but I couldn't look at the flag this morning," said the actor and called for a double gin.

"I'm stuck with a bloody author this morning, if you don't mind," he continued. "Introducing his new book on my programme."

"Any author who has to introduce his own book shouldn't have bothered writing it," said Brendan.

"Understandable, Brendan," said the actor, "but he's going to read from it as well."

Brendan lifted his pint to his lips, drained the glass, and ran the back of his hand across his mouth. "Reading your own stuff," he said, "is a form of mental incest."

Shortly after that exchange Brendan shouted a greeting at a small man in a felt hat, and walked away from us. I recognized the man as Brian O'Nolan, a famous columnist on the *Irish Times,* whose writings appeared under the pseudonym Myles na Gopaleen, or Myles of the Little Horses. He was also famous as Flann O'Brien, the author of four novels in English, as well as the famous work in Irish *An Beal Bocht,* since translated as *The Poor Mouth.* James Joyce said of O'Nolan, "A real writer with the true comic spirit." And Brendan is quoted as saying, "I read him with relief and jealousy."

When O'Nolan left the pub, Brendan returned to our company, laughing. "O'Nolan just told me he saw a huge Buick outside the American Embassy in Merrion Square, and that it reminded him of a pregnant whale blowing a mouth organ."

Thus, a wave of laughter followed O'Nolan's exit into the warm sunshine.

But our glasses were bordering on empty and I doubted if we had the price of three pints between us. "Jaysus, but a ball of malt would go down well," said Brendan, a ball of malt being what a double whiskey is called in Dublin.

Just then a young man entered the pub dressed in the resplendent gray-and-red uniform of the Knights of Malta. In his outstretched hand he held a cardboard box bedecked with small paper flags on pins, these flags bearing the Maltese cross and being sold for whatever you'd care to give, to support the charitable works of the good Knights. You slipped your money into a slot in the box and the Knight placed a flag in the lapel of your coat.

The young man looked at us and rattled the few coins in his box. "Merciful Mother," intoned the actor, "what in God's Holy Name is that?"

"With any luck at all," said Brendan, "it would be the money for the balls of Malta."

◊ BILL BARICH ◊

Same Everything

Marysville, in May, at 6:00 a.m. The pleasing quiet of early morning. I wanted to get up with the sun, so I could be out in the fields when the machinery began to turn and the dust began to rise, watching workers once again impose a sense of order, of dividend, upon the land. Now, parked on the shoulder of a dirt road, I can hear the same gentle rustle of wheat I heard yesterday—the earth's subtle whispering in odd counterpoint to the noise of tractors and cultivators. Odd, too, how manifestations of urban life appear quite suddenly in a landscape as plain as 19th-century Kansas. Down a two-lane blacktop nearby comes a demon teen in a chopped-and-lowered Nissan truck, his radio blaring. The wheat recovers quickly, though. It's as if a bullet had been fired through it, causing the plant stems to part momentarily, even reluctantly, before returning to normal. In fact, the fields and orchards have a secret-keeping quality. If I were young again and in love with a girl, I'd want to draw her into the wheat; now, in spring, into the green wheatfield, where the breeze would be as warm as breath on our skin.

At a little country store in Yolo I asked a young clerk if he knew what was growing on a farm across the way. He looked puzzled, as if he'd been asked something he should know but didn't—that look of students who've failed to do the most rudimentary homework assignments. For a moment, he moped at the cash register, hoping I would go away, but when I didn't he went to the back and into a storeroom; and then a heavyset, red-faced man, who limped and wore an apron

---

◊ *Bill Barich lives in San Francisco. His most recent book is* Hard to Be Good *(Farrar, Straus & Giroux).*

and had the not-entirely-welcoming countenance of a person inter-rupted in the midst of a task—stacking cans, sweeping spilled flour from the plank floor—marched forward, sweating mightily.

His eyes were fierce at first, but when I asked my question again they turned soft and almost loving, as if he, too, had been sent back to a schoolroom, to a time when everything around him had added up—a time, say, when no Nissan trucks sped down County Road 194, when no men in Marysville would dare to claim they'd been beaned in the head with a baseball bat by angry black gang members, as one fellow had done recently in the local paper; and so, hitching up his pants, he spoke with assurance, sweetly. "It's barley, I believe," he said. And I could see that he wanted more such questioning, but I had none to give.

◇

In a bar last night, this exchange:
"All men are assholes."
"It's women who make them that way."
A third customer, intervening, "What you got here is a chicken-and-egg situation."

◇

A visit to the Sikh temple on Bogue Road. It's a bright blue-and-white building with minarets; Christmas lights are strung around the out-side. A brick wall runs around the temple, separating it from prune orchards on three sides. I entered quietly, wandering about until I came to a small room, where several men were sitting on the floor. They were old men, mostly, and they looked as if they had retired from their earthly labors and were now dedicated to the job of preserving the memories of their youth in Punjab. Some had turbans, but others were bareheaded. They all appeared to be wondering what sort of devious impulse had brought me into their company.

A man of middle age rose to greet me. He had a scraggly black beard and wore a gold-orange turban and a silk pajama suit. He carried himself with great dignity. In his posture and bearing, I saw the strut of British colonial officers; there was something in him, too, of a favored pupil, who is always on the brink of stepping forward to claim a prize. His manner was polite, a little bemused, a little distant.

He didn't seem eager to have a visitor; on the other hand, he was willing to deal with this person who had dropped into his lap from outer space. He had been eating Chico-San rice cakes and drinking tea. A few kernels of puffed rice were caught in his beard.

When he introduced himself, I heard his name as Bengal. He was the head priest of the temple and had two assistants. He thought there were between six and seven thousand Sikhs in the Yuba City–Marysville area. Services were held at the temple twice daily, for morning and evening prayers. On Sunday, there was a longer service that lasted two or three hours. Afterwards, a big meal was served in a communal dining room.

Bengal said that his English wasn't very good; yet he had lived in Yuba City for some years. If I wanted a lot of information, he said, I should come back in the evening when men who spoke fluently and with decisive knowledge would be available. Then, he offered me a cup of tea, and one of the old men brought it to me in a styrofoam cup. It was very rich and sweet, thickened with condensed milk. "We always do it that way," Bengal told me, beaming proudly. He had a habit of tilting his head in such a considered position that I thought he was about to recite. His black eyes would flash, and I would be reminded of Indian men and women in Kama Sutra poses.

The tea was hot, so I drank it in slurps, just as Bengal did. When we were finished, he led me into a simply furnished bedroom, much like a monk's cell, and asked me to wash my hands at a sink installed in a wall. There was no soap. I held my hands beneath the tap for a minute, then wiped them on a towel that hung from a child's pegboard, where a bunch of manic ducks were pictured romping.

"Ducks," I said. Bengal seemed to enjoy this, and his eyes flashed even more brilliantly. I had heard that the weather in Yuba City was similar to the weather in Punjab, and I asked him about it.

"Yes!" he cried, jabbing a forefinger into the air. "Exactly the same."

"Is it true that you grow the same crops?"

"Same everything!"

At a door to the temple proper, its inner sanctum, there was a cardboard box filled to overflowing with orange kerchiefs. "Cover your head, please," Bengal advised me, though he gave no instructions on how I might wear the kerchief. It rested limply on my head, and I had to put a hand on it to hold it in place. Again, Bengal was enjoying himself; anyone could see that he had an ample supply of mirth. I wondered if his apparently limited command of English were an affectation, part of his function as a priest, a means of keeping his Sikhness intact, protected from the American emanations of K-Marts and Jack-in-the-Boxes. He opened the door, and we entered a big assembly room that had the feel of a high-school gym. The ceiling was strung with tinsel and ornaments. The floor was covered with brown carpeting, and a throw rug lay before the altar, on which a holy book rested. It was easy to imagine it glowing.

On the wall behind the altar were pictures of gurus, seven or eight of them. They had a strange beauty, a kind of swirling mastery. I had a distinct sensation they were watching me. "Number One, Number Two, etcetera," said Bengal, counting them off. He was beginning to tire of me, I think. He told me that men and women were always separated in the temple, but the thing he wanted most to impress upon me was that the Sikhs would take in any person—"*Any* person!"—for seven days, providing food and shelter, regardless of the person's race, creed, or nationality. But the person had to agree not to smoke or drink.

"How long have Sikhs been in the area?" I asked. Bengal shrugged; he didn't know. He led me back to the room we'd been in earlier. More old men were present now, sitting cross-legged on the floor. Bengal quizzed the eldest, who was a withered, nut-brown fellow in a vintage Harris tweed sport coat. He was missing several teeth and could have been anywhere from 80 to 120 years old. I was struck again by the unassimilated nature of the group. The way they sat and conversed, the ritual gossip, the tea and the rice cakes—it was village life transplanted to another continent.

Bengal bent to his informant and listened to him whisper. "Aha," öhe said. "Since about 1906." There was no way to verify the figure, and, besides, Bengal seemed to be losing patience, so I thanked him for the tour and told him I wouldn't keep him any longer. What a smile came over his lips! Such happiness! It was as if he'd been borne into the atmosphere on a magic carpet. He gave me a soft handshake and a friendly nod—yes, very good, you are going now! And I left feeling how nice it was to visit a religious place, a house of worship, and not have any attempt made to impress or convert you. The Sikhs, I thought, would not be distributing pamphlets about salvation, going door-to-door in Yuba City, any time soon.

◇ BRANCHES ◇

MÒ

◇

end; branch; recent;
last; final

◇ WORDS ◇

◊ LEO BRAUDY ◊

Photography & Fame

In 1859 Baudelaire denounced photography for the way it gave merely a picture of nature rather than anything from the realm of the imagination, the true place of art. But he was fighting an already lost battle and may have presciently foreseen how his photograph by Eugène Atget would carry his image as the poet of darkness down to generations who had read few of his actual works. By the later years of the nineteenth century, all the inner Napoleons, neglected geniuses, and spiritual adventurers — let alone the frankly ostentatious public men — had to put on more of a show to catch the attention of both the audience to which they played as well as the one they sought to reject. A turning away from publicity or visual fame in search of a spiritual ideal by both European and American artists could still be a vital protest against the commercialization of art. But the increasing visibility of the avant-garde, for example, indicated how difficult the gesture was to maintain with any purity. Hardy's final novel, *Jude the Obscure,* the tale of one man's futile struggle to be recognized for the immensity of his artistic aspiration, perhaps not too coincidentally appears in 1896, the year after Louis Lumière opens the first motion-picture theater. The two events furnish an appropriately Janus-like yoke for the twinned incitement and frustration of the desire for personal recognition that so preoccupies artists in the nineteenth century and so many others in the twentieth.

In the latter nineteenth century the special transcendence promised by the movies still lies ahead. But other engines of fame were

◊ *Leo Braudy is Leo S. Bing Professor of Literature at the University of Southern California. This essay appeared in* The Frenzy of Renown: Fame and Its History, © *1986 Leo Braudy, published by Oxford University Press, which recently brought out his collection of essays,* Native Informant.

gathering momentum. In America *Who's Who* was founded in 1898 and the Hall of Fame at New York University in 1900, while throughout America and Europe photography was already well established as the prime way to bring oneself to the attention of one's relatives, friends, and followers. The silence of the photograph allowed a combination of distance and intimacy that was a more domestic version of the Revolutionary portrait of the hero gazing off in the direction of his destiny. By turning human beings into objects of silent contemplation by themselves and others, it embodied the possibility that spiritual virtue might be made visible if properly posed and properly perceived. Unlike the general dressed in military splendor, the new public hero could stand out both spiritually and realistically at the same time, while the photograph froze a moment for eternity.

Photography took hold especially in America, where the insistence on the visibility of all those who aspired to public recognition drew its sanction from the openness with which the country itself was created and its optimistic insistence on an appeal to the suffrage of a democratic audience. Despite the eighteenth-century surge of portraiture for democracy and newly industrialized techniques for producing engravings and mezzotints, it could still be said that the people who voted for Adams or Jefferson or Burr or Madison didn't really know what their candidates looked like. But one of photography's most important effects was to take the art of imaging out of the hands of those skilled enough to paint or engrave as well as those rich enough to buy and place it at the disposal of virtually everyone. In an emblematic event toward the end of the century, Theodore Roosevelt at the age of 27 set out from his ranch in the Dakota Territory to catch some men who had stolen a boat. The weather was wintry and the chase, wrote Roosevelt, took "three days of acute misery." But there was a camera on hand to record the journey and the victorious young rancher standing with his gun over the culprits. The next year Roosevelt returned to New York to reenter a public life he had left behind after the death of his wife and his mother.

There is of course no strict causal connection between Roosevelt's snapshots and his decision to run for mayor of New York or his later public career. But I do want to suggest a causal atmosphere that in the nineteenth century urged the ambitious American public man to include and draw strength from his visual self-consciousness, just as the weak young Roosevelt worked on his body as well as his emotions to strengthen both for his career. Representative democracy and an ever-expanding access to visual publicity went hand-in-hand. Of course, as Ben Franklin was one of the earliest to remark, the new power of visual media might also involve a new sort of entrapment for both the observer — under the sway of what he is so pleased to see — and the observed — imprisoned by the desire to be seen. One solution had been the gaze of destiny that looked away from the viewer into the fateful future. But the new democratic audience wanted empathy as well as distance. In the aloneness of photography, the public man could be nonsocial but yet theatrical, inheriting the tradition of Washington and Napoleon but emphasizing as well the aspect of having been come upon, discovered, raised from the log cabin into the public eye. Both politically and imagistically sensitive to his audience, such a public man also continually looked for hints about what details might be considered most independent and appealing. You're a wonderful man, wrote a young admirer to Abraham Lincoln, but you should grow a beard so that the ladies will love you as well. And so Lincoln did. The photograph was the midwife of a moment's meaning. Through it the public man and woman, *any* man and woman, could directly entice the gaze of the viewer. The absent as well as the dead would be present again, and, in a manner only aspired to by writers and artists, the immediate and the eternal promised to be made one.

(Grace Bedell wrote to Lincoln with the suggestion on 15 October 1860. On 19 October he writes back wondering somewhat coyly if it would not be considered "a piece of silly affectation" if he began growing whiskers now after never having had them before. The first bearded photograph is dated 26 November and it has been argued that Lincoln began to grow his beard after the election, perhaps because there had been no previous president with a beard. But the thickness of the 26 November beard seems evidence of an earlier growth. His first photograph by Brady at the Washington studio shows a thick beard and head of hair much thinned and shortened in later photographs.)

Photography appeared at just the point that the old generation of the Founding Fathers was dying out and a new heroic commitment was attempting to forge itself. French and English innovations in both the taking and the reproducing of photographs were quickly refined. Not even the nineteenth-century railroad industry seems comparable to the image industry in the rapidity of technological advance. In 1839 L. J. M. Daguerre revealed to the French Academy of Sciences the process he and Nicéphore Niepce had developed. By the mid-1840s Mathew Brady's Daguerrean Miniature Gallery was well established in New York. Hardly 20 years after a sculptor had to hammer the life mask off the head of Jefferson, a photographer (Brady claimed it was himself) had gained entrance to the home of the dying Andrew Jackson to take a less painful image. By 1851 there were approximately 100 daguerreotype studios in New York City and Americans took three out of the five top medals at the Crystal Palace Photography Exhibition in England, including one for overall excellence awarded to Mathew Brady.

As the enormous number of individual and group portraits that remain to us from the nineteenth century indicates, the individuals who flocked to Brady's gallery stood at the beginning of a great wave still rolling. Their desire to retain those images was more than just a personal quirk. It also seems part of an overwhelming cultural need that photography half-discovered and half-stimulated in order to furnish memory with precise visual details of face, dress, posture, and all the ways one appeared to others. There was an immense vogue for individual and group portraits. New processes abounded, and every home inventor experimented with new ways of transferring life into something that resembled permanence. Everyone who could afford it (prices ranged from 12.5 cents to $2 in New York at one period) could have a daguerreotype of themselves, and Brady especially began to cater to public interest in possessing the images of the admired greats as well. In 1850 he published *The Gallery of Illustrious Americans*, with lithographs made from his studio's daguerreotypes, including his 1849 White House portrait of James Polk, the first of an incumbent president. In 1860 the *New York Times* celebrated "what manner of men and women we Americans of 1860 are" by printing a selection of his portraits.

Brady and others continued to do individual and celebrity portraiture, but already the unique and unreproducible nature of the daguerreotype was urging inventors on to discover ways of turning the individual image into a multitude. The *carte de visite,* a paper calling card with photograph and signature that could be ordered in whatever quantity the client wanted, was introduced in France in 1854 and quickly caught on in America. The *carte de visite* not only added a visual image to the social habit of leaving one's calling card, but, almost from its introduction, it also became a prime means for public figures to strengthen their political or military campaigns with a shower of personalized, pocket-sized portraits. Suitably enough, Napoleon III was an early customer of Disderi, the *carte*'s inventor, while Abraham Lincoln said that he owed his election both to the Cooper Union speech that introduced him to the publishers and politicians of the East and to the *carte de visite* made of him on that occasion by Mathew Brady. The faces and figures of prominent Americans (the *cartes* were usually full figure) could from the 1860s on be included in the albums of their admirers and supporters, as if they were members of the family.

The emotional intimacy that the photograph helped foster between the famous and their audience was also reflected in the movement away from former standards of how prominence was conveyed. The portraits of Washington and other military leaders of the Revolution were still indebted to classical and Renaissance depictions of human glory. To the extent that Franklin's plainness was emphasized or that he and Jefferson were characterized as inventors or natural philosophers, their portraits did depart somewhat from the traditional motifs of public fame. But nothing in artistic portraiture really anticipated the almost total break with the traditional look of a European public face expressed in Brady's photographs of Lincoln. This was a look unadorned by the motifs of fame and glory that even the French Revolution had only transformed instead of obliterating (and which Napoleon III was spending a good deal of energy from 1852 on trying to revive). It was a look of neither a military man nor an Eastern politician in the Roman patrician style nor a nicely turned out dandy or aristocrat. Here was a homely face on an oversized body wearing rumpled clothes, with perhaps a domestic shawl over his shoulders. It was the plainness of Franklin combined with the stature of Washington—the ordinary man, the representative man, transformed into the extraordinary by both his belief in principle and the demands of history. As Nathaniel Hawthorne described him in print, so he seemed in image, a face and figure that almost magically seemed to take up a preexisting space in the imagination of the viewer, which he had been yearning to fill:

There is no describing his lengthy awkwardness, nor the uncouthness of his movement; and yet it seemed as if I had been in the habit of seeing him daily, and had shaken hands with him a thousand times in some village street; so true was he to the aspect of the pattern American, though with a certain extravagance which, possibly, I exaggerated still further by the delighted eagerness with which I took it in.

Almost as soon as Lincoln took office, the conflict between North and South began. To win the war and keep the country from splitting apart was "a task before me greater than that which rested on Washington." For the Revolutionary generation Washington represented independence and autonomy from the European yoke, drawing on its imagery to herald a new cause. But Lincoln had the task of keeping the country together, the North and the South, the blacks and the whites, and in his own person convey one palpable image of the integrity of spirit and action to which anyone might rise if summoned by history. In the campaign biography of Lincoln written by William Dean Howells, when he was a 23-year-old reporter, the language of panegyric still reveals the style of greatness Lincoln had hewed out for himself.

The emigrant, at the head of the slow oxen that drag his household goods toward the setting sun — toward some Illinois yet further west — will take heart and hope when he remembers that Lincoln made no prouder entrance into the State of which he is now the first citizen. . . . Lincoln's future success or unsuccess can affect nothing in the past. The grandeur of his triumph over all the obstacles of fortune, will remain the same. . . . [I]t is the Presidency, not a great man, that is elevated, if such be chosen chief magistrate.

Howells's biography was hand-corrected by Lincoln, and it is unlikely that Howells's imagery did not also reflect something of Lincoln's view of himself. The day after Lincoln arrived in Washington, he made a trip to Brady's Washington branch, now more grandly called the Gallery of Photographic Art, to have his picture taken. It was to be the first of many trips to the studios of Brady and others in the area. As Adams and other Founding Fathers had decided to make Washington a visual symbol of American unity and pride, so Lincoln exploited the new medium to impress his own image of solemnity and seriousness of purpose on the eyes of the nation. The pictorial invariableness of his dress — a funereal coat and pants that,

Hawthorne wrote, looked worn so much that they "had grown to be an outer skin of the man," together with the tall stovepipe hat that made an extremely tall man look taller—invested him with an air of destiny. Those who knew him complained that his photographs never did justice to the animation that lighted his otherwise listless features when he talked or told a story. But perhaps he realized better than they how the photograph conveyed something of his own direct appeal along with the magisterial distance of a Washington. Even his insistence on going to the fateful performance of *Our American Cousin* at Ford's Theater fits into what seems to be his sense of the need to appear before the people. Lee had surrendered only a few days before and Grant was to appear before Lincoln and his cabinet the next morning. The play, which Lincoln had seen before, celebrated American spirit and energy. A new unity, he hoped, would be born from the war, and central to the public display of the presidential box was a large engraved portrait of George Washington.

◇ BILL BERKSON ◇

Poetry & Painting

Towards the end of her lecture *What Are Masterpieces and Why Are There So Few of Them,* Gertrude Stein had this to say:

> I write with my eyes not with my ears or mouth. I hate lecturing because you begin to hear yourself talk, because sooner or later you hear your voice and you do not hear what you say. You just hear what they hear you say. As a matter of fact as a writer I write entirely with my eyes. The words as seen by my eyes are the important words and the ears and mouth do not count. I said to Picasso, the other day, "When you were a kid you never looked at things." He seemed to swallow the things he saw but he never looked, and I said, "In recent years you have been looking, you see too much, it is a mistake for you." He said, "You are quite right." A writer should write with his eyes and a painter paint with his ears. You should always paint knowledge which you have acquired not by looking but by swallowing. I have always noticed that in portraits of really great writers the mouth is always firmly closed.

Poetry and painting—the "interrelation of the arts" happens because everyone has to take their ideas out for a walk. We enjoy the adaptability of ideas beyond the physical circumstances that may have occasioned them. Who needs ideas, or how important are they in actual practice? It's said that Degas told Mallarmé that he, Degas, had some wonderful ideas for poems, and that Mallarmé let Degas in on a professional secret: "But, Degas," said Mallarmé, "poems are made with *words,* not ideas."

Some people suspect that it's mischievous or arcane when two arts, except maybe words and music, cooperate, marry, or intermingle. But

◇ *Poet and critic Bill Berkson is professor of art history at the San Francisco Art Institute. His most recent collection is* Lush Life *(Z Press, New York).*

poets have loved painting with a vengeance ever since Dante said to Giotto, "How come you make such beautiful paintings—and such ugly kids?" The point is, no form of behavior exists exclusively. Maybe imagemaking is the closest thing to writing. Painting has a skin. Both painting and poetry occupy fictive spaces in the physical world. But then again, it may be because poetry and painting are more incomparable to one another than to the other arts that their affinity is sealed.

Many poets have had jobs helping painters, have sat for them long hours, naked no less, in unnatural poses on lumpy sofas. Poets write about paintings as parts of the world, inhale clouds of turpentine for deeper insight into technicalities, marry the painters male and female, live with whatever favorite works they can scrounge (and pay off divorce settlements with them later)—but that's all only human, it's no cabal.

You can do a lot with educated eyes. What I mean by "educated" is simply how pictures, among other things, can teach you about how to see, and about what's visible when you look hard enough or most openly. At a certain point, past the shock of actually seeing, you want to do something about it. That's what makes an artist begin being an artist in the first place. At one time or another you get hit like with a rock. I have a theory that the course of anyone's artistic life is determined largely by the attempt to retrieve that original rock, or what the painters used to call The Dream. Such a prime matter is easy to forget, like dreams. But when you look hard enough or most openly, you are reminded by some sensation like color or light that reflects or refreshes your living space. Just as when you leave a movie and it's been good (fascinating) and your eyes have been glued to the screen, in the street you see people or a slice of sky, and the sensation is continuous. Your ordinary vision is suddenly invigorated and heightened. That sustenance has some staying power. I know I owe some of my alertness for its presence to looking at paintings.

Everyone looks at pictures, and many painters are not dyslexic. Any poet who isn't also a painter or a draftsman has to admit that there's some envy involved in the bargain. Gertrude Stein said she was hopeless when it came to trying to draw objects, she saw no relation between the piece of paper and the object she wanted to draw. And that's been exactly my experience, too. I doodle, I trace, I fake it, but I can't draw, so to speak, from life. So in looking at and thinking about painting, I have this more or less common vicariousness. It's no sob story. One shouldn't get too entranced by the materialism of art.

Some painters seem baffled by poets because they think poets don't work as hard. Is poetry a residue? Similarly, a poet may fantasize no end about the manual luxury in painting—that no matter how bad you feel, or how "nothing," you could just pick a brush, slap some colors around, and given a few skills, arrive at a beginning at least—as opposed to the awesome blank page facing the awesome clogged febrile word-brain. It's nice to dream like that and then get back to base: paint on canvas, words on paper.

There's an "everything" principle—the universal "everything" principle—that poetry and painting share. It has to do with including. Fairfield Porter says, "There is an elementary principle of organization in any art that nothing gets in anything else's way, and everything is at its own limit of possibilities." Any divergence from the "everything" principle is obfuscation, which often is necessary as a ground swell, to add surface. Surface is the great revealer. Both poetry and painting have surface, but with poetry the location of surface is harder to pin down. With paint, color, the issue of revelation becomes paradoxical. As Robert Smithson reminds us, "The word *color* at its origin means to 'cover' or 'hide'; matter eats up light and covers it with a confusion of color." In poetry, surface may be a matter of complete apprehension of materials across the junctures of word or phrase and interval (or blank). Surface, finally, is what connects the dots. Take this from Schuyler's "The Morning of the Poem":

So many lousy poets
So few good ones
What's the problem?
No innate love of
Words, no sense of
How the thing said
Is in the words, how
The words are themselves
The thing said: love,
Mistake, promise, auto
Crack-up, color, petal,
The color in the petal
Is merely light
And that's refraction:

A word, that's the poem.
A blackish-red nasturtium . . .

In Michael Blackwood's movie of Philip Guston at work, you get to see the beautiful gesture Guston makes as he walks very slowly back towards the painting to put on more paint. He's sort of swimming through air like a Chinese dancing master, and the hand not holding the brush is blocking off from view a certain area of the composition as he zeroes in. It's still a composition at this stage, and on the soundtrack Guston is saying, "Well, everybody has notions. But notions are not reality. Reality is when you feel to take pink paint and you put it down and for some mysterious reason, some magical way, it becomes a hand — then that's painting. The public, the looker, thinks you have to have some blueprint for it — and there isn't a blueprint."

When Poetry meets Painting, in Padua circa 1306, Giotto and Dante are drinking and gesticulating about the positions of the figures in Giotto's *Last Judgment.* In 1959, when Poetry meets Painting, art is more on the side of the painters but the painters are being generous with it because poetry is less always about having seen paintings and is acting more like itself, more like painting that no one's dreamed of yet.

When Poetry meets Painting, we begin to wonder about Art. It seems poets would never say "Art" without knowing painters, but the painters can't talk about it without knowing poems. Real painters do know poems. To be more specific, I met painting in the spring of 1959 in the form of de Kooning's landscape abstractions at the Janis Gallery in New York. Before that, art meant the Metropolitan Museum near my home where as a child I saw a reconstructed Egyptian tomb and displays of 15th-century armor. And color slides of Gorky and Mondrian in college.

In New York, then, the signal gesture was de Kooning's expansiveness and speed, which suggested spatially the kind of surface excitement poetry was beginning to take on as well. A year later, seeing Philip Guston's work — especially his drawings with their slower accumulations of image — I was struck in a different way. The mass-effect of his line was more like a confirmation. In the case of de Kooning I felt, "Oh God, I'd love to write like that," but I'd have to hurry up. I wasn't fluent at that level. Whereas, with Guston I felt "I *do* write like that" — having some inkling of his process, a fellow inchworm! — "and there's something in it, too!" Something similar

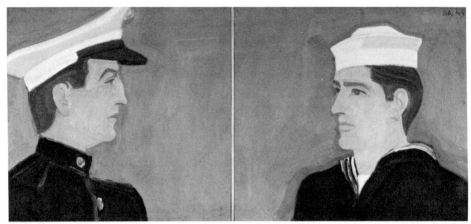

◇ *Alex Katz,* Marine and Sailor *(Frank O'Hara & Bill Berkson), 1961, oil on canvas, diptych*

occurred in reading and knowing Frank O'Hara, and loving his incredible acumen. I tried to approach it but couldn't hold on. I had to realize I didn't work that way, attractive as it might seem. My drive was more stubborn, contemplative; and more like Guston, I wasn't so convinced about what the subject matter was. I couldn't say, as O'Hara did, "What is happening to me goes into my poems," which implies an instantaneous sweep approaching the speed of light. But I *could* say, with Guston, "I want to end with something that will baffle me for some time" and "I just want to nail something so that it will stay put."

So the early sixties became an extended invitation for me into the facts and mysteries of hometown New York art. That "splendid state of confusion" was due partly to the residue of heroism, fifties-style, in the air, although by then it was becoming millions-in-business-as-usual. The city was the center of a general cosmopolitan alert that lasted about another ten years. In the early sixties, criticism's idea of the purity of any separate art — poetry, painting, or dance — seemed like a joke just as it does now. (It became a bad joke for a while in between.) One saw how art and social behavior could be seen as extending from one another and talked about in the same terms — what Alex Katz calls "good urban manners" in alignment with "high-style art." The illuminating essay on that score was Edwin Denby's about de Kooning in the thirties:

Talking to Bill and to Rudy for many years, I found I did not see with a painter's eye. For me the after-image (as Elaine de Kooning has called it) became one of the ways people behave together, that is, a moral image. The beauty Bill's Depression pictures have kept reminds me of the beauty that instinctive behavior in a complex situation can have — mutual actions one has noticed that do not make one ashamed of one's self, or others, or of one's surroundings either. I am assuming that one knows what it is to be ashamed. The joke of art in this sense is a magnanimity more steady than one notices in everyday life, and no better justified . . .

It was Edwin too, along with a few other poets, who was quickest to understand exactly what the younger artists were up to — the ones who were emerging or had just emerged. Here is one of Edwin's sonnets from that time:

Alex Katz paints his north window
A bed and across the street, glare
City day that I within know
Like wide as high and near as far
New York School friends, you paint glory
Itself crowding closer further
Lose your marbles making it
What's in a name — it regathers
From within, a painting's silence
Resplendent, the silent roommate
Watch him, not a pet, long listen
Before glory, the stone heartbeat
When he's painted himself out of it
De Kooning says his picture's finished

I hope the main connection is becoming clearer. How one can speak, for example, of such a poem as having a scale, beyond the compactness of 14 short lines, similar to the live aspect of size in painting.

How painters react to poems is fascinating. At one point, in the seventies, I could say that Philip Guston had become a kind of Ideal Reader for my poems, because, lettering and then drawing around some of them — I don't actually know which he did first — he opened up certain poems for me, as to subject. One drawing he made in 1973 incorporates a poem called "Negative," which is about an encounter with a large glass door. As Guston said, "Poems and drawings give each other new powers — energies."

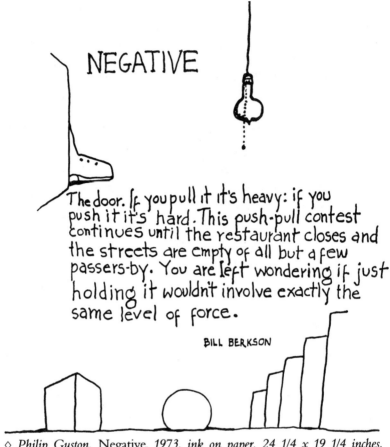

NEGATIVE

The door. If you pull it it's heavy: if you push it it's hard. This push-pull contest continues until the restaurant closes and the streets are empty of all but a few passers-by. You are left wondering if just holding it wouldn't involve exactly the same level of force.

BILL BERKSON

◇ *Philip Guston,* Negative, *1973, ink on paper, 24 1/4 x 19 1/4 inches, collection: Bill Berkson*

I've lived in California for 20 years—a long time—and oddly enough, there still aren't many California artists that I care about as much as the ones I keep leaving behind. There are some obvious exceptions: California artists whose work I've written about from time to time. But if my eyes have been codified somewhat and not adjusted, I don't think it's a matter of prejudice. Jane Freilicher came from New York to teach for a few weeks in Santa Barbara. She said that getting her first glimpse of the landscape out here she realized what the indigenous painters were up against, if they wanted to confront the values of traditional painting: "that awful palette!" Al Held told me he spent weeks looking out the window of a grand

◇ Lynn O'Hare, Untitled, 1976, gouache, 6-1/4 x 9-1/2 inches, private collection.

studio on Telegraph Hill and finally made a deal with a printer's collective in the basement: "I spent the rest of my time there painting in a corner with a bare lightbulb." It happens that I am married to a painter who grew up in California, Lynn O'Hare. Lynn's paintings are not so much about local color as about how objects can command your point of view or how when light and vision are occluded, the obstructed view proffers a new object of attention. Here's a poem I wrote excited by one of her paintings that had a trellis full of flowers in it:

◇ DON'T KNOCK IT

for Lynn

Over piled leaves by the cement porch
trimmed & shook from a blue rug: Hair.
The tangle upwind where it fell from,
where closer a branch makes a hard decision, shock-
definitive. Painting's trellis tide
stemless seamless splurge & spray of
openhanded blue, pink top

constant heart's labyrinthine shuttle.
Can't resist the way it floods, revvying one up
for air: "The flowers are coming!"
A New Yorker's sense of distance: Elbow-edged
you take up a Brussels sprout & peel it.
The right white gates span receptive
to your jubilant rush.

Some painters just delight you. Some confirm your eyes for the everyday. Others actually provoke a subject matter or conception that resurfaces in poems. Some can affect your aspirations like the deepest thought or a sunrise. A painting and a chance remark—both by Alex Katz—got me started on this poem called "Baby's Awake Now":

◇ BABY'S AWAKE NOW

And now there is the lively sound
Of a panel truck heading due southwest
Along Elm Road, edge of dusk—
The densest light to see to drive by

The underbrush has brown fringe
And small silent birds.

I saw the rainbow fire.
I saw the need to talk.
I saw a unicorn and a red pony.
And I didn't want any deviled eggs.
I drove home with my collar up.

We're alive. You do alarm me to the fact.
The light is on the window in the air,
And breath comes faster than the hounds
To sanction what remembered, what stuck.

Writing art criticism is less interesting but obviously it's pertinent. It's very demanding. I've written art criticism for 30 years off and on, but never as consistently as some other poets like John Ashbery or Peter Schjeldahl. It's hard to stay fluent with criticism and even harder to keep from getting apathetic about it. Its provisionality is both enticing and maddening. There's the problem that it hardly ever comes clean as either observation or writing; like most journalism—and that's what most art writing is—it doesn't hold up over time.

What's the good of art criticism and why does anyone do it, not to mention who reads it? For one thing, art criticism is a job that pays fairly well, particularly if you do a lot of it. Poets hardly ever get paid for doing what they do best, so they take, usually, the odd jobs they can get and bear. Aside from economic considerations, criticism is a public opportunity to be articulate about something that most people ordinarily let slip away into tangential mutterings: your supposedly silent, non-verbal, on-site responses to works of art. I think of it doubly as commercial expository prose and/or (as Carter Ratcliff once remarked) "language somewhere in the vicinity of what it's talking about." What makes poets' criticism valuable, I think, is that they are interested in these situations of looking not as frames of judgment but as observation for observation's sake: they write to find out what can be said in relation to what they see and hopefully to be communicative of some common pleasure in seeing. Can you say what you see? Can it be described? Or is the feeling of two-way recognition between the looker and the work more interesting to tell about? Pleasure in writing criticism is often connected with the surprise of vernacular—the words that sensibly spring to mind when the mind's eye is on a sizable patch of orange paint seen some hours or days previous. Poets are less interested in evaluation and motive. They know that the best one can hope for is the equivalent vitality of a parallel text, and to that they bring a technical proficiency as befits the job.

Art criticism presumably knows what it's talking about. It has a referent and a topic, more determinately than most poems. The words go across the topic making discriminations. In writing art criticism, I like to put my perceptions, via an occasional headlong (or packed-in) verbal construct, out on a limb. If the limb breaks, I tend to hit the factual aspects of the work under discussion with a thud; if I land on my feet, I can bounce back into—or usefully out of—my tree.

Most criticism makes me mad. Most critics are Philistines in the sense that they ignore the cardinal rule of art practice, which is never to give the game away: under the pretext of seriousness or just by coming on excessively shrewd, they either divulge the mystery or insist there is no mystery. It is important to protect the mystery. Professional manners in criticism involve not giving the game away, respecting the secret of art's manifold dialectic, and at the same time, knowing when to divulge the obvious.

◇ *George Schneeman and Bill Berkson,* Bacia, *1969, ink & collage (photo: Rudolph Burckhardt)*

One gives poetry readings, but the art criticism reading, so far as I know, hasn't happened yet. I'll give it a whirl. This is a paragraph from an article I wrote about Franz Kline about three years ago, which I like well enough, mainly because it stays so specific to my way of looking:

Kline simplified but allowed plenty of noise. His hard finishes show a permeability to vision like the night air. His directional lines make for dual sensations of passage and grip. (Some mid-fifties pictures show similarities in scale between impasto textures and the coarse grain of heavy linen fabric, which account for the palpable tractions.) A black-and-white surface gathers sharply and wells towards the observer; moored to the edges it nudges them to expand. The blacks connect to edges or to other blacks, while the whites divide and scintillate. Black and white together or separately careen edge to edge as prodigiously stretched lines. There are things white does that black will never do, and the other way round, like consonants and vowels. Two blacks in the same stretch are distinct and make a difference — not a third color but a shade. In *Lehigh V*

Span (1959–60), a long, tapering black plows through a traffic of tones (including shimmers of green, pink, blue), as different whites press forward, projecting more and less solidly than a wall. Given the scale, it's peculiar how close you can look and still see a unified image. The light, as Adrian Stokes said of Turner's light, "takes actuality to itself." Among the sheared contours, there's a quasi-mathematics — lateral divisions into threes and fives — as in the parts of a sonnet. (There are rhymes as well, like blank/yank/flank/plank.) The light spreads the same way the paint is smeared, though with an extra elasticity. Motion is concretized, a characterization, not an issue of performance, not the painter's gesture as such. It's the picture, not the man who made it, that seems to say with Godard, "I want to do things, not just name them."

One of Frank O'Hara's poems begins with the line "Picasso made me tough and quick and the world." There is a sense in his poems of inheriting modernity — and modern art in particular — as an expanded ethos. In the wake of that modernity — in what is now called "postmodern" — we're left with a glacial moraine of endless options — terrible, monstrous, great, and so on. It certainly now seems less a century than a field. Since modern art gave us "everything" — i.e., all the existing forms are *here* — naturally no one feels that those given forms are enough. The poem-paintings of the fifties and sixties reinforced a ground-zero common sense for poets and painters alike. Now poet-painter collaborations seem to be a lost art, perhaps simply because the day-to-day relations have become more scattered.

Wonderfully, there is no logic why poetry and painting should meet at all. It is not poetry dressing up to be "like" painting, or painting being pro- or anti-literary. Those comparisons are really speechless. I sometimes feel called upon to write a whole other lecture entitled "Why I Am Not a Painterly Poet." The real connections lie elsewhere, with materials which criticism is ever hard put to recognize, because criticism most often doesn't, as art will, talk about everything at once.

◇ HENRY NOYES ◇

China Books Begins

The year 1959 was a turning point in our lives, a year when we were called upon to use all the ingenuity and experience we had accumulated in a lifetime. On October 1, by coincidence China's National Day, our longtime friend Paul Romaine phoned me to say, "Henry, I hear you're no longer working at Pettibone Mulliken."

"That's correct. When I applied there three years ago for a job in the tool-and-die department, I neglected to put down my university education on the application form."

"They fired you for that?"

"No, not really. The real reason, I was a shop steward, filed and won too many grievances; and also locked horns with the works manager in bargaining sessions. Now I've had to file my own grievance with the Machinists' Union and the Labor Relations Board. But they're slow to act."

"You think you'll get your job back?"

"Not a prayer. The cards are stacked."

"Then I have something here that might interest you: a letter from Imported Publications and Products in New York. They supply me, as you know, with books and magazines from the Foreign Languages Press in Peking."

"What's the deal?" I was excited without yet knowing why.

"If you come down to the shop this afternoon I'll tell you more."

◇ *Henry Noyes was born in 1910 in Canton, the son and grandson of missionaries. He left China in 1919, studied at the Universities of Toronto and London, chaired the Creative Writing Department at the University of Missouri, and founded China Books and Periodicals, Inc. in 1960. He lives in San Francisco. These excerpts appeared in* China Born: Adventures of a Maverick Bookman, © *1989 Henry Noyes, published by China Books and Periodicals, Inc.*

Paul Romaine ran the only independent bookshop in downtown Chicago. He handled bestsellers and popular fiction to pay the rent, but his chief interest was in progressive publications and his store was known as the best place in town for avant-garde books and magazines. Despite the inquisition of Senator Joseph McCarthy, symptomatic of the deepening freeze of civil liberties in the Cold War period, Paul continued to handle radical writers of the thirties: John Steinbeck, Agnes Smedley, Jack Conroy, Clifford Odets. As liberal leaders of the New Deal became McCarthy's special targets for political assassination, left-led coalitions and united fronts dwindled. In Chicago the Abraham Lincoln School was defunct. Henry Wallace's Progressive Party shrank to a holding operation of the isolated left before bowing off the stage of US political history like earlier third-party movements. The American Peace Crusade had spent its energies in one giant rally at the Coliseum. The Congress of Industrial Organizations was being shredded from the top down by loyalty oaths and anti-labor legislation passed by an intimidated Congress. Romaine's bookshop was one of the few progressive institutions to survive the fifties — the New Dark Age, as Paul called it — and he continued to handle *Moscow News, China Reconstructs,* and the *Peking Review;* also, to display them in his window on La Salle, the Wall Street of the Middle West. He had such an affable, pipe-smoking disposition that even officers of the law stopped in to browse and ask him questions like: "What the hell is Marxism-Leninism? And who is this Mao Tse-tung?"

Paul's wife, Marguerite, welcomed me with a cynical smile as she stood with arms akimbo behind the cash register: "You're a notorious character. Read what the *Chicago Tribune* writes about you, in case you missed it." The clipping she held out accused me, in usual *Tribune* style, of taking part in a worldwide conspiracy, and asked: "Why should a professor otherwise want to work in a machine shop?"

"Why indeed?" Marguerite mocked.

"Why not?" I took her up half seriously. "Gertrude and I decided to work with our hands to round out our characters. The days I could make a living as a freelance writer and organizer of large meetings for progressive causes ended with the New Dark Age. Besides, Chris and Nicky are great kids, but they eat like pigs and need new shoes every three months. And seriously, I miss the day-to-day association with fellow-workers who usually say what they mean and mean what they say."

"Paul's got a proposition for you." Marguerite nodded up at Paul's office, a mezzanine pigeon loft from which he could keep his eye on customers and also watch the passing crowd of bankers, stockbrokers, and lawyers in La Salle Street.

Paul was not a word waster. He motioned me to a seat with a twist of his pipe and handed me a letter. "From Margaret Cowl. She's a remarkable person. Single-handed she's organized the import of publications from the Latvian and Lithuanian Socialist Republics, the USSR, and also China. She has the right kind of guts. Her father died when she was only fourteen. She went to work in a garment factory, hid in the toilet when the child-labor inspector made his rounds, and for years supported her mother and younger brothers and sisters."

The letter invited Paul to take over the import of publications from China, since Margaret, at 65, was about to retire and wanted to slim down her imports. "If you can't do it yourself," she wrote, "can you recommend somebody who's qualified?"

Paul came straight to the point. "You're the only person I know who's qualified, meaning that you are deeply interested in China and have wide contacts in the progressive movement." He gave me an encouraging smile. "You've used my China section like a library for years. You're a natural, China born . . ."

"But wait," I objected. "I don't know a thing about the book business, accounts, marketing . . ."

◇

Our problems were not only with legal restrictions and regulations [with the Treasury, Customs, banks. . .], however, but with political forces from right to left. Our preliminary base, inherited from Imported Publications and Products, consisted of the eight radical bookstores affiliated with the Communist Party. But one by one, these began to defect from supporting China to supporting the Soviet Union only. *Long Live Leninism* was actually the parting of the ways. Several articles, combined under this title, were featured in the *Peking Review* No. 17, 1960, which was the first publication we had received from China. We had hardly got over the excitement of opening the first packages, shipped airmail direct from Peking, when our phone started to ring. From left to right, callers wanted this issue. "It's controversial, you know." Why, I wasn't exactly sure at the time. It presented Lenin's well-known thesis on imperialism: that war was inevitable unless the peoples of the world were strong enough to prevent it, presumably through revolution. In supporting Lenin's thesis, the Chinese polemicists characterized the rearmament of Germany and Japan as US imperialism's way of breaking down the peace and laying the basis for a third world war.

Several weeks later an airmail shipment of *Long Live Leninism* arrived in book form, with a white linen cover and a red jacket with Lenin's portrait in black and white. It became our first bestseller and was sold out in a month. I heard from Margaret at this time that a top-ranking Party official in New York was urging her not to handle the book because it was too controversial, besides being sectarian and damaging to the peace forces. When I asked, "What is your reaction?" she replied, "Who am I to decide between my Chinese and Soviet comrades?" Soon afterwards I had a call from the educational director of the Illinois State Communist Party, who said he wanted to bring a leading ideologist in his party out to the store. "Fine," I said, "I'll be happy to show you both our books. But if he wants to discourage me from handling *Long Live Leninism,* please tell him he'll be wasting his time." There was a hasty click at the other end of the line.

"Peace at almost any cost" seemed to be the new slogan of left-wing parties both in the United States and Europe. But Mao Tse-tung was telling the Chinese not to be intimidated. People made the atom bomb; people should agree never to use it, and then to destroy it once and for all. On the other hand, Khrushchev was saying that the atom bomb is not a toy for children, thereby justifying his refusal to share it with China and other fraternal countries and torpedoing the unity of the "socialist world."

The rift between China and the USSR widened through polemics that China first directed at the Central European communists and then at the USSR itself. Since the US Communist Party sided with what the Chinese called Soviet revisionism, the radical bookstores we served showed less and less interest in handling publications from China, and then open hostility. "My people hate the Chinese," one of their managers blurted out when he canceled his orders for Chinese magazines. "No, we don't want any more stuff from China!"

"Even the children's books?" I asked sarcastically. "How can a professed Marxist-Leninist hate a whole people, especially as many as 800 million?"

Political splinter movements from the CPUSA—the Provisional Organizing Committee, Hammer and Steel, and, later, Progressive Labor—supported the Chinese side of the polemics, but their influence was limited and they could not fill the gap in book sales left by the departure of the communist bookstores. It was time for us to enlarge our market, or close our doors.

In Chicago our clientele was small, confined mainly to teachers and students. I decided to travel the country by Greyhound and investigate other possibilities, particularly the West Coast. On a $99 ticket I could travel the whole country as long as I did not backtrack. I decided to concentrate on the periodicals, since they carried the latest information about China and would play an immediate role in ending the myth that it was the "unknown." In five weeks, I lined up 43 newsstands in major American cities to handle *Peking Review, China Reconstructs,* and *China Pictorial:* in Denver, Seattle, Salt Lake City, St. Louis, Los Angeles, Omaha, San Antonio, New Orleans, San Francisco of course and other cities. . . .

In San Francisco, Louis Swift of L-S Distributors had agreed to handle the Chinese periodicals for wholesale distribution. Louis, a victim of polio, was a living example of how a disadvantaged person could overcome a serious handicap and help others in the process. He sat at his desk in the front office and shouted orders that could be heard in the back stockroom, and even in the basement. On his wall was the golden key to the City of San Francisco, which Mayor Christopher had presented to him as one of the city's most distinguished citizens. Louis Swift had a winning smile behind a rugged mustache and beard, gray hairs yielding only in patches to white. "San Francisco is the place for you," he advised, and at the same time commanded by inference that we should transfer CB&P to the West Coast. . . .

We had scarcely set up shop in San Francisco when Herb Caen, the best-known gossip columnist on the West Coast, came strolling in to inspect us and our books. Two days later we were given an official welcome in the Caenfetti Column of the *Chronicle,* which described CB&P as "Peking's foot in the door" and a firm that had ambitions to expand rapidly. The paper had only just hit the newsstands when we began to receive calls from enterprising realtors offering us whole buildings with railroad sidings to help us expand. The owner of the corner café, however, rushed in to say we should sue Herb Caen for libel. "Imagine calling you Peking's foot!" But Louis Swift, who had tipped him off about our arrival, called to say, "Send Herb Caen a thank-you note. Now you are kosher!"

Our new location in the heart of San Francisco's Mission District on 24th Street was at the epicenter of the Bay Area, convenient by freeway and bridge to the Stanford and Berkeley crowd and more locally to the many San Franciscans — longshoremen, ex-members of the armed forces, overseas Chinese, students and teachers — who had a personal or academic interest in the People's Republic. We also received orders, chiefly on the telephone or by post, from merchants, bankers, and civic leaders who favored opening trade channels. Before World War I, 40 percent of the docks in San Francisco Harbor serviced the China trade; a whole dockside area was still called the China Basin. Since the trade embargo of 1951 by presidential decree, most of the surplus docks were being turned into boutique complexes and amusement centers for tourists — or closed. Robert Gomperts, president of the World Trade Association, who dropped by our store to welcome us to San Francisco, estimated that 90 percent of the businessmen on the West Coast were pressuring the President to end the embargo. We received calls from textile importers, paint and varnish exporters, wheat merchants, travel agents, all asking what our magic formula was for opening trade with China. They even offered us junior partnerships if we would give them a hand. Our reputation and clientele broadened out.

From 1964, the San Francisco Bay Area was the right place for us to be. It was a germinal period in American culture and we found ourselves at the center of new movements fertilized by a confluence of intellectual and political cross-currents. Groups, as well as individuals, were interested in China's approach to socialism and many of them turned our store into a material resource center, beginning with the free-speech movement. In Berkeley, Mario Savio and the "free speechers" were demanding a complete restructuring of the multi-university and the society whose interests it served. People came first, he insisted, especially the young. One of the first quotations from Chairman Mao to become current in Berkeley, three years before the Little Red Book arrived from Peking, was his tribute to youth: "The world is yours, as well as ours, but in the last analysis, it is yours. You young people, full of vigor and vitality, are in the bloom of life, like the sun at eight or nine in the morning."

Why should students "full of vigor and vitality" waste four years in classrooms with 500 other auditors listening to a professor reading lectures from 15- and 20-year-old notes? A new incentive to change the old academic world brought students from all over the Bay Area to browse at CB&P and find ideological support for their campaigns — even the extremists who found in Mao's attack on stereotyped writing a justification for launching a free-speech movement. "We're fed up with academic euphemisms. Four-letter words are earthy, gutsy, full of the life of the streets" — so went the campaigns in the student press. "We're going to use 'fuck' in our papers whether the Board of Regents likes it or not."

At about the same time a group of seven "Diggers," unbeknownst even to themselves, were launching the psychedelic movement which was soon to embrace and overpower the free-speech and four-letter-word campaigns and incite the nation's youth with incense, pot, hash, the Jefferson Airplane, and much more. Taking their name from a communal and anti-Establishment group in England three centuries earlier, the San Francisco Diggers adopted a three-principle philosophy. They advocated peace on earth and, more immediately, the end of the Vietnam War and the withdrawal of American "advisers." They were ultra-democratic in practicing brotherhood and sisterhood of the Buddhist as distinct from the Christian orders, and they believed in smoking dope and baking brownies laced with marijuana. In their more sober moments they read books on the Chinese revolution, guerrilla warfare, and communism, sitting in lotus positions on the floors of CB&P and the Psychedelic Shop on Haight Street near the intersection of Ashbury. Since they were always short of ready cash, they felt no urge to buy, and as long as they didn't smoke dope or burn incense in our store, we let sitting Diggers read. We, like them, were infected by the tolerant spirit of San Francisco's patron saint.

Peace, love, freedom, brotherhood and sisterhood were words put back into meaningful circulation. The media could only report their excesses. But new mimeographed handouts, New Age weeklies, poetry broadsides chanted in restaurants and distributed free on the streets, and rock music expressed the new way of life, the new Tao of freedom. If any section of the people was oppressed, how could any other section be truly free? Liberation — women's lib, sexual liberation, black and brown liberation — was a powerful wind blowing away old stenches and stereotypes.

In spring 1967, we received an airmail sample of the *Quotations from Chairman Mao Tse-tung*. We had no notion at the time that this Little Red Book was to give a powerful boost to all the young liberation movements and our sales a great leap upward. We thought we were taking a big chance in ordering a thousand copies, the largest order for a single title we had ever placed with Guoji Shudian. Two days after we received airmail shipment, all thousand were sold. The Little Red Book became a status symbol for anybody opposing bureaucratic authority. Waving it was evidence that whoever owned a copy was at least a rebel, if not a self-styled revolutionary. Our store was flooded with status-seekers from all over the country. We cabled Peking to loft 25,000 more *Quotations* to us by air freight. They were gone in a month. We ordered 100,000 more. It was our big breakthrough into the book world. We sent a postcard announcement to every bookstore in the US and received over a thousand orders. By the end of 1968 we had distributed over 250,000 and in the following 15 years we were to sell over one million.

The extravagances of the "Great Proletarian Cultural Revolution" in China had already been served up by the media. The wild youth of China were shown night after night on prime news time in unruly mobs wielding the Little Red Book. Negative analysis on the radio and in the press, aimed by newscasters to discourage American youth from such outrageous behavior, backfired. Mao Tse-tung was the only national leader at the time encouraging youth to have confidence in their power to change the world. "Go ahead, bombard the headquarters of reaction," he was urging. And young people around the world were responding, "We hear you!"

It was a period of massive civil rights struggles in the South with sit-ins in drugstores, bus boycotts, the Supreme Court decision for equal rather than "separate but equal" education. Above all, however, it was a period of growing dissatisfaction with the war against the Vietnamese people and with the Establishment that waged it with the lives of young Americans. A disproportionate number of these, shipped home in flag-draped caskets, were black or brown. It was a period of peace marches, united fronts of diverse political and religious elements. It was a period when the Black Panther Party organized a new national movement which seemed to threaten the existing order of white supremacy with its program for peace in Vietnam, socialism in the United States, and diplomatic relations with the People's Republic of China.

By the end of the sixties, CB&P had become a model people's bookstore. In a dozen major cities, similar movement bookstores had been opened to meet the reading demands of a generation that was organizing new political associations and setting compasses for new social horizons. They shared a conviction that wars of aggression and nine-to-five subservience to moneymaking were not the way of life, the Tao, which they wanted to travel.

◊ JAMES D. HOUSTON ◊

The Hip Plumber

The hip plumber is underneath my sink, squeezed in between the flung-wide cabinet doors, working with his wrench to unscrew the trap so he can unplug the drain.

"Sometimes," he says, "when I am up under here all by myself, in the shadows with the pipes and the smells, I think what the hell am I doing in a situation like this? And then I just relax and say to myself, It's okay. It's okay to be here. This is where I am *supposed* to be. If I wasn't supposed to be here, I wouldn't be here. You know what I mean? What I am saying is, I surrender to that place and that time, and then I am at peace with it, I become one with it. Hand me that flashlight now, so I can see what the hell is *in* here."

I hand him the flash and he peers around at the stuccoed underbelly of the sink, the chalky corrosion stains.

"I don't take any of this seriously," he says. "I mean, it has to be fun. I have to enjoy it. I go out on one of these big jobs, where some contractor calls me in to do the whole kitchen and bathroom, and these other guys are out there, the roofers, the sheetrock guys. They're glum. They're walking around doing what they do, but they can't wait for the day to end. And me? I'm singing, I'm smiling. They say, Hey, you don't have any right to smile, doing this kind of shitwork. In their view, see, anybody who smiles must not know what he's got himself into. They think something is wrong with me because I really do enjoy what I'm doing. But hey, it's all one, isn't it? Work is worship. That's what I tell them out there on the big construction jobs. I say, Work is worship. They just look at me."

◊ *Novelist James D. Houston lives in Santa Cruz, California. This essay appeared in his most recent book,* The Men in My Life, *© 1987 James D. Houston, published by Capra Press, Santa Barbara, California.*

151

Now he has the pipes loose, and he is feeding the snake-cable down into the long drain, a few inches at a time, feeding, cranking the spool-handle ferociously, then feeding a few more inches of cable.

"You see, I am just a puppet. This came to me nine years ago. I saw that what I had to do was surrender myself to . . . whatever you want to call it. God. Brahman. The Great Force. The Oversoul. You name it. I call it God. But you know what I mean. You surrender to it. You are a puppet, and it works through you. Each morning I wake up, and I think to myself, Okay, what is important. Feel good. That is the first thing. Then, share it. Share what you feel. And surrender to whatever comes your way. Look at this snake. You know what it's doing? It's flopping around down there at the bottom of your pipe where all the gunk has accumulated. There is nothing wrong with your drain pipe, by the way—although I might re-plumb this trap for you one of these days, if you're into that. You have about a ten-inch loop here, and all you need is four, otherwise you have water standing on both sides of ten inches, plus these two extra fittings you really don't need. Who installed this stuff anyhow?"

I tell him it came with the house. He inspects the loop, eyes wide in the half-dark. He shifts his position. He gives the handle another crank, with another smile, the fun-lover's grin, playful, a prankster.

"What I'm saying is, the drain pipe is innocent. The drain just does what it has to do, which is be a pipe for the water. And the water does what it has to do, which is swirl as it descends, so that over the years it coats the inside of the pipe with all the little pieces of stuff that come down out of the sink, and this makes a kind of doughnut inside the pipe, a doughnut with a hole through the middle that gets a little bit smaller year by year. The doughnut gets bigger, and the hole gets smaller and smaller and smaller, until it is down to a very fine point—which is just like meditation, you see. But then one day, bip, the little hole closes. The drain stops draining, and the snake goes down there and opens it up, like the kundalini snake of breakthrough perception! And whammo, a channel is cleared and the water is flowing again!"

◇ ANONYMOUS ◇

Some Boyfriends

Didn't talk much. We did go upstairs during rainstorms and make love though. There's lots of thunder and lightning in the Midwest. Anyway, that was enough for awhile. Then we went to Colorado and got hailed on. That, it turns out, was too much.

◇

He asked me to marry him and I said no. Angry and hurt, he told me that I was "no prize." A few days later he said that he realized that he was no prize either and in this sense we were well-matched, wouldn't I reconsider?

◇

Joe was the kind of man you take home to your parents and leave there.

◇

Clive has incredible patience. He once taught our cat how to turn off the lights.

◇

My last boyfriend and I were together for five years. He taught me how to be celibate.

◇

When I first met him, I offered to mend his favorite jacket. Back in the privacy of my own apartment, I spread his coat on my bed. Then I

◇ *These fragments appeared in* The 100th Boyfriend, *compiled and edited by Bridget Daley and Janet Skeels, published by the Real Comet Press, Seattle.*

took off all my clothes and laid down next to it. Wrapped those tweed arms around my torso and breathed for a while, smelling his neck on the collar, his sweat in the armpits. After a couple hours of this, I did mend his jacket, sewing three of my own hairs into the lining. I really wanted to hang onto this guy.

◊

Then there was Mr. X, my housemate at the "Fiesta House" on Fiesta Street, who enjoyed shooting Fiesta brand rubbers across the room from his erect cock.

◊

Otis loved a woman who drove off a cliff. Or not.

◊

He was more of a True Love than a Boyfriend. He used to list me as next-of-kin on employment applications — sometimes as his sister and sometimes as his stepmother.

◊

He stood at the Xerox machine, copying long passages of Kant. The machine was piled high with his books. He wore a light cotton shirt and baggy white pants. He turned to say hello, scooped up his nickels from the copier and put them into his pocket. The coins slid down his leg and rang when they spilled out on the floor by his shoes. He blushed. He was definitely my kind of guy.

◊

After a year and a half of going out, Jack and Nancy rented a house together. She stayed one night, then moved out in the morning. Though Jack had never brought it up, she sensed that eventually she might be expected to have sexual intercourse if she lived there. As a recently born-again, Nancy avoided proximity to sinful opportunities. She repeatedly challenged Jack to "try Christ," to accept Jesus as his personal savior. One day he tried it, but after several hours gave up and told Nancy he still felt like an atheist. After she consulted her pastor and Bible study group, they broke up.

◊

Sometimes my lover pisses me off so much that I think I should tell my husband about him.

◇

One New Year's, Laurence and I went to a party in the 'burbs. With 15 minutes left until midnight, Laurence grabbed my arm and hustled me out the door. "We're going to shoot," he whispered, running to the car. All the way to his place, I worried about what he would shoot. Heroin? Speed? When he got to the house, he ran in and got it — the gun. "Shit," I thought, "he's going to shoot me!" Then, all at once, the sound of shooting was everywhere. The whole neighborhood was bringing in the New Year by firing into the sky, inadvertently putting out street lights and windows in the process. That was New Year's with Laurence.

◇

You know those tall Jewish men with dark eyes, a little bit of gray hair and big noses? They're the best in bed. So patient, do anything to please. Must be the guilt. The worst ones are rich Americans on vacations in Paris. They give you an Estée Lauder lipstick or a pair of stockings in the morning like it's World War II or something.

◇

For a long time this pretty cute guy tells my friends he likes me and everything. So I say OK, give him my number. Saturday night, I'm all dressed up and ready and he never shows. I wait until about 10, by then I figure he's not coming so I go to a party.

I tell a girl there about getting stood up. She says, "Hey, don't you know? He's in jail. He got real smashed, went out on the balcony of his apartment, and threw beer bottles at a cop car." I should've known then that the relationship would never work.

◇

For a while, it seemed like most of them were named John, tall blonds with moustaches. Then I noticed that several of my boyfriends had grown up without their fathers. But the instant G. took off his glasses to kiss me, it became perfectly clear. I knew the gesture so well it made me shudder. The real common denominator was bad eyesight.

◊ JOHN W. WILSON ◊

The Partners

It's three o'clock in Palo Alto, and, outside the windowless fourth-floor boardroom on Page Mill Road, a hazy winter sun is already slanting toward the range of hills that bounds the Santa Clara Valley on the west. The partners of Merrill, Pickard, Anderson & Eyre have gathered around an oval table that almost fills the room for their weekly ritual, the face-to-face confrontation that shapes their high-stakes investment decisions.

Three of the four were venture officers at Bank of America before spinning out. Now their independent private partnership has some $90 million under management. Steve Merrill, in his early forties, was the leader of the B of A group; he carries an air of confidence as well as a self-deflating sense of humor. Jeff Pickard, barely forty, approaches things with analytical detachment. He says little, but when he has something to contribute, he gets to the point. Chris Eyre, in his mid-thirties, the most ebullient of the four, balances the ingrained optimism of his Mormon pioneer heritage with a cautious approach to every investment. Jim Anderson, a recruit from Hewlett-Packard, is the youngest at thirty-three and the only one with a technical background. He rivals Merrill in debating skill, but seems to oscillate during the discussion between positive and negative poles, as if the optimistic engineer that he was and the skeptical investor he is trying to become were engaged in their own private debate.

There are others in the cherrywood-paneled room: John Russo, a research associate, and Steve Colt, newly recruited as a partner, are

◊ *John W. Wilson lives in Larkspur, California, and is senior editor of ComputerLetter. This excerpt appeared in* The New Venturers, © *1985 John W. Wilson, published by Addison-Wesley Publishing Co.*

156

attending as observers, but occasionally chime in. Before the meeting gets serious, Anderson is the victim of a mild roasting over his suggestion to install mobile telephones in the partners' cars, and Eyre is congratulated for finally getting out of his first venture with a profit of $83,000. "That'll pay for a car phone," remarks Merrill.

◇

The rest of the meeting is largely given over to discussion of The Learning Company, an educational software specialist looking for $2 million. Steve Merrill has just returned from the annual Consumer Electronics Show, and he has seen enough of the competition to satisfy himself that this company indeed has an outstanding product line. Whether its management team is strong enough and whether it can grow fast enough to produce a satisfactory return are questions still to be answered.

Merrill cautiously builds a case for making the investment. The others offer a few caveats, but in the end seem to go along. With only a few abridgments, this is how the partners work toward consensus:

MERRILL: Let me give a quick summary of the company. It was started by a Ph.D. educator out of Berkeley and a few of her friends. They wrote one program that's turned out to be very well recognized in academic circles as a great program, but the company was a disaster as far as I can tell. Jack Melchor and a group of his friends put in $300,000 about a year and a half ago, but the thing kind of floundered after that. Jack got some good people on the board, and they went to work trying to get things back in order, primarily concerning themselves with finding a CEO. They found Marcia Klein, who has done quite a good job of focusing the company on its products, defining its purpose, restructuring some of the marketing agreements and pricing—very basic stuff. So they did $1 million in their first year, made a little money, and they are now running at $2 million and projecting $8 million in two years. They are raising $2 million now. I went around at the show, and I led the tour. I didn't rely on her to pick out competitive products. I must say, I was absolutely flabbergasted at how terrible those products were compared with hers.

ANDERSON: Well, the others are all entertainment.

MERRILL: It's a dangerous kind of research, but I think it's a fair assumption that they have built the best reputation in education circles for quality software for children. And that is their philosophy. They want to build a product line, stick exclusively to education. Ann [Piestrup, the founder] sets the tone for the company. She is an educator, a crusader, and she believes in certain kinds of education and she's probably right. Only recently, and because I think she's been programmed a bit, has she also started talking about trying to make money at it. But there's no question where her heart really lies when push comes to shove. And that has to permeate the company to a certain degree. The second characteristic that permeates the company is that these people are all very nice and very decent and very bright and therefore probably not very tough and maybe not too effective in the dog-eat-dog world of selling software.

PICKARD: Does that include Marcia?

MERRILL: That's a question. Marcia clearly has gone in there and been able to work with that environment. The few checks I've done on her, they said that's one of her capabilities, she seems to be able to span that environment and the outside world very well. I could do some more checks on her. Even if you were satisfied that Marcia is aware of the need to do that and be tough in the outside world, what will she do to her credibility inside the company? She can't change the entire culture of the company. I don't want to get this thing out of proportion, but the fact is they are not the kind of opportunistic, aggressive people who are running Spinnaker [at the time, the leader in educational software].

EYRE: If they are marketing to get shelf space at the local ComputerLand, that's one thing, but if they are marketing through schools . . .

MERRILL: A third to a half of their business will be through schools. The plus side of this, and one of the arguments in favor of this company, is it's exactly that kind of culture that would not work in a video game environment or even in a business software environment, but it's exactly suited to the educational software business. All the other people are trying to act like video game people and apply it to the educational field, and that's a field it's not going to fly in.

ANDERSON: Who are the other managers?

MERRILL: If you look at the whole management team, there is really only one man. This is not a group of feminists, that's not the problem.

ANDERSON: You know my bias. [Anderson's wife is a manager at Hewlett-Packard.] I think if you have a group of women with a track record in industry that's one thing, but the problem is they haven't been in industry.

MERRILL: They don't have much of a management team. They have got to hire the number two person in the company, which is going to be a marketing person, and a number three, the finance person.

ANDERSON: So they are still building the company?

MERRILL: Absolutely. It's not a Class A management team. It may be a group of Class A educators applying their talents to educational software.

ANDERSON: The next question is, even at a $5 million valuation, how much money can they make? Let's say they exceed their plan and do $10 million in '85, what's that worth?

MERRILL: $25 million [a fivefold increase in the value of the company, reflecting a fivefold increase in sales]. But the most appealing thing about this from a gut point of view is that, ignoring the numbers, this kind of philosophy will be very attractive to the kind of company that would be interested in this deal. They're going to like these people and they'll pay a premium over what the numbers show.

ANDERSON: One appeal is that products in education just keep on going. People are still buying Tinker Toys.

MERRILL: That's a bet. It certainly applies more here than anywhere else in software.

PICKARD: It would have to. I have no feel for their ability or anybody else's ability to come up with new products in this area.

ANDERSON: That's a good question. Wasn't Imagic the one that had the formula they were going to test-market everything and do all that market research?

MERRILL: These guys have a product that's already won.

PICKARD: To me, measuring the risks on this thing, one of them is how much we're betting on new products.

MERRILL: I think any way you look at it, we're betting a lot on new products. They couldn't quantify that, but they are not saying they will get to $8 million by converting existing products.

EYRE: The other thing you're saying is that hopefully this marketplace is a little more stable and, if you get a product there and people like it, they'll hold on to it for a while—as opposed to a video game.

MERRILL: The financial issue here is very simple. The bottom line is price-cutting. They're selling these things for forty or fifty bucks apiece and the cost of goods is $4. Is this business going to be one where a high-quality product can command a premium price? And second of all, what is the price of talent? Is it going to turn into having to give a $1 million advance to the authors or can they build a stable of in-house talent to generate products of high quality without paying through the nose for it? Probably the answer is, there are enough people out there in the educational field who want to work on these things.

ANDERSON: There's something about it I like, I have to admit. But the thing I'm uncomfortable with is whether we're in effect betting against Spinnaker. If Spinnaker is successful, and they're suddenly a $100 million company, and we're sitting here at $10 million to $15 million, and it's a capital-intensive industry . . . . I just wonder if we can survive.

MERRILL: That's a risk.

EYRE: Isn't the real question here whether these guys are going to be an author or a publisher?

MERRILL: My perception is that with their talent pool and their orientation, they strike me as quality authors.

EYRE: If you're going to be a publisher, you have to have a huge line to cover the costs.

ANDERSON: Is this going to be time-intensive? We still have to build a team here.

MERRILL: Yeah, it's relatively time-intensive. Not as time-intensive as it might be. We don't need a CEO. I wouldn't want to make this bet if I wasn't comfortable that Marcia was going to work out. But Marcia needs help.

ANDERSON: So you'd go on the board?

MERRILL: Yeah, we'd have to go on the board.

PICKARD: Where do you stand on this? Are you advocating it?

MERRILL: No, I'm having a discussion on this case. I still have some work to do. I guess the question I am asking myself is, should I spend more time on this or drop it.

ANDERSON: Two observations I'd make. This is starting to sound more and more like a price-sensitive deal. And secondly, it concerns me a little allocating your time to a board seat on a deal that has at best a 3 or 5 times upside to it. I'd like to have you working on a deal with a little more blue sky [meaning one with more upside potential].

EYRE: I'd be a lot more crazy about the deal if we could simply park some money in it.

MERRILL: Or if they would give us a price break. But they are very price-sensitive.

ANDERSON: How much is she raising?

MERRILL: $2 million.

ANDERSON: What is she doing with it?

MERRILL: Marketing, promotion, new management. It's a partnership decision, not mine. It would be an easy thing to do. The bottom line is, it's low risk but it's not going to be a huge winner.

PICKARD: Is anybody else looking at it that if they go on the board you'd feel comfortable parking some money there?

MERRILL: Unfortunately, I don't think there is.

ANDERSON: You know what bugs me? Something tells me if we got the right couple of managers in there, it just takes off and they suddenly dominate educational software and the market blooms and the sun comes out and all is wonderful.

MERRILL: It's still not going to be a $500 million company. But what you do is you cultivate this little jewel and somebody comes along and says we want to be in the software business and we want a quality acquisition.

PICKARD: You're going to do some more work on it, right?

MERRILL: Well, I sort of get a sense that we kind of like it. I don't hear any strong objections. Every deal we do doesn't have to have the potential of being a $500 million company.

◇

And so it went. Decisions were not so much made as discovered, as if the partners were sorting through a haystack of conjecture and warnings to find the kernels of opportunity that had to be there. Steve Merrill's optimism ultimately prevailed. Shortly after the partners' meeting, Merrill Pickard offered to invest about $1 million at a relatively low valuation. In the meantime, though, Dick Kramlich of New Enterprise Associates had also discovered the company and offered to finance it at a higher price. Rather than bow out entirely, Merrill Pickard scaled back its investment to $500,000 and agreed to accept John Glynn, an experienced venture capitalist, as a director in place of Steve Merrill.

The Learning Company made solid progress for a time, but then Marcia Klein, the new chief executive, became ill and was forced to leave active management. At the same time, the market for educational software began to soften as sales of home computers slipped far behind industry forecasts. The Learning Company successfully launched a new product that appeared to reinforce its reputation for quality and it conserved cash at a time when competitors were falling by the wayside, but it had trouble meeting its sales plan. Like most venture capital investments, it appeared to be neither a failure nor an amazing success, simply a promising company with an uncertain future.

◇ ALAN DUNDES ◇

Arse Longa, Vita Brevis: Jokes about AIDS

AIDS is certainly no laughing matter. But if, in fact, only the most serious and anxiety-producing topics generate humor, then humor should provide an essential safety valve in the midst of this particular tragedy as well. AIDS jokes, taken as a whole, constitute an authentic folk view of the disease. Since most of the initial victims of AIDS were homosexual, the cycle began with a tone of overt homophobia. Perhaps the earliest joke in the cycle was:

Do you know what "gay" means?
Got AIDS yet?

Told before 1983, this joke implies that in time all gays will contract AIDS. From one extreme homophobic perspective, homosexuality was an evil and AIDS a divine form of punishment. Later, when AIDS began to surface among heterosexuals, this view-point had to be modified.

Another early joke commented directly upon the "shame" of admitting one's homosexuality:

What's the worst thing about getting AIDS?
Convincing your parents you're Haitian.

◇ *Alan Dundes is professor of anthropolgy and folklore at the University of California, Berkeley. His collection of essays,* Folklore Matters, *was recently published by the University of Tennessee Press. Sources for the folklore of AIDS include: Casper G. Schmidt, "AIDS Jokes, or Schadenfreude around an Epidemic,"* Maledicta 8 (1984–86), 69–75; Alan Dundes, "At Ease, Disease — AIDS Jokes as Sick Humor," *American Behavioral Scientist 30 (1987), 72–81; Gary Alan Fine, "Welcome to the World of AIDS: Fantasies of Female Revenge,"* Western Folklore 46 (1987), 192–97; and Joseph P. Goodwin, "Unprintable Reactions to All the News That's Fit to Print," *Southern Folklore 46 (1989), 15–39.*

This refers to the so-called four Hs, the four groups most at risk: homosexuals, heroin-users (or other drug-users sharing the same infected needles), hemophiliacs (who contracted the disease from transfusions), and Haitians. Presumably, since parents know whether or not a child is a hemophiliac, the AIDS victim rather than admit to being heroin-addicted or homosexual, would be forced to choose the fourth group. There is a racial cast to this joke: since most Haitians are Black, it might seem additionally difficult for a white child to convince his white parents that he was Haitian.

There are other examples of racist AIDS jokes:

> What's sickle-cell anemia?
> AIDS for spades.

This joke reflects the same kind of mentality that argues that AIDS is divine retribution for homosexuality; in this case, AIDS is a heaven-endorsed means of eliminating a racial minority. Another racist text:

> They're going to have to change the name AIDS — all the Blacks keep applying for it.

These jokes all come from oral tradition, a tradition that is free from censorship (as opposed to the media), and therefore one in which racism and sexism flourish to the extent that American society is racist and sexist. The majority of AIDS jokes, however, are anti-gay, not anti-Black. One of the sickest is perhaps:

> Did you hear about the homosexual who finally decided to come "out of the closet"? He told his parents he had bad news and good news. "The bad news is I'm gay; the good news is I'm dying."

Here again is articulated the homosexual's fear of coming out of the closet, of informing his parents of his sexual preference. In this case it is not death before dishonor, but death cutting dishonor short. (In some instances, individuals with AIDS have asked their physicians to conceal the details of their illness, and the actual cause of death is omitted from their obituaries — so as not to cause "embarrassment" to their familes.)

Homophobia is explicit in many other AIDS jokes:

How do you know your garden has AIDS?
When your pansies start dying.

Why is AIDS a miracle?
It's the only thing in the world that can change a fruit into a vegetable.

A pro-heterosexual and anti-homosexual bias is made perfectly clear in jokes comparing herpes and AIDS:

What's the difference between herpes and AIDS?
One's a love story; the other's a fairy tale.

What do you call someone with both herpes and AIDS?
An incurable romantic.

The use of such slurs as pansy, fruit, and fairy underscore the homophobic bias in these jokes. The point is that they are as much about attitudes toward homosexuality as they are about AIDS.

Many of the homophobic AIDS jokes refer specifically to anal intercourse:

Do you know what AIDS stands for?
Anal Intercourse Deterrence System, or Anally Injected [or Inserted] Death Sentence.

Who brought AIDS to the United States?
Some asshole.

Do you know why there is no cure for AIDS?
Because laboratory scientists can't teach rats to buttfuck.

The last joke may also articulate the public's impatience with medical researchers, who surely ought to be able to discover a "cure for AIDS."

In 1985, actor Rock Hudson admitted he had AIDS — and quickly became the subject of jokes. Samples from this subset of the cycle reveal familiar themes:

What's the difference between Staten Island and Rock Hudson?
The first is a ferry terminal, the second a terminal fairy.

Why did Rock Hudson's car insurance go up?
Too many rear-enders.

When Rock Hudson checked into the clinic in France, the doctor said, "I'm going to need the names of your last 100 male lovers."

Rock Hudson replied, "What do you think, I've got eyes in the back of my head?"

Since Rock Hudson was a film star, it was deemed appropriate that some of the jokes refer to current movies:

Did you hear about the new sequel to *Rambo* starring Rock Hudson? It's called *Rambutt*.

Did you know that Sylvester Stallone has AIDS? He was in *Rocky II*.

Other Rock Hudson jokes pretended to give his epitaph:

What is it going to say on Rock Hudson's tomb? Born in the East, reared in the West.

Do you know what it says on Rock Hudson's tombstone?
    Asses to ashes,
    Lust to dust,
    If you had tried pussy,
    You'd still be with us.

When AIDS began to be reported among heterosexuals, including women, the joke cycle shifted to take this into account.

Other jokes reacted to the extensive media effort to publicize condoms. One involved a reprise of an earlier Polish-American ethnic slur cycle:

Two Polacks were shooting up one day. After one finished, the second took the same needle and used it. Said the first, "Are you crazy? Why did you use the same needle I used? Don't you know I have AIDS?" The second replied, "That's all right. I'm wearing a condom."

Another manifestation of women's participation in the AIDS crisis is found in a 1986 legend. (A legend is a story told as true, set in the modern real world.)

A man picks up a beautiful woman in a bar and they spend the night together in a hotel. Next morning the man awakes to find the woman gone. When he enters the bathroom, he finds a message scrawled in lipstick on the mirror: "Welcome to the wonderful world of AIDS!"

This legend suggests an extreme form of a female-revenge theme. The woman's answer to the inevitable question "Why me?" is to infect as many sexually active males as possible. The rationale is presumably "If I am going to die, I might as well kill as many 'guilty' no-good males as I can." Since it was a male who originally infected the woman, she feels justified in taking her revenge in this way.

The male fear of contracting AIDS from a woman is expressed in a 1988 joke, which, curiously enough, combines AIDS with Alzheimer's disease.

> Mr. Johnson, concerned about his wife who has undergone a series of tests at a local hospital, calls her doctor to get the results of the tests. The doctor informs him that by coincidence there happened to be two Mrs. Johnsons who were tested at the hospital on the same day and their records unfortunately got mixed up. One of the Mrs. Johnsons has Alzheimer's disease and the other has AIDS. The husband asks, "What shall I do?" The doctor inquires, "Is your wife at home now?" The husband says, "Yes, she is." The doctor advises, "Take her for a drive a couple of blocks from home and leave her off. If she finds her way home, don't screw her!"

The mention of doctors reminds us of another important facet of the AIDS epidemic, namely, the treatment and care of AIDS victims by medical professionals. Normally, doctors and nurses are presumed to be brave with respect to treating patients with contagious diseases, or, at any rate, to take all necessary precautionary measures, but the plight of medical practitioners with respect to AIDS is the subject of the following 1988 joke:

> A young man goes to a doctor for a physical. After completing the exam, the doctor tells him he has AIDS. After an emotional outburst, the young man asks the doctor, "Is there anything I can do?" The doctor tries to console him by saying that he will get the best medical care available, and that he must start immediately on a diet limited to flounder and pancakes. The young man interrupts, "Oh! Flounder and pancakes? Is that a cure for AIDS?" "No," replies the doctor, "but it's the only thing we can slide under the door."

Whether this joke reflects actual anxiety on the part of medical personnel or is simply a joke told to underscore the danger of contagion — even doctors are afraid — is not totally clear.

In another version of this joke, the theme is not at all one of the doctor's fear of further contact, but rather of insisting that blame for the disease belongs to the victim himself — for having indulged in the sexual activity that is presumed to have caused the condition. The first part of the joke is the same, but the answer to "Is there anything I can do?" is different:

> The doctor says, "You should travel to Mexico where you should drink the water and eat unwashed fresh vegetables. And you should put salsa and chili peppers on everything you eat." The young man asks, "Oh, is that a cure for AIDS?" "No, but it will teach you what your asshole is supposed to be used for."

In this brief exploration of AIDS jokes, we have seen many of the painful and distressing aspects of the disease dealt with. We have also seen how new folklore comes into being as a necessary psychic response to crisis. AIDS jokes may well have helped communicate the very real dangers of the disease; these jokes may actually have performed a valuable service — like public service announcements on radio and TV. On the other hand, to the extent that AIDS jokes add to homophobia, they are to be deplored, even though later jokes seem to have emphasized heterosexual transmission.

In any event, the jokes exist, whether one likes them or not, whether one finds them the least bit amusing or not. Furthermore, there is no real way of stopping them. The folk will always produce folklore. And it is important to seek to understand why the AIDS folklore was created in the first place and why it continues to thrive. To sum up, AIDS jokes may not give us hope, but they may somehow help us cope.

1.0 That Architecture is a language seems

obvious. Architecture is an activity of structure. It has meaning. This meaning is communicable via structures and conventions that are akin to grammars. Architecture presents one world as an idealization of another--it involves the distance of signification. It is a product of intention.

In this intention is the blind teleological urge that looks to language for a sense of direction. Architecture turns to language because of language's ability to generate meaning, not just reflect it. Given a program, the architect needs to know how to proceed; he needs a plan for the plan, some guiding light that can direct his efforts. If Architecture is language, the literate practitioner then should only have to open his mouth for architecture to appear.

But Architecture has also, always, been more than a language. It has been concerned not only with saying something, but with what is said. It presents one world as an idealization of another. Consequently, when Architecture can find no consistent "thing to glorify," or no single world to explain, it must temper its desire to be seen as a language. It must accept a role that is less vast: where Language structures and deciphers the meaning for an entire world, Architecture must lower its sights to the potential meaning of lesser constructs: individual "worlds" that have forgotten the desire for such hegemony. Architecture in a self-aware age must demote itself from language to text.

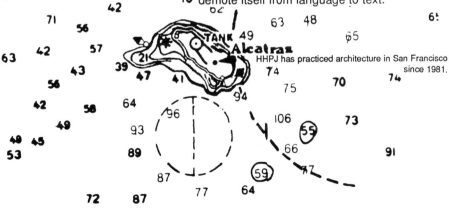

HHPJ has practiced architecture in San Francisco since 1981.

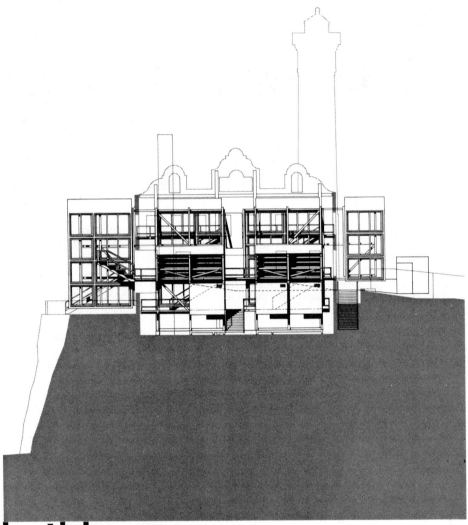

In this case the figure is complicated by being no thing, but rather, and no more than, an instrumentality. Language, properly figured, becomes a Work: a text. Otherwise it is seen as a property, a quality, possessed by those things it once explained, or created. Now, however, it can only maintain with these a sort of contiguous relationship. In this light, text becomes an idea more useful to Architecture. It reorients our attention from Architecture having a property or capacity — language — to its being a certain kind of thing

◇ *Wes Jones is a partner in Holt Hinshaw Pfau Jones, architects in San Francisco since 1981.*

– a text.

2.0

Language succeeded as a metaphor for Architecture when there was an all encompassing "classical" world that set the context for creative activity. In that world, Architecture's role of giving concrete, permanent form to the intangible ideals and outlook, the cosmology, of the period was mirrored exactly by the understanding of language as a mapping of that world into the cognitive realm. Today this "mapping" is simply no longer possible: as literary theorists question the neutrality of the means, social and physical theorists question the "reality" of the object. Both the transparency of language to its "meaning," and the objective continuity of a "world" to which this meaning might refer, have been questioned — with the result that the gap between language and its object is becoming increasingly obvious. As language becomes more opaque, its instrumental nature becomes more apparent. Language becomes motivated: **the ground, subject to intention,**

becomes figure and gets in the way.

3.0

The idea of language, as a noun, lacks value: language is always a means; a text uses this means to create, to state, a value. We know the idea of value is central to Architecture. It is the force which sets up the oscillation between Art and Utility. Thus we are led to the essence of Architecture, to something that cannot be isolated and studied separately. And text works well in this regard also: it is inhabited by the same rich play of meaning as Architecture. A text is a statement of or about some truth; it creates at the site of this truth a local absolute dividing it from the larger context of possibility. **Here it contains —**

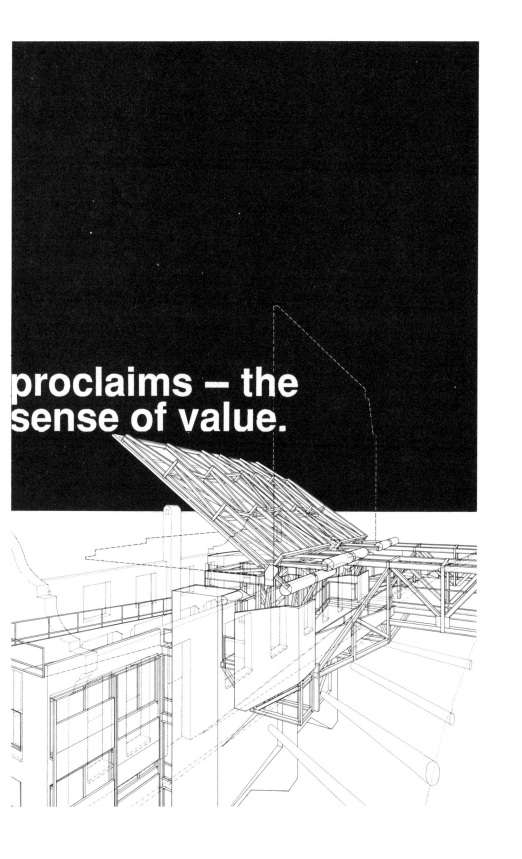

proclaims – the
sense of value.

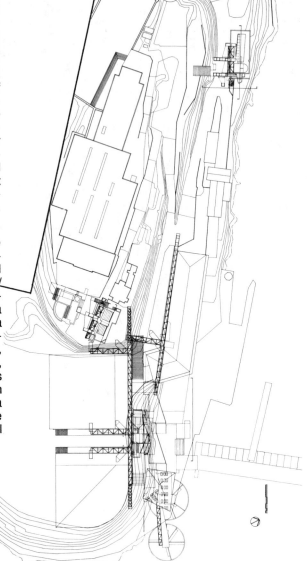

But a text is at the same time in-complete. To the extent that it prefigures/expects the supple-ment of commentary, it denies the wholeness of the truth it declares. The text is an approxi-mation of ideality. It is localized by brevity, but the universality of its claims invites later expan-sion. It is a statement about one subject that expects to be com-mented upon in illustration or defense of another: an open-ended structure about closed truths. In expecting critique it carries the sense of self-aware-ness that is so celebrated today.

These senses of the idea are underlain by the structural prin-ciples contained in the original Latin root for the word: a text is/was a weaving. A woven struc-ture invests its object with a sense of deferral. A word or idea which is woven carries its mean-ing as a sort of field condition, rather than as some simple, lapidary understanding. It is, as we saw, never complete; though it speaks of absolutes or of a sense of finish, its edges are always just out of reach or still being created.

4.0 Text, texture

Architecture – all are the same strategy,

but applied to different materials. The definition and understanding of each is complicated by its woven character, the declaration of a seamless whole built up from the discontinuous relationship of discreet strands. For Architec-ture these are Art and Utility, for the text they are truth and commentary. In both cases the idea exists in the space between, ceaselessly shuttling back and forth between strands that claim precedence.

◇ SAM HAMILL ◇

The Degradation of Money

I could face all this, the hell with it, if I had the means (that is, only the daily bread for my wife and me) to devote myself to the work I want and know I can do—so that I wouldn't be working like a crippled man. The degradation of money. Yesterday I had the most humiliating idea I may ever have had in my life: to stop writing for a period otime—five or ten years, I don't know—to find a job that would allow me to save a little money, and then do what I want. A ridiculous thought; for living things there is no deferment.

—George Seferis, *A Poet's Journal*

But there is not a single poet in the United States who makes a living as a poet. The open marketplace envisioned by the founders encourages economic discrimination against women and minorities. It values the "worth" of a good baseball player to the tune of millions of dollars per year. It may make a millionaire of an adolescent with a guitar. It may make a mediocre journalist rich and turn a romance novelist into an international celebrity. But there is not a single poet in the United States who makes a living as a poet.

I recently placed a poem with a respectable literary magazine. I worked on that poem for 13 months. Not daily, of course, but with regularity. And I'd spent 40-odd years preparing for it. I was lucky to have placed it where I did: it will appear in a magazine that actually pays for poetry. I received, gratefully, a check in the amount of $5 for,

◇ *Sam Hamill is editor at Copper Canyon Press, Port Townsend, Washington. His collection of essays,* A Poet's Work: The Other Side of Poetry, *in which this piece appeared, was published by Broken Moon Press (Seattle), which also brought out his essays on Japanese poetry,* Basho's Ghost, *and his poems and translations in the Zen tradition,* A Dragon in the Clouds.

perhaps, 150 hours of actual writing time, or something less than 3¢ per hour for my labor.

> Why does one write poems? Why, although they are such secret things (for one who writes them), does one consider them more important than anything else in life? This vital need.
>
> —George Seferis, *A Poet's Journal*

> When I get a little money, I buy books; and if any is left, I buy food and clothes.   —Desiderius Erasmus

Evidence of the degradation of poverty is everywhere evident in poetry. One finds it in the poetry of Richard Hugo, who worked on an assembly line at Boeing for nearly 20 years, during which time he wrote some of his greatest poetry, poems paying homage to the poor, the degraded, the oppressed, and the misbegotten. The poverty Hugo experienced as an assembly-line worker was not simply financial, but rather a poverty of spirit which contributed to chronic depression and a sense of alienation he never overcame. One finds it in the poetry of Muriel Rukeyser, in her cotton dress and burly compassion, expressed in her commitment to redefining social priorities. One finds it in the intelligence of W. S. Merwin's drunk banging in an old abandoned furnace, in the poetry of Thomas McGrath and Kenneth Rexroth and Denise Levertov, in every poet of the working (and unemployed) classes.

Tu Fu was so poor during the An Lu-shan Rebellion that his young son starved to death. The greatest poets of ancient China lived either by patronage or by their begging bowls.

Ezra Pound conspired with everyone who would listen to sell subscriptions to buy Eliot's way out of his bank-clerk position, to buy him time to write.

Old Mrs. Melville wrote a friend, "Poor Herman! First he wrote a book about fish which no one wants to publish, now he's gone back to writing poetry again."

Orwell wrote from firsthand experience of catching and eating rats in *Down and Out in Paris and London*. We remember Kafka, and the old blind beggar, Homer. We remember the parable of the rich man and the camel and the eye of the needle. We remember that Kung-fu Tze, Socrates, Jesus of Nazareth, Mohammed, Gandhi, Lincoln, and King all were poor.

Neruda and Vallejo were poor. Theodore Roethke was finally undone by bitter memories of his humble origin—poor Roethke! More than the money, he envied the status of the rich. We remember how often we have been taught that being poor and honest has a dignity that no other way of living can ever earn.

Nazim Hikmet and Yannis Ritsos and Mahmoud Darweesh spent years in prison for what they said in their poems. We remember Pound in his cage, sleeping on newspapers and wrapped in a single blanket; or the poverty of Osip and Nadezhda Mandelshtam, of Brendan Behan, of Albert Camus, who as a child loathed the stairways of his tenement out of fear of rats. And we remember the poverty of Bertolt Brecht.

Everywhere we look, there are models.

I have been asked to be one of the evaluators for several small literary grants to be made by a state arts agency. The money for these three $1,000 grants and one $3,000 grant comes from the city and the state, and from matching funds from the National Endowment for the Arts. The young woman who administers the program apologizes profusely because she cannot pay me for reading and evaluating 97 manuscripts. The arts agency pays her a salary sufficient to save her from the humiliation of food stamps, but she must live in a cheap apartment and live frugally. The agency reimburses me for the mileage for my trip, two hours each way, to and from the city. But the time I spend, both in meetings and in evaluating the 97 manuscripts, I must donate.

Writers are expected to make these sacrifices. Doctors and lawyers and grocers and psychiatrists make similar sacrifices for the good of the community, but with one paramount difference: they earn a decent living from their primary work.

The degradation of money. I teach in prisons and public schools and universities not simply for the money I earn, although I cannot survive without it, but because I love the subject and my students.

A typical poet in North America finds it necessary to relocate every year for the first few years after college, and every several years for a couple of decades after that. The poet becomes disconnected, never developing a true sense of place or of community outside the community of the printed page. The typical poet teaches, partly because teaching leaves the summer free to write, partly because the subject is a passion. But teaching drains. The writer-in-residence is rarely a candidate for tenure because it is far less expensive to make that position temporary, keeping the resident artist on the lowest rung of the pay-scale. Even within the confines of the artificial community of would-be scholars, the poet is heretic. And the poet outside academia? That poet is a scholar-out-of-office, a professor of desire.

The young writer is in college. At some point, he or she writes home, "I think maybe I will dedicate my life to poetry."

The family soon writes back, "That's nice. But what will you *do?*" Meaning, "to make a living," or to save the family name from embarrassment.

I have a friend, a poet about as well-known as an American poet can be, whose wife told me this about their marriage: after meeting and approving the union with the poet, her family took her aside. Would it be all right, they wanted to know, if they introduced the poet to their friends not as a poet, but as a professor. After all, it is so much more dignified.

> Our public life is a jungle where everyone is out to slaughter the other with guile, slander, cowardice, shamelessness. These people make you feel as though you were chewing fog.
>
> —George Seferis, *A Poet's Journal*

At this writing, I am 47 years old and am "employed" about four to five months per year at a salary that approaches $10 per hour. I have six years of university education, read several languages and research in nearly a dozen more. I have been lucky enough to have been honored by several grants and awards. But I have no health insurance, no medical coverage, no dental coverage, no retirement fund, minimal insurance on my home, and no money in the bank. For the past 20 years (with two significant exceptions), I have survived from week to week. But I have enjoyed far greater wealth than I ever dreamed possible.

The general public distrusts art. A 1985 Associated Press article pointed out that 57% of the public disliked abstract art, while a whopping 70% visited an art museum less than once a year. "Thirty-five percent said they never visited art museums, 27% never attended concerts, and 39% never went to the theater." The article broke down groups by education, by income, and by region. Less than half of all college graduates support subsidies for the arts. Fewer than one in three high school graduates support subsidies for the arts. Our federal budget designates more money for military marching bands than for art.

Nowhere in the article was literature even mentioned.

Because money for literature is scarce, and because the general public measures quality by money, the poet is constantly faced with the prospect of being expected to "play poet" as though it were an amateur competitive sport. Private and university presses regularly run contests with the first prize being publication of the "best" book. Which leaves literally hundreds of poets sending out manuscripts with cover letters explaining how they have been "runner-up" in contest after contest. It would be all too easy (and probably just) to dismiss these poor careerists as victims of poetic justice, except that contests degrade not only the naïve participants, but poetry as well.

Robert Graves has stated that he writes for "a few friends" rather than for a public. The poet's chief loyalty, he says, "is to the Goddess Calliope, not to his publisher, or to the booksellers on his publisher's mailing list." And certainly not, I would add, to the judges of a poetry contest.

Poetry is not a contest. Anyone believing contests show anything but trends should have a look at the Yale Younger Poets list. Does anyone read Howard Buck? He was the first. John Chipman Farrar, David Osborne Hamilton, Alfred Raymond Bellinger, Thomas Caldecott Chubb, Daryl Boyle, Theodore H. Banks Jr., or Viola White? Marion Boyd, Beatrice E. Harmon, or Elizabeth Jessup Blake? Eleanor Slater, Lindley Williams Hubbell, Mildred Bowers, Ted Olson, Francis Claiborne Mason, or Frances Frost? Louise Owen, Dorothy Belle Flanagan, Shirley Barker, or Henri Faust? Each is a poet, each wrote good poetry.

Careerists scramble over token university positions. Many of these writers see a position in a university as a step toward national recognition, which it often is. But the attitude built into contests inclines them to disregard their critics while embracing easy flattery.

Contests chart the calm blue seas of fads. Back in the days when poets served severe apprenticeships under the stern gaze of elder poets, it may have meant something to have "studied under" so-and-so. But we have too often chosen the democracy of the Writing Program with its composition by committee rather than enduring the tyranny of genius. "Genius," Blake said, "is not lawless." Nor is it expressed by committee. MFAs, a "terminal" degree, produce more MFAs. Today, the academies certify hundreds of new American poets every year, far, far more poets being "drafted" into semi-official poetry societies than football players drafted into the pros. Many of them have been winners or runners-up in contests sponsored by The Associated Writing Programs, by literary magazines, university English departments, private presses, and/or nefarious vanity publishers.

In recent years, there has been a new wrinkle: the invention of the "literary lottery," a contest in which the participant pays to enter, then prays to be among the anointed. I'm told a decent publication can get two or three thousand entrants. Charging a $5 "reading fee," one has a budget of, say, $8,000 from reading fees alone. Since one can put out a pretty well-made book in an edition of a thousand for approximately $3,000–5,000, even after postage and advertising our "editor" has raised several grand. The losers may then be among the "runners-up" who are cordially invited to enter again next year.

> What really dissatisfies in American civilization is the want of the interesting.
>
> — Matthew Arnold

When Scott Walker decided to move Graywolf Press from Port Townsend to St. Paul, our local newspaper ran a sympathetic story. Walker told of his love for the Northwest, and for Port Townsend in particular, but, he said, he simply couldn't raise funds here. In Minnesota, he explained, there would be more grants, there would be corporate and private funds to help. Our local paper was very sympathetic; losing Graywolf Press, it said, would be a loss to us all. But our paper had never reviewed his books. When Graywolf was struggling to find funds, neither our local paper nor the major dailies in Seattle, among the worst in the country (the Seattle *Post-Intelligencer,* a Hearst paper, doesn't even have a book page), came to his aid. But they all mourned his moving.

What does the economic situation of the poet have to do with the art of letters? Simply this: the poet's marginal position within the community, the lack of a permanent position, and the lack of future economic stability constantly undermine the poet's sense of self-worth. We are told in many ways that our most valued work has no "value" to the culture at large. When the poet, in order to have the all-important time to write and to study, works for a pittance and lives in motels or moves from college to college, one of the most important connections in culture is severed, and the poet becomes a low-grade highbrow entertainer, a fly-by-night gadfly to be used and passed on by institutions.

Poets have no right to expect to be paid for their labors. They have no right to expect enthusiastic audiences. They have, in fact, no right to expect any material return of any kind for their work, work that is correctly defined as the economy of the gift. But if the other arts are valued by the culture at large, the calling, the avocation of the poet, like that of painter or composer, should be honored; the poet, like the painter or composer, needs money to buy time in order to work.

Poetry is not a vocation. When universities certify young poets, they degrade both the poets and the poets' work. It is an honor to teach a child how to listen and how to speak in rhyme; it is honorable and useful work to teach at all (just as I, sitting here at my desk in the early morning, thinking, drinking coffee, am now involved in a discourse, am setting up a dialectic, am both teaching and learning, engaging my life with yours, imagined reader, in the shared hope that the realizations resulting from this discourse will be mutually beneficial). But the work of teaching is another vocation.

Nevertheless, we are belittled by the arrogance of ignorance in others, just as the farmer is degraded by the ignorant assumptions of those who never learn to read a water table or to understand an animal or to make a simple piece of furniture with their hands. Just as the "women's work" of the past was belittled by men too self-important to learn how to darn a sock or to bake a loaf of bread.

In point of fact, the American economic system is degrading to all artists and to art itself. The true artist is faced with perpetual adolescence in the American economic reality, and often lives from hand to mouth, embarrassed and frustrated by poverty, frequently insulted by public perceptions and misconceptions about what art is and is not, always on the lookout for the handout, for the patron, a spiritual pagan in the Church of the Almighty Dollar. This condition has existed since the early *polis*.

But the poet stands outside even the community of artists, for the musician, the painter, the actor, the sculptor, the clown — all these may hold out hope that someday it will become possible to eke out a livelihood from the various crafts of their respective disciplines, while the call to poetry more closely resembles the vows of poverty one takes in order to enter a religious community. No poet in this country can realistically expect to ever enjoy a regular income as a result of mastering the craft of composition. Removed to the margins of culture, poets remain in economic shadows.

What is the "comparable worth" of a poet compared to a local minister? And compared to a cop? Who shall "police" our grammar? The poet labors many years, preparing for the gift of inspiration; from this inspiration, the poet makes a gift. But neither poet nor poem is divorced from the morality of the marketplace. There is, as Seferis said, no deferment for the living.

Perhaps this complex problem has no solution; certainly, it has no simple and obvious one other than the re-education of the general public. The entirely necessary and honorable work of the National Endowment for the Arts and various state arts agencies is not sufficient; they are underfunded and provide convenient targets for the likes of Jesse Helms and his ilk. But pouring more tax dollars into state and federal coffers will not, of itself, solve the problem. There are more arts bureaucracies than ever before. The problem will be solved by Boeing Aircraft contributing to the welfare — not charity, but *welfare* — of the poet as it already does the painter. The situation will be resolved when it is defined in the high school and college classroom, when it becomes a suitable subject for "home economics."

Poetry exists as a gift economy, interdependent with the shadow work of the artist, and with the "hard economy" of the greater culture. No one can survive by the economy of the gift alone. No one can live by the hard economy alone. Everyone, at one level or another, is engaged in shadow work.

"In the economy of the spirit," Valéry said, "thrift is ruinous."

◇ BRANCHES ◇

MÒ

◇

end; branch; recent;
last; final

◇ DEEDS ◇

◇ GARY SOTO ◇

The Savings Book

My wife, Carolyn, married me for my savings: Not the double-digit figures but the strange three or four dollar withdrawals and deposits. The first time she saw my passbook she laughed until her eyes became moist and then hugged me as she called "Poor baby." And there was truth to what she was saying: Poor.

I remember opening my savings account at Guarantee Savings on May 27, 1969, which was a Monday. The previous Saturday my brother and I had taken a labor bus to chop cotton in the fields west of Fresno. We returned home in the back of a pickup with fourteen dollars each and a Mexican national who kept showing us watches and rings for us to buy. That day my brother and I wouldn't spring for Cokes or sandwiches, as most everyone else on our crew did when a vending truck drove up at lunch time, tooting a loud horn. The driver opened the aluminum doors to display his goods, and the workers, who knew better but couldn't resist, hovered over the iced Cokes, the cellophaned sandwiches, and the Hostess cupcakes. We looked on from the shade of the bus, sullen and most certainly sensible. Why pay forty cents when you could get a Coke in town for half the price. Why buy a sandwich for sixty-five cents when you could have slapped together your own sandwich. That was what our mother had done for us. She had made us tuna sandwiches which by noon had grown suspiciously sour when we peeled back the top slice to peek in. Still, we ate them, chewing slowly and watching each other to see if he were beginning to double over. Finished, we searched the paper bag

◇ *Gary Soto teaches at the University of California, Berkeley. His most recent collection of poetry is* Home Course in Religion *(Chronicle Books). This piece appeared in* Living Up the Street *(Dell).*

and found a broken stack of saltine crackers wrapped in wax paper. What a cruel mother, we thought. Dry crackers on a dry day when it was sure to rise into the nineties as we chopped cotton or, as the saying went, "played Mexican golf."

We had each earned fourteen dollars for eight hours of work, the most money I had ever made in one day. Two days later, on May 27, 1969, I deposited those dollars; on June 9 I made my first withdrawal — four dollars to buy a belt to match a pair of pants. I had just been hired to sell encyclopedias, and the belt was intended to dazzle my prospective clients when they opened the door to receive me. But in reality few welcomed my presence on their doorsteps and the only encyclopedias I sold that summer were to families on welfare who so desperately wanted to rise from their soiled lives. Buy a set, I told them, and your problems will disappear. Knowledge is power. Education is the key to the future, and so on. The contracts, however, were rescinded and my commissions with them.

On June 20 I withdrew three dollars and twenty-five cents to buy a plain white shirt because my boss had suggested that I should look more "professional." Still, I sold encyclopedias to the poor and again the contracts were thrown out. Finally I was fired, my briefcase taken away, and the company tie undone from my neck. I walked home in the summer heat despairing at the consequence: No new clothes for the fall.

On July 13 I took out five dollars and eighty cents which, including the five cents interest earned, left me with a balance of one dollar. I used the money for bus fare to Los Angeles to look for work. I found it in a tire factory. At summer's end I returned home and walked proudly to Guarantee Savings with my pockets stuffed with ten dollar bills. That was September 5, and my new balance jumped to one hundred and forty-one dollars. I was a senior in high school and any withdrawals from my account went exclusively to buy clothes, never food, record albums, or concerts. On September 15, for instance, I withdrew fifteen dollars for a shirt and jeans. On September 24 I again stood before the teller to ask for six dollars. I bought a sweater at the Varsity Shop at Coffee's.

Slowly my savings dwindled that fall semester, although I did beef it up with small deposits: Twenty dollars on October 1, ten dollars on November 19, fifteen dollars on December 31, and so on. But by February my savings account balance read three dollars and twelve cents. On March 2, I returned to the bank to withdraw one crisp dollar to do God knows what. Perhaps it was to buy my mother a birthday gift. Seven days later, on March 10, I made one last attempt to bolster my savings by adding eight dollars. By March 23, however, I was again down to one dollar.

By the time I finally closed my account, it had fluctuated for five years, rising and falling as a barometer to my financial quandary. What is curious to me about this personal history are the kinds of transactions that took place—one day I would withdraw three dollars while on another day I would ask for six. How did it vanish? What did it buy? I'm almost certain I bought clothes but for what occasion? For whom? I didn't have a girlfriend in my senior year, so where did the money go?

To withdraw those minor amounts was no easy task. I had to walk or bicycle nearly four miles, my good friend Scott tagging along, and afterward we'd walk up and down the Fresno Mall in search of the elusive girlfriend or, if worse came to worse, to look for trouble.

My savings book is a testimony to my fear of poverty—that by saving a dollar here, another there, it would be kept at bay.

I admit that as a kid I worried about starving, although there was probably no reason. There was always something to eat; the cupboards were weighed down with boxes of this and that. But when I was older the remembrance of difficult times stayed with me: The time Mother was picking grapes and my brother ate our entire lunch while my sister and I played under the vines. For us there was nothing to eat that day. The time I opened the refrigerator at my father's (who was separated from our mother at the time) to stare at one puckered apple that sat in the conspicuous glare of the refrigerator's light. I recalled my uncle lying on a couch dying of cancer. I recalled my father who died from an accident a year later and left us in even more roughed up shoes. I had not been born to be scared out of my wits, but that is what happened. Through a set of experiences early in my life, I grew up fearful that some financial tragedy would strike at any moment, as when I was certain that the recession of 1973 would lead to chaos—burned cars and street fighting. During the recession I roomed with my brother and I suggested that we try to become vegetarians. My brother looked up from his drawing board and replied: "Aren't we already?" I thought about it for a while, and it was true. I was getting most of my hearty meals from my girlfriend,

Carolyn, who would later become my wife. She had a job with great pay, and when she opened her refrigerator I almost wept for the bologna, sliced ham, and drumsticks. I spied the cheeses and imported olives, tomatoes, and the artichoke hearts. I opened the freezer—chocolate ice cream!

At that time Carolyn put up with my antics, so when I suggested that we buy fifty dollars worth of peanut butter and pinto beans to store under her bed, she happily wrote out a check because she was in love and didn't know any better. I was certain that in 1974 the country would slide into a depression and those who were not prepared would be lost. We hid the rations in the house and sat at the front window to wait for something to happen.

What happened was that we married and I loosened up. I still fear the worst, but the worst is not what it once was. Today I bought a pair of shoes; tomorrow I may splurge to see a movie, with a box of popcorn and a large soda that will wash it all down. It's time to live, I tell myself, and if a five dollar bill flutters from my hands, no harm will result. I laugh at the funny scenes that aren't funny, and I can't think of any better life.

◊ JOHN HAINES ◊

Mudding Up

A clear afternoon in mid-September, 1947. You will know the kind of day I mean: a warm, tawny light over the hills, the sky is flawless in its clarity, and already in the windless air leaves drift down from the birches and aspens.

In the broad field above the river bluff the hay stubble and the uncut grasses are washed to a dry, translucent yellow. Here and there a few stalks of fireweed and dock stand rusty and strong; their feathery seed-bolls are tattered, blown empty in a late August wind.

A quietness over the land. The noise of summer, of high water and road traffic, of mating birds and foraging insects, has mysteriously vanished. One braided channel of the river is only a stone's throw from the edge of the field; yet near as it is, the shallow restlessness of that water over stones and gravel is somehow diminished and distant.

A day when a shout, an axe-stroke, or the single cry of a raven, rings clear and remote. The humming of a few late wasps in the browned marigolds, the drone of a bumblebee, surging and resting, fills the hollow of all creation.

◊

Allison and I are mudding up the walls in the old Richardson stable, making it tight for the winter. We have been at work three days, and this is the last.

Each afternoon we have walked across the road from the roadhouse, to find our tools laid aside late on the previous day. It has been some

◊ *When he is not "in residence" somewhere in the Lower 48, John Haines lives on a homestead at Richardson, 65 miles east of Fairbanks, Alaska. His most recent book of stories and essays is* Stories We Listened To *(The Bench Press, Seward, Nebraska).*

191

years now since horses were stabled here. The low, big-timbered building has sunk down in the sod, the original chinking has fallen away, leaving here and there a gap for wind and frost. But the metalled roof is sound, the stalls are still in place, and the earthen floor is deep in old, rotted hay and long-trampled manure. This fall Allison has turned the stable into a chicken house, and he wants his hens to be warm in the long dark that is coming.

According to age and agility we have divided the work as we have moved ever higher up the gray, weather-cracked wall. I stand now on a rung of the wooden ladder, working with trowel and mortar board. Allison is on the ground below, mixing the peaty soil with water into a square-sided five-gallon tin opened lengthwise to make a shallow trough. With a practiced stroke he stirs the brown mud-mortar back and forth with a stump of a hoe.

◇

"Was you in the war?" Allison stopped in his mud-mixing for a moment, and glanced up at me out of the shadow he stood in.

"Oh, sure," I answered him, "three years in the Navy in the Pacific."

"See much action?" He squinted up at me from under the brim of his cap.

"Oh, yeah, enough — more than enough."

I am none too talkative at best, and on that calm afternoon, a long way from the absurdities of global politics, of military rank and imposed duties, the Pacific War not long past was maybe the last thing I wanted to talk about. But not to be rude, I added, "Mostly, you know, it was just boring — a lot of waiting around for something to happen."

Allison resumed his digging and stirring. "Well," he said, after a short while, "I guess I missed all that."

"How about the First War?"

"Missed that, too," came the answer.

"Just as well," I said, "either way, it wasn't a lot of fun."

But for a moment or two I was back in the war, at sea, standing watch, earphones clamped to my head, scanning a radar screen for a strange flare, a hostile blip, and between watches and battle alerts waiting for the whole thing to end.

And then, not long after the war, I was back in school, standing before an easel, or sitting at a drawing board, trying to fix in form, line, and color something of a world I had yet to understand any part of.

And briefly I was with a girl I had left behind on coming to Alaska. I could see us now, distant and caught in a cold, slant light, coming out of the city library on a winter afternoon. We were on our way to her house, and each of us carried an armload of books. We were talking together and looking forward to an evening of reading and study.

And all of that passed through my mind and was gone. I came back to this present moment, and to the thing before me, to a simple task of repair I could take pleasure in learning to do. And to whatever was part of that: the glint of mica in the sandy clay soil, the ragged peat moss sticking in the log seams; to nothing more than the split and knotted, weather-grayed wood of the wall in front of me. I saw my hand on the trowel, and the wet-brown mud heaped on the board I held; and below me by the stable wall, Allison's broad and ruddy face in a stray shaft of light. I heard the soft scrape and slop of the water and earth he stirred back and forth in the gleaming tin trough.

As concentrated as I was on the moment, savoring every detail, did I sense that this quiet, rural world of Richardson, with its few surviving people and its old-fashioned implements, remote and settled on a stretch of gravel road, was vanishing even as I came to know it? It may have been that in some hidden part of myself I knew this, knew that I in some way was a part of the change taking place. But for now there was this moment, this day, and the promise of others to come: a vague, but tangible dream realizing itself in the cool, diminishing light of a first fall.

◇

Time passes. The work goes quietly; my mind drifts on ahead by days and weeks. It is afternoon once more; the veiled sun lies much lower in the south, spending its cold, gray light over the river and the fields. A light snow now lies on the ground, no more than an inch over the frost-shattered stubble of grass.

Allison and I have come to the stable to slaughter three of his chickens for the roadhouse kitchen. As we cross the road and head for the door of the stable, Allison, talking half to himself, remarks that the hour is right, and the hens will be settling to sleep in the early dusk and chill of this brief autumn day.

We quietly enter the stable, sliding back the wooden bolt in the heavy plank door. In the hay-scented, semi-gloom of the interior we approach the hens who are roosting on beams in the old horse-stalls. We stand still for a moment as from the shadowy space above comes a subdued clucking and shifting of feathered bodies. Allison reaches up with his gloved hand, takes one hen by its legs, pulls it from its perch, and hands it to me. He does this surely, and with no loss of motion.

We leave the stable as quietly as we came, taking care not to alarm the rest of the small flock. The one rust-red hen hangs tense and compact from my hand, the head with its pink comb turning from side to side, the bright, dark eye cocked in wonder. Still half-drugged with sleep, the bird does not cry out or flap its wings.

Outside the stable, in the cold air, we approach a spruce block standing before a pile of cordwood. A double-bitted axe with a worn and polished handle is propped against the block. With Allison directing me, I hold the chicken firmly and lay its head and neck on the block. Almost inert until now, the hen suddenly tenses and tries to free itself, but I grasp it all the firmer, holding its wings and feet with both hands. Allison takes a short swing with the axe — the head flies off, and at Allison's command I throw the bird to the ground. We watch as the suddenly headless hen stands up, begins to flap its wings and run swiftly over the wet ground, blood spurting from its severed neck. And then a soft, quivering mound of rusty feathers collapses on the shallow, red-spattered snow.

I have killed more than one wild bird and eaten it, sensed in myself some passing regret at having taken the life of a creature; but this is the first time I have slaughtered a domestic chicken. It is a lesson, as not long ago the mudding of the stable was a lesson. And so, what with the stealth and the axe and the blood, my sensibilities have been awakened in a way they had not been before. During these 15 minutes or so of concentrated activity, from the opening of the stable door to the swing of the axe, I have watched Allison and myself with a kind of fascinated horror.

We return to the stable for the second bird. And again the head flies off to the sound of the axe in the block, and again the headless bird flaps and runs and falls. On our third visit to the stable we find the hens awake and clucking in alarm, and Allison has some trouble catching one of them by the legs. We succeed, and once more we stand by the bloody block and watch that briefly quickened bundle of rusty feathers subsiding in the snow.

And then that work is done. We leave the axe in the block by the stable. Carrying the dead hens by their legs, Allison with two and I with one, we walk through dry, standing weeds and cross the graveled road and yard to the kitchen. That evening Allison's wife, Babe, will draw and pluck the birds. There will be roast and fried chicken for the table, chicken soup for the house, and one bird sent to a friend in town.

Already in the field behind us it is dusk and colder. Soon it will be night.

◇

Now in the shadow of the stable wall the air took on a deeper chill. Allison looked up from where he was standing over his trough, his face ruddy with work and the cold. With that one startling blue eye of his he sent a keen and searching glance over the upper wall, and remarked that our job was nearly done.

I pushed the last of the mud on my board into the moss-chinked seam of the log I was working on. Deliberately I smoothed the cold mud, working it into the gap with the blade of my trowel. When I had finished, I leaned back from the ladder to look, and felt a small rush of satisfaction. The log seams looked neat with their brown, drying mud-streaks. Rough-fashioned though it was, the stable would be tight and warm for the winter.

With my board and trowel I climbed back down the ladder to the ground. While Allison emptied his trough and cleaned his shovel and hoe, I scraped the mortar board, knocked it to free one last, clinging lump, and wiped the trowel on the dry grass stubble at my feet. As we had done on the previous day, and the day before that, we set our tools aside under the shelter of the stable wall.

Evening was coming on. Now that the afternoon work was over, I was conscious that my hands were cold, that my entire body was chilled from standing so long on the ladder. I took off the damp gloves I had been wearing, and shoved my hands into the pockets of my jacket. To judge from a sudden sharpness in the air, there would be frost that night.

As we walked back toward the roadhouse, I replied to something

Allison had said by way of thanking me for the help I had given him. It was nothing, I said; I had learned something in exchange.

We stopped for a moment by the roadside. A truck pounded by, big and single, raising a cold cloud of dust that slowly drifted away in the windless air. In the following quiet, Allison and I agreed that in a day or two I would return to help him saw up some firewood. Behind us, to one side of the stable, a long rough pile of spruce timbers lay in the grass; in the roadhouse yard another cord or two, loosely stacked, waited for the big, gas-powered saw.

I turned from Allison at the edge of the road. I would not join them for supper that evening; I had chores of my own to do at home. We said goodbye, and while there was still light in the woods I began walking the long stretch of road through the flat toward a familiar hill that rose before me, a high, yellow mass still sunlit on its crest.

The early evening was quiet and chill. No birdsong came from the woods to either side of the road. I could hear the river, subdued and distant through the trees; heard, too, in the brief time it took me to cross, the calm flow of water in Banner Creek under the tarred plank bridge. The only other sound was the crunching of my boots in the loose gravel of the roadside.

From somewhere now I caught the scent of woodsmoke on the evening air. Someone I had yet to meet was cooking supper off there in the woods away from the road. The thought reminded me that I was hungry, that I had not eaten since noon. It would be close to seven o'clock, I guessed. I had no watch, but I was learning to read the light, coming low now through a slot in the hills downriver.

No traffic on the road, no wheels, no dust. I walked along, one foot before the other, alone on the turning, graveled roadbed. As I walked, I looked often into the dim woods on either side of the road. I looked for nothing in particular, but only to name the trees, to read the shadows under the birches and aspens. I was thinking of supper, of wood and water, of things far and near that came and went in my mind.

At the high point of the bluff, where the road began a slow curve and descent, I stopped to look out over the river in the growing dusk. Light lay over the water, on the islands and the hills in the distance, so pervasive and steeped in its yellowness, it was hard to tell if that light came from the evening sky or welled up from somewhere in the autumn earth itself.

I listened to the pebbly sound of the river falling through diminished channels below me. And for a long moment I felt myself a part of that landscape with its shaggy, black islands and pale sandbars, one with the coppery gleam of water coiling and darkening, the distant country of night.

I turned and walked on. Soon the homestead hill and the deep shadow of the creek bottom came into view. I crossed the road, began to climb toward the small, unlighted house on a cleared shelf of the hillside.

And evening followed.

◇ BLAIR FULLER ◇

A New Ocean

At five in the afternoon one day in the fall of 1963 my "guide" took the sleep mask from my eyes and helped me to sit up on the deep couch on which I'd been lying since eight that morning. He told me that the mixture of LSD and mescaline that I'd been given had now passed through my system. How did I feel?

I could not answer him. The drugs had tilted my brain and breached a barrier, and visions from my subconscious had been pouring unstoppably into my conscious mind. Some had been literal, or had made me laugh — the desk I'd worked at in the Ivory Coast, a snapshot of a friend's expanded waistline — but most had been so heavy with significance and reproach that they had squeezed my heart to groaning. My father's wide eyes and yearning, boyish smile, shadowed by the brim of his fedora, had fixed me. At his death several years before, our difficulties had been unresolved. A Chanel suit belonging to my separated wife hung flatly in a dim and empty closet. My four-year-old daughter's thin legs and pretty shoes had skipped back and forth, back and forth. My hair behind the temples, and the cushion that had been under my head, were soaked with tears.

My guide led me to a chair before a window and drew its curtain wide. "How does it look to you?"

"Awful." An asphalt parking lot stretched to a tree-lined street down which cars appeared to be moving at violent speed. Solitary people were squinting against the slanted autumn sunshine.

"Do you want to go out there?"

◇ *Blair Fuller has written three novels and the recent collection of stories,* A Butterfly Net and a Kingdom, *published by Creative Arts Book Co., Berkeley, California. An editor of the* Paris Review *since the fifties, he was a co-founder of the Squaw Valley Community of Writers, an annual writer's conference. He lives in San Francisco.*

"No, I don't."

He wrapped a blanket around me, for I was shivering, and left the room. Beyond the closed door I heard the murmur of a consultation, and I could picture him with the blonde woman doctor who had checked me physically and had replaced him at my side when he needed relief, and with the wiry psychoanalyst who was the program's director. There were others of the staff, but I could not identify the voices.

Some of these others had medical or therapeutic credentials, some did not, but titles and qualifications seemed unimportant to them. They were of all ages and complexions. Something they believed could change the world had been discovered, and anyone of useful intelligence would probably have been welcomed by them. Not long before, John Kennedy had spoken about Space as "the new ocean," saying that we must sail on it simply for that reason, because it was a new ocean, and this group shared that spirit. So far, they had every reason to be optimistic about these inner-space voyages.

The friend of mine who had proposed insistently that I take the drugs, who knew the extent of my depression since my separation from wife and child nearly a year before, had worn a most unexpected, beatific smile from the day of his session onward, and he was not exceptional. The short-term benefits to troubled lives had been excellent, and no one had broken down.

My guide came back into the room and said, "We're going to give you something more. O.K.?" He was pale, and his dark stubble looked days old.

"Good."

A vertical cannister of CO_2 was wheeled in and a breathing mask attached over my face. A valve was turned and the sound of rushing air filled my mind. I breathed deeply and was suddenly weightless and flying, relieved of my body. Without friction, without any sense of speed, I shot straight up into the constellations, and there, in the star-dotted blackness, I arrived at peace. My heart was freed, and in a silence in which there was no temperature, no gravity, no wish or will or conflict, no need, I felt an overwhelming, blissful gratitude.

I rested there a while and then I started down. The Earth was far away, a speck and then a dime against the blackness, but it quickly grew. The continents and the oceans became distinct, the tan deserts, the ice at the poles, and the dark forests of Canada, Russia, and Africa.

I began to see the conglomerations of towns and cities, and to sense the variety of people, especially those where I'd lived — New York, Paris, Abidjan, and San Francisco. Nearing the ground I recognized with starts of joy some faces in the crowds, and I saw with the force of revelation that my father and my wife, and others whose specters had distressed me, were the same size as the rest, as robust and as frail.

As I slipped into my body and the floor became real under my feet, I felt my essential sameness with all these thousands of beings around me who were speaking in hundreds of tongues. Their warmth invaded me, and when I opened my eyes I was shouting with excitement at joining the world of humans.

My guide greeted my arrival and others came into the room to pat my back. After a time, one of them took me out into an evening of commonplace miracles.

I watched the ash-yellow oatfields rippling in a windless sunset and found that I could see the sap moving in the branches of the liveoak trees, even in the capillaries of the leaves. After dark, the lighted bridges crossing San Francisco were bemusing, as were those wonders of human order, traffic lights. In many of the people we encountered I saw beauty of body or spirit, and every one of them seemed a miracle of gathered energy. Now so would I be.

My friend of the beatific smile had talked about "psychoanalysis in a day," but this was something much better, I thought. There was no need for "analysis." I was free.

Next morning I learned from a waitress at the counter of a strangely quiet, twenty-four-hours-a-day restaurant that John Kennedy had been shot in Dallas. He had been taken to a hospital. That was what was known.

I had never seen such things as the scrambled eggs on the faintly patterned, brownish plate, or the nicks in the tines of the fork. Yet I ate. My mind attempted sporadically to interpret the news, and, at other moments, images from the day before took over. A man standing beside me spoke up in a loud voice, proposing a date to the waitress, and she turned pink and hurried away to the kitchen. This episode seemed no stranger than the food or the coffee.

The follow-up appointment with my guide was for eleven o'clock, still an hour away. I started walking without purpose and stopped outside a barber shop, for in it I could see a TV set turned on.

Both of the barbers were idle, one sitting in his chair, the other leaning against the back of his. Closest to the set was a black shoeshine man, an older man, sitting. Their concentration was such that I momentarily felt I should not disturb them, but I went in and was motioned to sit down.

The TV camera was at the hospital. Just after the barber had begun to snip my hair the announcement came that Kennedy had died.

The shine man pointed at my shoes, but I shook my head. He said, "They couldn't let him live. Not after Bay of Pigs. Couldn't let him live his *life.*"

The broadcast went back in time to Kennedy's arrival at the Dallas airport with Jackie. Smiling officials greeted them. He was handsome and jaunty. Everyone was full of daylight.

"See him there?" the shine man said. "He's too much for them. Too much. They can't abide it."

The broadcast showed pictures of the motorcade, of the cars coming into Dealey Plaza. Then it was broken into and a voice told us that a suspect had been arrested, and that his name was Lee Harvey Oswald.

"They get someone. Oh, yes."

The images shifted to the hospital again, to Washington about the governmental consequences.

The shine man said, "He let them look real bad. CIA. Military, too." He wiped his eyes with his knuckle. "*Lee Harvey Oswald,* indeed."

I paid the barber and walked to my appointment.

My guide had not yet come in and when he did, brisk and clean-shaven, he seemed too glad to see me. We sat at his desk and he asked some clinical questions. Had I slept? Had I dreamed? Was I experiencing flashbacks?

Then he dropped that manner. "Are you really O.K.? I thought of you first thing after I took in the shock, whether or not you'd be all right."

"I'm O.K."

"I was afraid you might lose it, the good stuff you finally got yesterday."

"I've got it still," I told him.

"You were tough," he said. "You wouldn't let go. I tried what I could to help you though . . . Then the news. It's your universe. And then." His face showed pain, but a more superficial frustration as well. His treatment had been interfered with. He said, "Maybe you'll want to take it again. Do some more exploring."

I was embarrassed to be talking about myself, my case. "Not tomorrow," I said.

"Oh, no. Maybe months from now, certainly not tomorrow."

It was a strange handshake. The muscles of his hand and his skin were extraordinary vivid, although there was nothing unusual about them.

I spent most of the next few days alone in my San Francisco apartment, the TV showing me the aftermath, the official events, the caisson crossing the Potomac Bridge. Sometimes I felt I knew where he had gone, out there in the cosmos. I could feel its weightless silence. For me it had been paradisiacal, but for him the timing was all wrong.

My apartment off Buena Vista Park had a small balcony which looked out on a sweep of the city's south side that included Twin Peaks, Diamond and Dolores Heights, and the bay toward San Leandro. Some of the Victorian houses facing me had been whimsically trimmed with bright paint. Wind chimes and bicycles hung on back stairway landings. I brooded on these clues to their inhabitants and on the backyard gardens below me, some neatly planted, others beaten down around a children's swing, a kiln, a trampoline. Mad and dangerous though some of my neighbors no doubt were, I admired their putting the next meal on the table, doing what they had to, and getting on with it. I was of them as I had not been before.

Fifteen years afterward I decided to find out what I could about the people who had run the program and those who had passed through it. I knew it had been shut down when LSD had been declared an illegal drug not long after my session.

I called the woman doctor who had sat with me part of the day. She had become a psychiatrist with a practice in Menlo Park.

On the phone she sounded professional and guarded, but said she would be glad to talk. I asked her if she'd like to meet for lunch, or any other time that suited, but she said, "You can make an appointment, if you like. I'll have to charge my fee." I was mildly shocked, but accepted her terms.

Her office was near where the "Center" had been, and it seemed a standard therapist's environment with comfortable dark chairs and a couch, and the curtains half-drawn. She was very much as I remembered her, a blonde woman, somewhat overweight, with a smile that at moments looked tentative, at others a touch cynical.

She told me that when they had had to stop the program there had been no money to follow up on those like me. She could not tell me anything about long-term results, except in isolated cases. "Now you'll be one," she said. "What's happened to you?"

I told her that I'd remarried and had two younger children, and that I'd continued to teach and write. I'd published a novel and shorter pieces, and with another writer I'd started an annual writers' conference. On the other hand, I felt I hadn't been productive enough. I had had a drinking problem, but I had quit five or six years before. "What about you?" I asked.

"You can see," she said, without much enthusiasm. She added wryly, "I still haven't lost weight."

There was not much news she could give me of the others who had been on the staff. So-and-so was still working at Syntex, another had taken a job in Los Angeles. In her responses there was a shade of tedium, but also sympathy.

I asked about the psychoanalyst-director.

"He's at a Vets Administration hospital in Maryland. I have the feeling that he's serving out his time."

Did she remember that Kennedy had been killed the day after my session?

"Oh, yes. Yes. That day changed a lot of things for us. For everyone."

"What changed?"

"You know as well as I do. Many things."

"Things always change."

Her mouth twitched impatiently, but she replied, "The mood. The feeling of the possible."

We said goodbye and wished each other luck.

Outside the building's sunny entrance I stopped to look at a liveoak tree, an old one with a great reach of gnarled branches and glistening dark leaves, which stood protected in the middle of a traffic island. I concentrated on it, and, after a bit, I saw the sap moving in its new, lighter limbs. The vision soon vanished and I could not revive it, although I was patient, blinking and staring intensely.

Then I let the effort go. Rather, it was swept aside by a rush of gratitude, part warm from memory, part fresh, a buoyant wave that lifted me from what had seemed a flat sea.

◊ CHRISTOPHER ALEXANDER ◊

The Perfection of Imperfection

In Mexico City there is a beautiful house called the House of Tiles. It is a huge house, more of a palace really, built by a famous count, near the very center of the city, two or three hundred years ago. The outside of the house is almost entirely covered with hand-painted tiles, mainly blue. In the distance the house shimmers with flickering color.

When I decided to go and have a closer look at the tile work, I found an amazing thing: The tiles are ordinary, about nine inches square, handmade and hand-painted. They cover the exterior walls, but the way they are laid is extremely surprising. There are ridges between them, huge valleys. Nor are they all in the same plane; many are not even vertical, meeting in the roughest possible way. By contemporary American standards, it would be considered a lousy job. And yet this is one of the most beautiful houses in Mexico City.

We have become used to almost fanatical precision in the construction of buildings. Tile work, for instance, must be perfectly aligned, perfectly square, every tile perfectly cut, and the whole thing accurate on a grid to a tolerance of a sixteenth of an inch. But our tilework is dead and ugly, without soul.

In this Mexican house the tiles are roughly cut, the wall is not perfectly plumb, and the tiles don't even line up properly. Sometimes one tile is as much as half an inch behind the next one in the vertical plane.

And why? Is it because these Mexican craftsmen didn't know how to do precise work? I don't think so. I believe they simply knew what is

◊ *Christopher Alexander is professor of architecture at the University of California, Berkeley, director of the Center for Environmental Structure, and the author of six books, including* A Pattern Language *(Oxford University Press). The graphics within the text are by Bob Baldock, a painter in Berkeley.*

◇ *Brick floor in arcade (low-cost experimental housing, Mexicali)*

important and what is not, and they took good care to pay attention only to what is important: to the color, the design, the feeling of one tile and its relationship with the next—the important things that create the harmony and feeling of the wall. The plumb and the alignment can be quite rough without making any difference, so they just didn't bother to spend too much effort on these things. *They spent their effort in the way that made the most difference.* And so they produced this wonderful quality, this harmony . . . simply because *that is what they paid attention to, and what they tried to produce.*

A modern American tile-setter, who has learned to get his satisfaction from the perfection of squareness, the perfection of plumb, and the perfection of the regularity of the tiles, *can never achieve the same result.* He cannot achieve it, even if he knows the field of centers and understands it.

The reason is simple. So long as his mind is occupied with the technical perfection, he cannot concentrate his mind on the field — and so the field will not happen in his work. There is not room for both. This is not because they are inconsistent. It is simply because you cannot concentrate on two goals of this magnitude at the same time.

In our time, many of us have been taught to strive for an insane perfection that means nothing. To get wholeness, you must try instead to strive for *this* kind of perfection, where the things that don't matter are left rough and unimportant, and the things that really matter are given deep attention. This is a perfection that seems imperfect. But it is a far deeper thing.

Although the process of order-making is a formal, geometric process, it is nevertheless a process that pays deep attention to problems of life. Its roots are in the existence of the wholes as centers in the world in their control of existence and their production of order.

Shallow concern with styles or images, which is typical of post-modernism, is another thing altogether.

It is useful to understand that, very roughly, the wholeness of any given part of space depends on the well-ordering or relative wholeness of the other parts of which this part of space is composed, and of those parts that are near it. Understanding this gives us a picture of a whole as an enormous system of wholes, layered, overlapping, large, and small. Somehow, the structure of a thing becomes whole, or not, according to the way these smaller and larger wholes are disposed.

The 15 properties of arrangement that describe the way smaller wholes form a system are structural — definite geometrical features that exist most strongly in things that are geometrically whole. The properties are:

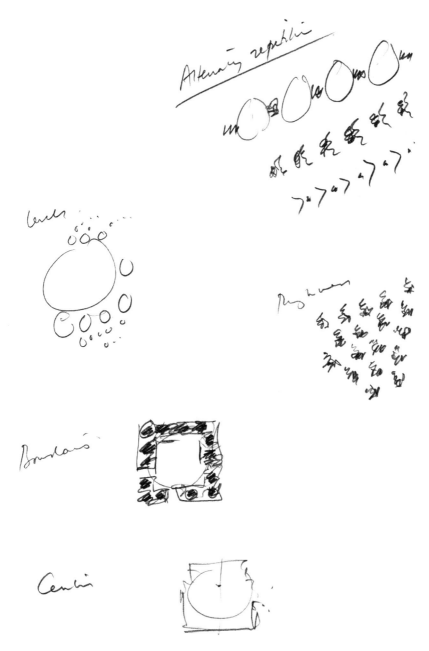

◊ *Alternating repetitions, levels of scale, roughness, boundaries, centers*

1. Levels of scale
2. Centers
3. Boundaries
4. Alternating repetition
5. Positive space
6. Good shape
7. Local symmetries
8. Deep interlock and ambiguity
9. Contrast
10. Graded variation
11. Roughness
12. Echoes
13. The void
14. Inner calm
15. Not separateness

Each of these properties helps establish the whole as a system of other interlocking wholes.

It is the texture or fabric of this interweaving that is wholeness.

In every project, at the stage before the site plan exists, we have two different systems of centers.

On the one hand, we have the system of centers that exists in the *site*. This system is created by the land forms, the roads, directions of access, natural low spots, natural high spots, and existing trees.

Second, there is the system of centers that is defined by the language that describes the project. In the case of the Eishin project, the language defined the main building blocks or centers from which the new school and university were going to be made. They included the entrance gate, entrance street, *tanoji* center, home base street, main square, back streets, and judo hall.

It must be emphasized that both systems exist at the time one starts the site plan. The first system exists on the site. The second system exists in the minds, and in the reality, of the people who are going to have the new school. Each of the two systems is real.

◇ *Sketch of Great Hall, New Eishin School, Tokyo*

Getting colors for the Great Hall in the Eishin school in Japan was one of the most exhausting things I have ever done.

While I was designing the building, I always had two feelings. First, that it was very dark inside. Second, that in the darkness colors were somehow glowing. I imagined bright colors — reds, yellows, blues — on the columns and capitals. But they were darkly glowing in the darkness, never bright. This was my starting point.

When I went to Japan, the building shell was finished. All the columns, capitals, beams, walls, and windows were there. The darkness also was there. So I stood for days in the dark hall, trying to imagine concretely what colors would create the proper feeling. It was incredibly hard work. Nothing obvious came. Most of the first colors seemed wrong.

Then, after several days, I spent almost a whole day sitting in the bath — my eyes closed — simply trying to see the inside of the hall. I sat for hours and hours. Finally, I began to see the inside of the hall and its columns as black. It was startling and unexpected — not something that had ever occurred to me. But it had the marks of an authentic vision. On the surface of the black, something glowed faintly.

I made a first sketch, very hastily.

The vision maintained itself. The chevrons on the column, which had been in my mind ever since some earlier sketches, now seemed dark red. By chance, as I had made the sketch in the train on the way to the site, the drawing was done in ball point. This had left faint bluish lines, even after I had painted the red and the black. The faint bluish aura was important, essential to the way the color glowed.

Now we began full-scale mockups in the building, painting huge pieces of paper and covering the real columns. It was very hard to get the right colors. The black I wanted is actually dark, dark gray, not black. Black was too harsh. The red was even harder to get. At first, simple reds had a terrible, bright, decorator-like quality, completely different from what I had imagined. Finally I began mixing a series of reds that had an extraordinary amount of black in them. I myself could not believe that they would seem red. They had so much black that I couldn't persuade my assistants to mix them correctly. They kept making them too red, not black enough. And yet, on the column, it was these blackish reds that glowed in the right way.

However, once again I realized that the inner vision was lacking. So once again I sat in the water of my bath with my eyes closed, looking. After many hours I began to see a shimmer of black and white — something entirely different in quality and feeling from what I had been trying to paint. But time had run out.

I had no more than a few hours left and was in a total panic. I told Hosoi I couldn't finish. He was very nice, and told me to relax. If it wasn't finished on time, it wasn't finished.

I went over to the hall, certain that I had failed. In my moment of failure I grabbed a brush and angrily, hurriedly splashed some colors on a mockup of the main beam, a sheet of paper 3 meters long and 70 cm high. On the beam, amazingly, the mockup fit perfectly. It was a new animal, something different from the dark, intensely glowing black columns, but with just the right life to hold its own against them, yet support them at the same time. It was solved.

Once again, the key was not the actual painting, the trying different things. It was the shimmering sense of black and white that I saw after immense effort, sitting in the bath.

About 10 years ago I made a coffee stand for our office. As I made it, I was aware that clients would be coming in and see it, and be impressed. Finally the thing I made was too clever. I wasn't trying to please myself; I was trying to please these clients and impress them.

If I had made it to please myself, I would have made it much less clever. I would have put it on two brackets, for example, instead of one. I would have made a little hole where the spilled coffee could be wiped off. I would have painted it red and yellow. But instead I made it with a single bracket, without a hole, in natural wood, and with that innocuous good taste that goes in architects' offices.

At the time I was only vaguely aware of this issue: I worried too much about our image and our office. I worried whether it would fit with the other things in the office. So my simple little exuberance, which I could have had if I hadn't been worrying about these things, was lost.

This simple little exuberance is hard to find, precious, and easily trampled; it takes enormous daring for it to show itself. It is the part that people can most easily laugh at, the part that can most easily be trampled, and the part that good sense most easily, most quickly censors.

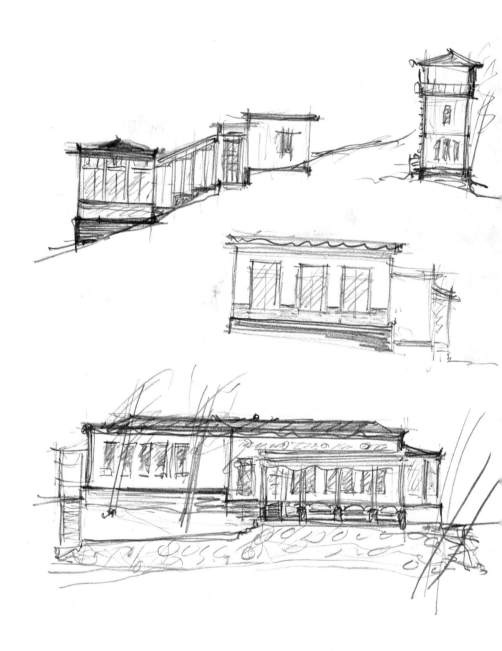

◇ *First sketches of a house in Berryessa, under construction*

Imagine that you are on a hillside, a dirt road, on a grass-covered hill. It is very quiet, a hot summer night. In the silence, far away, over the hill, you hear the sound of a flute. You strain your ears. You slowly recognize a haunting melody carried on the wind. Learning to see wholeness in a thing, when we are making it, is not unlike the process where I strain my ears to catch that haunting melody.

Our carpentry shop in Martinez is an ordinary structure with massive wooden columns and beams. After making it, I saw that it was fine, simple, and straightforward, but somehow lacking.

I spent several days trying to imagine the building filled with life. After a few days I began to get a clear vision of the building with a great white star on the central bay.

In the office I tried to explain it to one of my apprentices, but I could not make him understand. At a certain point I picked up an old piece of styrofoam. With a penknife, without making any measurements, I very quickly cut a big star from the sheet. I hacked it out as fast as I could. The star was crude and jagged, not all the points were pointed. The arms had different lengths and angles. I went outside and put a single nail through it, to hang it up. The whole thing took no more than 40 seconds. It brought the building to life.

Then a surprising thing happened. I had assumed that this crude star was just a mockup, that we would use it to cut a perfect star. In its place we began trying various exactly regular nine-pointed stars. My apprentice and I tried for three months. None of the stars we made had the same life in them.

Finally, I gave up. I acknowledged that the irregular, jagged star has some kind of life in it perfectly in tune with the building and that I had been lucky to find it. It was best to leave it alone.

A while ago I went to a Haydn mass in Salzburg's great cathedral. The high point was the Sanctus. A full choir, slowly increasing rhythm, deep sounds of the organ and the basses, and high song of the trebles, the filled church, the air tense as if on the edge of some awakening. At this most awe-inspiring moment, a young American pushed forward to a telephone mounted on one of the columns of the nave. He picked it up and listened. The telephone was tied to a tape recording giving interesting facts for tourists. He listened to the tape recording of dates and facts while the Sanctus blazed around him.

This man became a symbol for me of the loss of awe, of our loss of sense. Unable to immerse himself in the thing that surrounded him, unaware of the size and importance of the sounds that he was hearing, he was more fascinated by a tape recording.

I realized that this young man summarized what my efforts have been about. All the efforts I have made, at their heart, have just this one intention: to bring back our sense of awe, to allow us to begin again to make things in the world that can intensify this awe.

◇ PETER COYOTE ◇

Sleeping Where I Fall

Breath

The smooth cedar floor is yellow and cool under my feet. It is hard to walk so slowly: place the heel gently down, uncurl the foot from back to front, struggle to maintain balance, attentiveness. Falling into the monk in front of you is embarrassing. The back of his head is shiny as glass and not ruffed with hair. His ears stick out at improbable angles. His robes rustle softly as he moves. His knees and legs could not possibly hurt as badly as mine do.

Breath

I have buggered the monk in front of me publicly. I am exaggerating, but I might as well have since I walked right into him, unaware of the fact that his crawl of a walk had stopped. Hooked to the conveyor belt of my own thoughts, I had ratcheted along, like a slab of meat, and meat-to-meat had bumped him. I could tell by his stiffening posture and by the flush of red that spread above his ears that he was angry, but was too cool to turn around and call me a stupid asshole. He would shame me with cool. He was a Priest and I was some long-haired hippie who had obviously stolen the robes I was wearing to fuck up his high. That's the way it seemed to me anyway, and you can see, perhaps, why I was there. I didn't know I *needed* to be there at the time. I thought it would just make me more powerful.

Breath

◇ Actor Peter Coyote lives in Mill Valley, California. In the mid-sixties, he did graduate work with Robert Duncan and Mark Linenthal at San Francisco State University; he then worked with the San Francisco Mime Troupe and with the Diggers. In 1975, he was appointed to the California Arts Council, on which he served eight years.

A cool September day in eighth grade. My teacher, a slender, sensitive man named Doug Ogilvie, places a shiny, pulsing leopard frog on my outstretched palm. Time stops. Dappled light is filtering through the cool green maple leaves outside, throwing mottled shadows on the frog's spotted body. A rapid pulse at his throat. His eyes are the dense, black concentrations of energy, hornets tacked down by their wings.

I am absorbed, leaning closer, already over the bannister, free-falling toward an elusive, gathering communion when Mr. Ogilvie drives a sharpened wire mounted in a pale pink dowel through the tiny depression at the base of the frog's neck, turning it into a cold dead puddle on my palm. "That's called pithing," he says, smiling kindly, eager to share the thrill of discovery with me.

I am in my attic closet. The rough pine rafters and splintery one-by-six roof planks smell of dust and resin. Scraps of black tarpaper appear randomly between the boards. It is familiar, but today it is different. There is a shelf at chest height running around the walls and sloped roof. There is a shelf across the center of the room which is now, unaccountably, much larger than normal. On each shelf are rows of small aquariums. They are full of water, and the sides are heavily algaed so that it is hard to see inside them, but floating in each is a fist-sized egg-shaped presence, bisected horizontally. The bottom half is a thick yellow, the color and consistency of egg-yolk; the top is clear and soft like the white. They float there in the bubbling water, completely still and yet very much alive, glistening — embryonic potential. In my attic. This image has stayed with me for more than 20 years. Entered my life softly in a dream, parked itself "in my attic." Slept longer than a cicada, singing more sweetly and evocatively, urging me to do something I haven't yet understood.

Breath

Luther's feet were the color of lead. The brown pigmentation was almost totally obscured by the chalky flaked surface, a combination of winter in New York, unimaginable accumulations of dirt, and the depredations of heroin. He moved as slowly as an alligator, removing his shoe and setting it beside him on the yellowed newspaper. His ankle was wrapped in a filthy bandage, but the abscesses it was designed to cover had leaked through in rusty stains and I couldn't discern what principle determined which abscesses were covered and which, like the ones running up his calf and shin, were to remain uncovered.

We were sitting somewhere off 118th and Lenox in what the newspapers refer to as a "shooting gallery." The windows and doors had been boarded up and the toilets and sinks removed, evidence of some ancient eviction struggle. The open drain pipe beckoned somnambulent ghosts with full bladders, who initialed the surrounding walls and floors like the alley dogs and cats who roamed in and out making forays against the rats.

The floors were covered with piles of papers, empty screw tops from water bottles, bent needles, and sprays of blood where syringes had been blown clean. Broken light bulbs were everywhere, stripped of their filaments, which were perfect for unclogging the tiny 25-gauge needles most prized by cognoscenti. Piles of shit were relatively neatly stacked in one corner, and since it was winter, they attracted no flies.

A cheery fire struggled for oxygen in an abandoned canning pot, and the flame gurgled contentedly on the remains of an old chair leg. It was almost cozy.

Luther had scored a bundle — ten dime-bags, glassine coin-collector's envelopes with measured amounts of Mexican salt-and-pepper heroin. He was cutting me in today as payback and because he needed an audience for his lectures. Luther always lectured. I guess it was because I was white and he intuited the chasms of information that could never be absorbed in only one lifetime on my side of the color and legitimacy line. Even though my skin was yellow and my teeth were stained, and the circles under my eyes were the requisite shady blue-gray, Luther's antennae could pick up traces of residual optimism; faint rays of hope that played around my imagination and declarations; traits that had been totally and effectively expunged from his personality. He knew I was "green" and chose to help.

"Always watch your water," he said, pouring a little bottled spring water into the brassy cap he had wrapped with wire to create a little handle.

"Water'll kill your ass quick. Watch your water."

Luther was a connoisseur, and an old connoisseur at that, so I paid attention. Some guys would come in and use rusty tap water to fix with. Luther would watch them, shaking his head, casting his one rheumy eye in my direction to make sure that I had observed this breach of ceremony. Luther's other eye was covered with a smoky, gray film that looked like egg white. I didn't like to look into it, but he claimed that he could see some things better with it than with the runny brown one that was open.

While Luther watched his smack bubble over the candle, his lower lip would run slack. He might have been asleep except as soon . . .

Breath

. . . except as soon as the water boiled he had set it down and dropped one of his little cottons into it. Luther would watch the cotton swell while I would try to contain my impatience. He was, after all, my host, feeding and sheltering me this chilly evening, but, Christ, he could be maddeningly slow. His ponderous black fingers would pick up and examine his syringe. He liked slender diabetic syringes, perhaps because they were easy to get, and modern-looking. I preferred my own — the traditional glass eye-dropper with a bulb made from a baby's pacifier. A collar to fix the needle to the dropper was cut from the narrow border of a dollar bill. That seemed poetically appropriate, considering the vast amounts of money that slipped down that minuscule drain.

After assuring himself that everything was in order, he would filter his dope through his shaggy brown cotton. Then began the maddening probe of his foot. He would tie off his leg, and poke around with his finger, past the scabs and sores, around the scars, pushing this way and that in the chalky skin until he might find a little vein, not much damn bigger than the needle. He would poke and pry, dripping blood here and there, until finally some blood flowed back and blossomed into his syringe. Assured of a good hit, he would sit there booting it, depressing the plunger partially and then drawing it back, prolonging the full discharge to test potency, he said, but I watched him, hypnotized by the ballet of blood and water surging into and out of his body like a tide, and I just thought he dug it.

Afterward he did not change much. His raspy breathing never slowed. His posture never altered. He would draw up clean water and spray it onto the dry newspaper, to clean his needle. Only his blinks got longer.

I still had good veins. I would deliberately save my arms, make it a little harder on myself, as a discipline and as a disguise so I wouldn't get tracks. I didn't want to wind up like Luther, who occasionally and disturbingly had to shoot in his jugular vein. That made me queasy because it looked like a man committing suicide. Some guys shot up under their tongues, and one guy swore that he would shoot into his cock when he had an erection, fuck like crazy, and then, after he came, when his cock got soft, the dope he'd stashed in there would flow into his system and get him high. "It's perfection," he would insist. He could have been bullshitting, I don't know, because I was not about to stick needles in my dick.

Breath

Cool green light, clean light, is reflecting off the planed surface, the raised sitting bench that frames the tatami mats we sit on. It is late afternoon and the *zendo* is in deep shadow. The figures across from me are dark shadows, still as paintings. Bird and cricket cries make tapestries in the silence, and the chimneys of the kerosene lamps, cleaned with vinegar, have no traces of soot. The large wooden Buddha sits surrounded by wildflowers and fire, untroubled by sore knees, untroubled by memory, something of a pain in the ass.

For the last three or four hours I have been racked with convulsions. It is not uncommon for American Zen students to have spasms, although no one really knows why. Suddenly the lower belly starts to twitch, and then, just like flapping a sheet, the twitch expands into shock waves that travel the whole spine, shaking the body violently, making breathing and concentration virtually impossible. It is exhausting and embarrassing.

On either side of me the monks sit in stolid repose. I can tell that they are thinking about me, cursing their fucking luck to be stuck next to this imbecile with the Tibetan hair and earrings, the slack posture, the filthy habits, the sallow skin, the disruptive temperament, the anger that blazes like sunlight through crystal, splintering in shards, covering the world with its slash-and-burn rage. Why am I doing this? I hate these people. The calm deliberative manner; the detachment; the modulated voices; the shining skin; the absolute selfishness of internal contemplation in the face of world-suffering. There are no black faces here, no spontaneous expressions, no drums and tambourines; no dreadful ecstasies.

They have a drum that looks like a small wooden whale. Someone hits it with a stick and we all chant to the rhythm. I like that part. Thirty or forty voices pretty well cover the spectrum. The drum has a deep, resonant ring to it, and the Japanese is pretty catchy. I have no idea what it means, but I know that people have done it for centuries, kneeling on tatami mats, groggy with lack of sleep, noticing how the tiny weaves in the mats trap shadows and highlights; noticing the dust-motes dancing in the slanted shafts of light that lean against the windows like buttresses. Century after century, six centuries before Christ's nonsensical virgin birth, people were doing this. It must mean something. Breath. I don't shake so much at service.

Mental events. Metal tents. Metal tense. Present tense. Memory, for instance, is always present tense. While the sun warms my knees, I am also present in another morning, in the Sangre de Cristo mountains, not too far from the Huerfano Valley of Colorado. The panting of my dog sing-songs along like prayer. Frost covers my sleeping bag. A clean desert wind whirls a hawk around and around, scattering the scent of sage along with last night's ashes. I open my bag and cluck and JoJo my dog slips in, turns around, and peers at the world from her protective cave. She smells like the desert, like sage and dew. Her alertness flows through me like warmth. We crawl out of the shadow of my truck, gathering twigs which I bundle into a small fire, feeding it carefully, until the snap of larger pieces of scrub piñon tells me it has staked out a claim. Out of bag, stretch, stand on the bag, pull my boots out, check for scorpions, and pull them on; pour water in my aluminum teakettle from San Francisco's Japantown, hang it from the iron tripod I've fashioned from re-bar, grab a Camel and look around.

The truck is a '49 Chevy ton-and-a-half flatbed. It has 20-inch wheels on the back: 8-lug Chevy rims balanced and welded into the center of California rims. Plank sides rise about three feet off the bed, and the rest is canvas stretched over metal strapping, like an old Conestoga wagon. My welding tanks are chained to the side, tool chest is bolted to the running board. Everything is boxed or bagged, stowed simply and cleanly. An owl's talon, a cluster of feathers, some bundled sage, and a piece of turquoise hang off the mirror. I have built this truck from the ground up: replaced kingpins, bushings, antiquated cables; rebuilt the engine, Loc-Tited and torqued every nut and bolt of it, balanced the clutch and flywheel for a smooth idle; painted it blue, with a small crescent moon and star just below the right-front side-mirror. This is Dr. Knucklefunky, named in honor of the scars and lacerations that criss-cross my hands, honorable wounds of repair. There is always one scabbed, reddened wound on at least one hand. The badge of contemporary gypsy life. The needle tracks on my legs and arms are healed, or faded to a pale shiny pink. The memory of the tiny, daily crucifixion is still fresh though; and feelings erupt like dust-devils, seizing me, whirling me about in dry anger or fear; chiding me for not taking my medicine; not taking care of "them"—the devils I've vowed to face down.

Hunkered down over coffee, warming cornbread in the coals; passing the smoke of burning sage over my face and hair, offering it to the sun, it occurs to me that I have not worn a watch for months. It occurs to me that I am happy. A Camel . . . Breath . . . And the smoke from that memory cigarette twines effortlessly with the pungent incense offered to Buddha, and the same sun, in the same month, years later, is no less generous, no less present. And the peripatetic path that led me to this moment, this breath, no less mysterious, no less real. How did I get here? Where am I going? I am already somewhere else. Breath. Breath. Breath. Death.

I am looking at my lap. My eyes would like to rest there. I raise my head to see how long I've been asleep. The table is still there, a glass of water with my works resting in it—the artist and his brush. The table is still scattered with the Polaroids of Chester's girlfriend giving him head—lots of photos of the top of her head, a few with her head twisted oddly sidewise, so that the camera can see the stub of his cock entering her mouth. Her eyes are angled up toward the lens like a flounder and the corner of his angled hip is strangely pale and blue. A premonition. I can't remember now why he took the pictures or why he showed them to me. You'd think *getting* the head would be enough, why look at it through a camera?

I look across the table and Chester is tangled in his chair, his head thrown back, his eyes closed, his mouth open. His skin is gray like the photograph. I look at him and something is wrong. There is only the barest tick of a pulse at his neck, and I realize that I have not heard him breathe. Then he exhales in a deep, guttural flutter.

"Hey, man, are you O.K.?"

My question remains unanswered. I get up and shake him. He doesn't respond. I look around the room for help, but we are alone. There is no phone. I lay him on the floor. Street wisdom tells you that heroin stops the respiratory system, but that if you just keep them breathing, they'll come around. I settle down for a long night. Place my lips over his and shudder. He is disgusting. His teeth are brown and the small hairs of his mustache have caught some food and lint. Oh well. It is hard to concentrate, but I breathe into his mouth and force the air out again. Occasionally, I get the rhythm off, because I catch myself, pressed against his lips, not breathing, as if I had dozed off. But I breathe. I carry his life like a damaged bird. I offer him my good intentions carried on the respiratory cycle like sung prayers, hymns to his self-deprecating humor, to his future couplings with the ghost in the Polaroid. I am breathing for his failed marriage and his two disappointed children in Detroit. I have seen them on a laminated wallet-sized picture: blond, amiable, plaid pants and red sweater, a nondescript blue wall behind them. On the wall, an oval-framed picture of their mother holding both of them in her arms. Was that sadism on her part? We discussed it for hours one night. Tonight perhaps. Ah, what's time anyway, I think, as I breathe and push, breathe and push, mindless as a baker kneading dough. Then I realize that his lips are frigid. Cold fear straight-arms me into a push-up above him, staring down at the bluest face I have ever seen. Wax.

My mouth is dry and cottony. Residual tremors glide through my legs. I poke around the table, lift papers, check drawers, until some instinct leads me to Chester's pocket. Sliding my hand along his leg, I find the two balloons he'd hidden. I was disappointed that Chester had died lying. He wasn't going to tell me about the balloons. I take them and put them in my pocket. I am going to take my works but I decide that that would be, could be, bad luck. I look around the room. The piles of amplifiers and dismantled electric guitars are still in place. His paintings of thick-lipped women brandishing scissors and orange lightning bolts still hang on the Chinese red walls we'd painted one rainy February. The sink is still filled with musty glasses and thick aluminum pots. The poster of Einstein making a funny face above the slogan SHIT HAPPENS. Everything is in place, still with a life of its own. Everything but Chester.

I back out of the room and close the door quietly. I open my eyes wide, to look innocent, and walk down the long hallway as if I am looking for someone.

"If you're walking down a hall, and you turn around and go back the other way, you are still just walking down a hall." — Old Zen Master.

"Just because you start cooking a hamburger doesn't mean you have to finish it." — Contemporary Zen Master.

Is anything really happening here? Does anything really happen anywhere? This is an important question to me, no less important for its apparent contradictions of common sense. Of course things happen — you read the sign yourself: SHIT HAPPENS. Roosevelt cuts off fuel to the Japanese, the retaliation killed my wife's mother's second cousin. That really happened. A boat with 3,000 Jewish children on it awaits a Presidential reprieve allowing the tiny refugees to enter a safe haven; the President turns to Palmer Webber, his advisor and later my father's business partner, and says, "What am I going to do with 3,000 Jews?" They are sent back and torpedoed out of the water, splash down in a pale hail to become plankton. That happened.

The Kennedys move their shanty-Irish roots and enthusiasms right into McLean, Virginia, the horsy center of Scotch-English Protestantism. War of the Roses games over the graves of Indians. Upstarts riding to the hounds, crowding the staid seats of power with bootlegger bucks and a killer's smile. Frosty Episcopal faces watch from behind leaded windows, sip ancestral single-malt from leaded-crystal goblets; dissemble over the chicken and salad at hunt picnics and muse on the state of things.

Curious constellations of power: Mafia dons and Yale old boys; the Secret Service, an admiral who ran a hospital, a mourning wife riding in the wrong ambulance while the body was fiddled to support the single-assassin theory. This happened.

You could say that was karma. You could say that using assassination as an adjunct of foreign policy — Diem; Castro, if they could have — would kick back, could knock out a frontal lobe at the wrong time. But Malcolm X and Martin Luther King didn't kill anybody. Talk about rubbing it under your thumb — even the mildest hopes were crushed that day, at the motel, no? That happened.

My daughter emerged into the world in a room surrounded by Hell's Angels and friends, good food and loud chatter, a stoned doctor. Both midwives would be dead before she turned three. That happened. The National Guard at Kent State fertilized the ecology movement by blowing away the last direct resistance to American military fantasies. I mean, it wasn't Mexico City, where the machine-gun bullets stuttered through the cotton sweaters and dacron blouses, scattering bloody shreds of flesh and cloth like confetti. I mean those Mexicans can party — knocked off 60 or 70 at a clip in downtown! Kent State was small time, but it happened.

And through it all, coagulating like a terminal blood clot, the underground water table patiently soaks up the lethal residues from abandoned mines in the West. The heaviest of metals—arsenic, lead, selenium—percolate out of the rain-filled abandoned mine-shafts; settle slowly in the aquifers that feed Phoenix (guess again, old bird) and Tucson—quietly poisoning the fertile blood of mothers; quietly skewing the statistical probabilities: cleft palates, harelips, stillbirths, ovarian cancers: bubbles of statistical surprise, and still the steady drip, like a parody of an IV bottle poisoning the patient we've sworn to save. Ask any of these mothers fresh and bitter in their disappointment, they'll tell you that it happened. They'll familiarize you with the daily litany of bedpans and sutures; the ghostly eyes of traumatized children, riddled with tubes and incomprehensible fears and agonies all for the sake of a single digit in an annual report somewhere. Try to tell one of these mothers or fathers that the fleshy shards of all their hopes are not really there.

Yet this persistent feeling remains . . . Breath . . . This scent of understanding, this delicate intuition that the background upon which all this variety is played out, the pregnant energy ceaselessly becoming worlds and hummingbirds, itchy loins and waterfalls, pale blossoms and meteor showers, the whole chaos of individuated, nameable stuff; the intuition persists that from the point of view of this background, nothing at all is happening. To say something is happening implies a point of view, and that's only one half of the equation, how it looks from here. The other half, the nothing's-going-on half, is rarely spoken for, barely peeped, hardly acknowledged.

Perhaps it is like magnifying the complex feelings men have about vulvas to insupportable proportions. Looking at a nude woman from the front, particularly one with luxuriant pubic hair, is highly erotic. The dark triangle stands like an arrow, directing your attention to the unseen center of attraction and its imagined delights.

But to look at the thing head on is far more ambivalent. I've never understood the pleasure some men derive from "pink" magazines which feature photos of women posing with their legs spread wide apart, spreading their labia with their fingers. Viewed in this way, directly and without any mystery, there is something disquieting and slightly disgusting. It is too complex to be merely inviting and that may be the attraction: the center of birth and disappearance. In

England I knew a woman who at orgasm screamed, "I'm going . . ." How much more so would we be forced to experience these feelings if we were to stare unblinking into the source-center of the universe?

I imagine a gigantic beast with a cauldron of fire inside its mouth and belly. Huge, leathery dugs flap on her chest while her vagina drips human babies, cities, rain-forests, and northern lights; diesel trains and beluga whales; books, lamps, trees, floods, ledgers, phones, and constellations. Her huge hands scoop everything up as fast as they can, stuffing them into her ceaselessly grinding teeth, devouring her issue at breakneck pace: a huffing, grunting, drooling, changeless, nothing-going-on machine . . . Breath . . . Where was I? Where am I?

It amazes me how totally I can disappear. The shadow of the *junko* on the wall has brought me round. The *junko* pads behind the rows of meditators carrying a big, flat stick gripped in his fists, parallel to his body. He is there to help sleepy people, though his compassion can be severe. If your back aches, or your shoulders, you press your palms together and, as he comes behind you, he will stop, bow, and lay the flat of the stick on your shoulder. You will lean over slightly to one side, and he will slap the thick muscle that runs alongside your spine. You will lean the other way and he will slap the other side. Then you both bow—you towards the wall you've been facing, and he to your back. That's the invitational.

At other times you will just be parting the exquisitely chewed and softened caribou skins that cover the eager breasts of an Eskimo girl. Her teeth seem filed to points. Her smile is delicious, literally, because her lips are stained with berries. The seal-oil lamp has heated the inside of the igloo comfortably, and the bed she has invited me to is piles of caribou and seal pelts. She is ripping Velcro strips away from my Eddie Bauer expedition gear. She has just wrapped her hand around the white man's harpoon when I feel the flat of her husband's sword on my shoulder . . .

It is in times like these that one's posture has slumped and the *junko,* in his vigilant helpfulness, has sidled up behind you to help you maintain concentration. Some of these guys are built like full-backs. You wouldn't expect that they could be so strong, sitting *za-zen* all the time, but the wholesome food, vigorous work, and contemplative life leaves a lot of extra energy to develop muscle mass.

You cannot run away at times like this. You've been caught napping, and Zen manners prescribe your taking the punishment like a man. My shoulders feel as if someone has been injecting ground glass into the joints for days. I bow sullenly, and the thud of the stick dislodges my prostate gland to the left. I lean the other way, and it is knocked back right. Curiously, as I bow, I am invigorated and refreshed. Much of the pain has left my back and shoulders. Where is that Eskimo? I search and search, but the entire Arctic has evaporated.

There is a story in the monastery about a senior monk who was seen climbing over the wall before dawn, after a foray into the distant town for sweets. The man who saw him happened to be the *junko*. A little later, the *junko* came behind the offender in *za-zen* and hit him so hard the whole *zendo* was shocked back into a lower level of consciousness, apprehensively alerted to an impending incident.

When the stick came to rest on the opposite shoulder, the sitting monk, who had never flinched or given any sign whatsoever that he was made of flesh, pinned the stick with a free hand. The two were frozen like statues. Anything might have happened. But each sent his message to the other. The *junko* removed the stick politely. He and the chastened monk bowed. Everyone exhaled.

◊ RUSS RIVIERE ◊

The 20-Breath Snake

Hook liked to tell this story: So there we were, on the headwaters of the Rio Custapec, above Finca Yaeger and a mile or so from the end of the road. Out of those deep canyons grow what must be the tallest and fattest liquidambars on earth. This was going to be the last collecting day at the last collecting location . . . the last day before I could get the fuck out of Mexico. After three months I really missed my kids. I was also very close to starvation. Alushe might be able to make it on the fare our boss, the Forest Pig, provided, but I myself needed burgers.

We, that is, Alushe, the Forest Pig, and myself, had just left the Mexican botanical team to its business of making breakfast. Quite the breakfast. They were frying eggs, they had fresh rolls, they had somebody's canned Canadian bacon, they had an assortment of fresh fruit, and they had some scornful snorts out of us. When you work for the Forest Pig, you don't need no stinking luxuries. We had already eaten. A couple of oranges was all we needed. Supplemented by the last of my personal stash of *animalitos.* They are the animal crackers you buy by the kilo. They taste like the Sunday funnies, but they have made the difference more than once in the minimum-requirement-of-blood-sugar department. Anyway, we had the jump on the Mexicans. That meant we could score the best plants while they indulged their weaknesses. I am certain that the Forest Pig had invited them on his collections only to humiliate them with his superiority. "Outcowboy the Greaseballs" was his philosophy in the field, and probably everywhere else as well.

◊ *Russ Riviere lives in Bolinas, California, and is director of field operations for the Forest Island Project.*

Now, it was typical that Alushe and me would start each new day with our ears laid back just like any other abused beasts of burden. This morning was a little different because, like I said, it was supposed to be our last. By this time, Alushe was almost as capable of climbing trees as myself . . . or at least of collecting in them independently. So we separated. The Forest Pig went up a ravine into the high limestone cliffs, on the make for ferns and orchids, Alushe headed off along the banks of the upper road, and I myself took the lower side of the road where I could see more clearly into the crowns of the trees. Steep slopes, you understand. I figured I had seven or eight climbs in front of me. There were more or less quarter-mile distances between us, but we were easily within shouting range.

At about 6,500 feet it was kind of chilly, and I had been assured by the Snakelero, who had stayed behind in San Cristóbal, that we would be outside the range of all possible arboreal *venenosas*. So, for the first time I was not worried about running into snakes. At that time I had a great respect for the Snakelero. My usual concern had become a big joke to everybody except Alushe, but their opinions meant little to me. Anyway, I waded up the trees that day with a will. And will is what it took after the fourth climb. I was exhausted. Not only by the day, but by all the other days and by too little sleep and too little food. I was sick to death of carrying all my equipment around, and I was sick to death of no gratitude from the Forest Pig. So, from a slightly mitigated bad attitude I regressed quickly back to my normal, bitching, swearing self. What was worse was the nobody to share it with. Except another *pinche* tree. But there was no choice. Just get it over with.

There was this little scree slope that ran about 50 feet down to the object tree from the trail, and I figured I could negotiate it without uncoupling myself from my equipment. I probably could have except for the exposed root that caught my right hook and sent me slamming backwards into the trunk at what was probably closer to 30 than 20 miles per hour. That was bad enough. After I caught my breath and looked up, I realized how much worse it really was. The tree was a lot bigger here than it was from the trail. Plus it was completely smothered in epiphytes, aeroids, and bromeliads for the first 70 feet, at which point—the first crotch—it was still four feet in diameter.

I could have cried. Maybe I did. The pain in my elbow was even more intense than my hatred for science, but neither one was as bad as not wanting to climb that tree. However, when it comes down to it, everything else aside, I am a treeman. Unless there is a bar handy, I *will* climb the sonofabitch.

Now, climbing your typical tropical rain forest tree is not like the flip, chunk-chunk cleanliness of your typical temperate tree. This is not to say that the Douglas Fir, for example, is not without its frustrations in terms of hard jutting stubs and body-shredding bark, but in the scale of human misery, the rain forest tree is supreme.

There was no possibility that I was going to trust free-climbing the vines to the first comfortable tie-in, because I had experience in that technique. Normally, it was the basic ant attack that made you lose your hold in desperate situations, but there was also the likelihood that *guitarones* or other murderous wasps would be on hand for ambushes. Not counting spider ants or scorpions. So I resigned myself to the long, but surely safer, technique of removing the vegetation as I climbed. This is done in sections. Overhead. Every three or four feet I would hack a ring around the trunk and rip the vines free. I don't know how to make this sound as difficult as it is. It is also hell on the habitat. Caustic sap is worth mentioning here. Some trees have it, some vines have it, and it can, in different and varying ways, bring great grief to men. Blindness and shrieking rashes are among the possibilities. And, of course, cutting anything overhead makes me nervous.

So there I was, hack-hack, voopa-voopa, chunk-chunk, rip-groan for maybe 45 minutes of sweat-straining agony. I had gone about 60 feet when I came to the bell, I mean where the diameter of the trunk went from about four feet to about seven feet. I was now convinced that I had not checked this tree out in a thorough manner. In the meantime, I had buried my climbing line under 20 feet of chopped vegetation, and it was hopelessly tangled. I had to let it go. Having to let go is an interesting phenomenon. All of us have probably experienced it. Letting go of the climbing line is not as bad as letting go of the wheel, which is fairly sudden, but it is almost as bad. However, there is a kind of purity in being reduced to nothing but a waistline.

Looking up, I got a pretty good shot of the crotch, which to my further discouragement was hairy beyond the normal. In order to throw my waistline through it and make myself secure for the upper ascent, I would have to clean the crotch out. The only thing I could do was to climb as far above my waistline as possible and hack at the crotch with my machete. This was a maximum-strain situation that would surely turn into one of minimum effectiveness. So I did the easier thing. I poked around in the crotch the way border guards in French Revolution movies look for the hero in the hay wagon. Satisfied (if that's the word), I then unclipped myself from the waistline. This left me clinging to a vine with my left hand, while my hooks were tentatively set in the trunk. I then swung the waistline with its heavy clip (I have knotted my head more than once with it) through the crotch. All I had to do now was to inch my way up one, two feet, reach around the blind side of the trunk, grab the clip, breathe with relief, core in, and continue. The inching up was successful enough, but when I reached around the trunk to grab the clip—Whang!

Shit! Another suck-ass wasp, I thought, forcing myself not to over-react. But when I looked at my hand, I saw the trickle of blood. Blood? I looked at the crotch, then at my hand. Then at the crotch. Blood? Then I saw it and can see it yet. Slowly, lazily, preparing itself for the next strike—the 20-Breath Snake—the almost mythical grin-ning little pit viper that instantly paralyzes birds, frogs, and rodents in trees, and that had just bitten me!

Now I have spent a great deal of time thinking about this very snake. The Forest Pig had told me more than once, and with what he passed off as humor, that if bitten by one of these guys you'd have approximately two minutes to live. Which was why the TselTal called it the 20-Breath Snake. There was no anti-venom for it, and even if there was, I knew we didn't have any. We were also 200 miles from the nearest airport, which would be fogged in anyway. Added to that was the fact that I was 70 feet up a tree on the uphill side, 150 on the downhill side; not tied in; and I still had to deal with this snake.

Decisions had to be made. Should I kill it with my machete and take the chance its upper half would fall in my lap? No. Even if the head missed me, I wouldn't want to go to Hell with no snake. Should I flip it onto the trail so that Alushe and the Forest Pig could see what killed me? I knew that the snake had a prehensile tail and couldn't move well on the ground. No. I would have to get too close to it. I remembered that I had paid up my life insurance and was gratified in a strange way. I thought all these thoughts in the amount of time it took me to yell, "SNAKEBIT!" at the top of my lungs.

Stay calm, keep your heart rate down, and get out of the tree before you fall out. That was my advice to myself. I backed down real slow, keeping my eyes on the golden, sloe-eyed ones of the snake.

After I caught myself from barking out any further, I took another look at my hand. It was already swollen. I sucked the blood off. What precious little there was of it. I expected that dark blood you see in punctures, but instead there was this short pink scratch. This was not your direct, two-fang hit. I began to smell hope.

If anyone asks you what hope smells like, you can say it smells like burgers.

A couple of dozen pure, calm steps and I was at the base of the tree and also at the bottom of the scree slope I had fallen down before. I probably should have stayed there, but I couldn't. I mean, I had to reach the road. So I did, charging all-fours up the slope.

As I reached the top, black fingers began to run through my brain. I started to pull a strap off my pack for a tourniquet, when the Forest Pig came charging out of his ravine. I instantly forgave him for all his asshole ways. If I had to die, I couldn't find better or more profound company.

"WHERE'S THE SNAKE?" he boomed, as he skidded by me, out of breath, eyes furiously darting. This was not the question I expected, but caught up in the moment like I was, I pointed to the crotch of the tree.

"You mean you didn't get it?"

I groaned; he grunted: "Where did it get you?"

I raised my hand.

Then Alushe came rushing in; the Forest Pig sent him to get water from the creek, the Pig himself being busy searching for the snake through field glasses.

It was still there, writhing on top of the foliage remaining in the crotch.

"*Negroveridis!* By shit, it's *negroveridis!*"

The Forest Pig looked around at me in order to share his enthusiasm.

He saw how far that was going.

"Don't worry. If you're not dead by now, you won't be. At least I don't think so. The problem now is how to get the snake. We have to have the snake!"

Alushe returned with the water, while the Forest Pig paced back and forth, building himself into that state of irreversible despicability that so marks his kind.

"We cannot let it defeat us!" he kept saying.

I soaked my hand, absorbed, as you can imagine, with the growing realization that I might be O.K., but I was not yet completely out of the action. I tightened my jaw and repeated no way, no way, to myself as the Forest Pig sidled up in his charmingest manner and said, "Take a close look at that little sucker."

I accepted the glasses. I pretended to possess some kind of scientific interest. I did not say, "How the fuck much closer can I look, you prick?"

"You know, I suppose," the Forest Pig went on, paying no attention to my silence, "that there are only three specimens of *Bothrops negroveridis* in the world, and no live ones?" Of course I did; we'd talked about it plenty of times. What else do these pricks have to talk about? I still didn't say anything, because I was absorbed by the snake. I struggled one-handed with the focus, hoping to see the snake's magnified eyes overlay my memory of them closer up. It wasn't much use. My steadiness was shot.

"I'm glad I wasn't wearing gloves," I said, mostly to myself. I must have moved my hand the precise moment the snake struck. Had I had gloves, I would not have known that I had been struck. I would have inched my body into the crotch, at which time I would have been hit in the throat. Not a pretty picture. It occurred to me that something fatey was going on. Some creeping affinity.

"How are you feeling?"

I eased the glasses down and turned my head to look full into the eyes of the Forest Pig. How could so large a man have such glistening little rabbit turds for eyes?

"Grateful."

In reality, my left hand was beginning to look like a catcher's mitt, my legs were rubbery, and the rest of my body was frozen with uncertainty. The real deal was between me and time, and there was nothing the Forest Pig could say to encourage or encroach upon my attitude. I was in a state of grace between the living and the dead, and I fully planned on playing it to the hilt.

No slouch at reading between the lines, the Forest Pig took back the field glasses. He looked into the crotch for a long moment. He said, "You know, we're dealing with a disoriented animal up there. He's a night hunter who has been disturbed in the daylight. It's cold and he has stiffened up. Probably why he missed you. Look at him, still on top of the nest ready to repel another invader. An extremely anxious situation for him, don't you think?"

"What makes you think it's a him?"

"There's only one way to find out, isn't there?"

We looked at each other dead on, and then, as if we had rehearsed the move, both of our heads turned toward Alushe.

Now, Alushe has had long practice in looking ignorant. He can look irreproachable if he wants, with his classic Mayan features, or he can look like he doesn't know one end of a shovel from another. In fact, I've never known anyone with so many ways of looking ignorant. But this time, he knew that we knew and that there was no honorable way out. Especially since the Forest Pig held the money.

The Forest Pig began the dialogue: "Baak I Laal."

Sly. Real sly to call Alushe "Big Brother." To use the term that signals that more has been shared than ordinary relationships can bear, and so if you cherish me and know me and value our future friendship, you will respond.

"Baak I Laal, we have to have the snake. Hook cannot do it, and I carry too much weight. You can do it and you have our help. Hook now knows the name of the animal, and I will watch through the glasses and tell you how to move."

Effective. The Forest Pig may be a fucking jerk, but he is always an effective fucking jerk.

"Baak I Laal," Alushe began in the formal oratorical style, "Baak I Laal, you say that we must have the snake. I am not sure but that the snake already has itself. Hook has no cannot. He has done it. You say that you are too heavy and cannot do it. That is true. It is not what you are for. Hook knows the name of the animal and that is also true, but he cannot tell. You say that you will watch me, but you cannot be me. I am not ashamed to say that I do not like snakes and that they do not like me."

After what followed—a good half an hour of watching the Pig throw rocks at the snake—Alushe and I were not surprised when he finally said, "We'll camp here." Out of breath as he was, there is no end to his snot.

"Not only do we not have the snake, we don't have the tree."

Although we were looking forward to the return trip, this new decision wasn't as bad as it could have been. The afternoon was cool and sunny, every detail was crisp and golden, and my appreciation for everything around me was immense.

We made camp quickly and with few words. I wasn't much help, but the small tents went up easily, and as Alushe built the cooking fire, the Forest Pig changed tack. I supposed that my high spirits were infectious and that the Pig's change of attitude was simply an emergence into common decency. Sure.

Our meal consisted of one can of fava beans, some dried mountain tortillas called *kosh osh,* and what was left of the *animalitos.* We squatted around the fire and ate with slow bites and darting eyes. The way the Donner Party must have. The Forest Pig was in the habit of counting mouthfuls so as to make even the lightest eater feel guilty. He rationed tequila the same way, but that night, as I say, was different. The food game didn't change, but he positively plied me with tequila. And I positively drank it. He spoke of higher responsibility — how knowledge is only gained by sacrifice et cetera. He told me what a neat guy I was. I guess that is what finally got me. With Alushe already snoring, I agreed to go after the snake the next day.

When I finally went to sleep that night, I dreamed clear, weird dreams. I will tell you here that there is nothing I can't stand as much as hearing somebody else's dreams. I would rather listen to their back problems. Mine are usually no different, but over coffee the next morning I told my dreams to the Forest Pig. No toothless old bag at Delphi ever got cloudier and uncloudier over a potentially fat customer than the Forest Pig got over me. No trench chaplain ever shoved a doughboy more eloquently out into no man's land.

I would have gone anyway.

◇

"All right. Don't worry. I'll have my field glasses on the crotch every second. All you have to do is flip him out. I'll take care of the rest."

I returned this short set of Forest Pig instructions with a slit-eye nod. Alushe had taken a seat on a rock to watch. He turned his head and gave me the mock, sideways spit. We use this as a code when something is genuinely the shits. It helps to buck us up. I agreed with him, and it didn't take no gesture to see it. I headed back down the groove in the scree my body had made the day before. Yep. Same tree all right. Same amount of nothing on it.

I would only have to scale the mound of drying vegetation that I had stripped from the tree in order to arrive at the clean trunk. It would take me less than two minutes to arrive at the crotch. Great. I started up. As I ascended, I became sorrier and sorrier. At the same time, the Forest Pig, looking on from the safety and security of the ground, started revealing his true nature by making faces. The closer I got, the more intense and slathering and raw his faces got. All of my hatred for him reemerged. As I neared the crotch, my progress slowed to almost nothing. I might as well have had a Studebaker sedan tied to my climbing belt. Sweat was pouring in my eyes.

"YOU'RE OKAY!" the Pig yelled. "NOT A THING MOVING!"

Including me, I thought, giving him the searingest look I could imagine. I let out every inch of slack in my waistline. The snake could only strike out half the length of his body, you see. But even that was no use. I just couldn't force myself to get any closer.

"I'M GONNA TRY FOR THAT CROTCH," I shouted at the Pig, who always pretended to understand. What I meant was that I would throw my climbing line through a higher crotch, apparent now in one of the upper branches. I would then climb the rope and come down on the snake. Which I would have done the first day had I not had to deep-six my climbing line.

I bundled enough rope to make the throw and enough to fall back down to me once through the crotch. Maybe a 20-foot throw. The first shot missed. That is the rule. I swore softly, recoiled the rope, and got ready again. My concentration was intense. The rope arced up this time, missed the target, and came down through the snake crotch. Exactly the worst place for it. I would have to pull the rope free. Which is to say, it was now possible to pull the snake into my lap. My mood deteriorated.

"YOU CAN DO IT!" the Pig called, recognizing the situation.

"YOU CAN DO IT!" I called back, among other things.

Now, it doesn't pay to lose your temper at times like these, but I couldn't help it. In my rage, I thunked around the trunk, getting as far away from the retrieval as possible. I drove my hooks into the tree as hard as I could. I also drove my right hook into my left Achilles' tendon. Right up to the hilt. Through my boot and an inch and a half of cold steel further. I yanked it out just as hard. In no way did I want the Forest Pig to know. The sweat burned my eyes and my boot filled with blood. I lost all reason. I charged into the snake crotch . . . through it . . . then above it. I cored in with my waistline and flipped my climbing line into the crotch I had missed before. The Forest Pig was screaming, but I wasn't listening. I dropped back into the crotch. I ripped into it with my boots and my machete.

No movement. Not one sign of life. The snake was gone. The anticlimax of it all made jello out of my legs, so I straddled the crotch like it was a fat pony and I watched the ants try to find a way into my pants. "He's gone," I said, more to the tree than to the Forest Pig. But the Forest Pig already knew. I half expected to see him throw the field glasses to the ground and stomp on the lenses. I collected a small branch to represent the tree. Fruits, flowers, leaves. Alushe came to the base of the tree to retrieve it. I climbed down.

◇

We loaded our equipment into the truck. Nobody said a thing. My boot sloshed a little with blood, but it didn't leak. I was somehow pleased that my hand hurt more than my heel. I climbed into the back of the truck without even removing my hooks and collapsed. At least I was on the way home.

"Just one more stop," the Forest Pig said after we had gone about two miles. Nothing he could say could really get to me anymore, but I did wonder how far Alushe and I could get in the truck before the Pig's body was found. We pulled into a small turnout at the edge of the German coffee farm. Probably quite a ways.

Alushe and the Forest Pig gathered up the machetes and collecting sacks. I stayed in the back. My heel had stiffened up, and I knew that once I took my boot off, it would be a long time before I got it back on. I pulled my body out of the truck.

"It's not far," the Forest Pig said, some small endemic plant that he knew would be in bloom. Alushe and I followed as the Pig made his way up the trail. It was a good trail. Wide, clear, and obviously used as a kind of *periferico,* or perimeter trail, by the coffee workers. The first mile was bad enough, but after that, each step was torture. I got dizzy. I sat down. Alushe knew right away that something was more wrong than usual. Nobody sits down in the jungle. At least, not me. We agreed that I would wait for them to return.

It was a good place to rest, right beside the greatest strangler fig I have ever seen. It was a giant macramé cathedral. Completely hollow inside, the tree reminded me of some rich and beautiful widow who made her home on the decomposed ashes of her long-dead husband. I fell asleep.

I wish I could say that when I woke up everything was different, but it wasn't. Alushe prodded me with his walking stick, so I had to begin the long walk back.

The Forest Pig took the point the way he always does when the trail is easy: Botanical Adventure Man, thrusting his way one perilous step further . . . into the unknown. Asshole. Alushe, behind me, was making shushing noises to remind me of my mumbling, when I saw the Forest Pig lift his elephantine leg over a branch that had fallen across the trail. What struck me was a small flash of electric green.

"Hey, uh, Jefe . . . this almost looks like . . ."

And sure enough it was. *Bothrops negroveridis.* The 20-Breath Snake. A teenager. Maybe it fell out of the tree. Maybe it crawled out onto the edge of this dead branch and the branch had broken. But here it was. Some kind of mystical gift to science.

The Forest Pig did a little dance around the branch. Dumbo around the china jar. Alushe was only slightly amused, but I myself was outright amazed. The snake was small, about nine inches or so, and the big problem was how to get it back to the truck. As innocent as he looked, he was not the kind of guy you drop in your pocket. The Forest Pig solved it. He broke off the part of the branch the snake was coiled around and walked it out of the woods. Or almost out of the woods. He had to stop every couple of hundred feet and turn the branch around, because the snake would wind his way toward the Pig's hand. This became a kind of comedy contest, and I knew who I was rooting for.

We were in sight of the truck when the snake dropped off the stick. It was like he had waited for the grass. The grass was just his color. He was not supposed to be able to move effectively along the ground, but then I had just received a big lesson in supposedlies. The fact was the snake was lost and I was glad. The Forest Pig ranted and rooted around for half an hour, and then Alushe, of all people, found it and flipped it onto the road. Easy pickins. The Pig got it into a jar and I rode all of the many hours back to San Cristóbal with this snake between my legs.

◊

The only living 20-Breath Snake in captivity died two months later in the San Diego Zoo. Wouldn't eat. A month after that I was able to get my boot on.

◊ HILDEGARDE FLANNER ◊

Bamboo: An Honest Love Affair

I became acquainted with bamboo in the twenties when my family bought an old place in the foothill suburbs above Pasadena. Among the company of trees, shrubs, and perennials, there was a solitary bamboo.

I was correct in assuming it was no ordinary kind. It had a dark green stem — or culm — stained with blotches. It also had style and elegance. I was never able to learn who planted it, though I tried repeatedly. Perhaps it was the woman who had planted the original garden half a century before, a woman who had traveled much in the Orient and had, perhaps, smuggled in a rhizome in the sleeve of an embroidered kimono. Perhaps it was the owner who had worked for the Park Department. In any case, by the time my efforts to discover provenance and person finally came to a blank halt, a good many years had passed, and the bamboo had grown into a tall, rich, graceful clump. Flourishing in the half-shade between two great cypresses, it was enchanting. It bent and swung and arched. Its heavy plumes spread when the wind blew.

Then one day, the director of the Arboretum at Arcadia, Dr. Russell Seibert, was brought for a visit by my husband, who was doing some architectural work for the Arboretum. Dr. Seibert declared our bamboo to be one of the most beautiful he had ever seen — and he was a specialist. He, in turn, brought by Dr. John Creech, who was in charge of the U.S. Plant Introduction Garden in Maryland. Dr. Creech walked around our bamboo with a motion picture camera and took its circular portrait. He announced it was

◊ *Hildegarde Flanner (1899–1988) lived in Calistoga, California. This essay appeared in* At the Gentle Mercy of Plants *(John Daniel & Company, Santa Barbara).*

Phyllostachys nigra variety *henonis* forma *boryana,* from China. We could call it bory.

I am grateful that I can associate my first ardent feeling for bamboo with my youth, with the time of beginnings, and the early years of hope, love, and creativity. It was, however, a rare and lonely attachment in those days, shared by no one close to me and catered to by no local nurseries. With the exception of Lord Redesdale's *The Bamboo Garden,* out of print, hard to find, and very expensive, the few books that might turn up were inhumanly technical. Two decades passed before the Department of Agriculture published a series of pamphlets by Robert A. Young which became the bible of the increasing number of bamboo fanciers. It was from these pamphlets that I learned of the Barbour Lathrop Experimental Bamboo Gardens near Savannah. In 1950, returning from a summer trip to France, I took a circuitous route home and drove down to see them.

I arrived on a Saturday and found the Gardens closed. This was a stunning blow, because I could not wait until the next day. But I could get in, just barely, and I did, by climbing over the locked gate. Once inside, I wandered in humid bliss among the glorious ornamentals growing there. When, shakily, I climbed out, I had forty Deep South mosquito bites on one bare arm. I was too startled to add up the bites on the other arm.

I recollect standing on the deck of my home above the old garden and looking into the extraordinary display of the bory, its wild movement in the wind or its mystical serenity on a quiet day. "If you should ever bloom," I said, "and die from blooming, as they say may happen, it would be terribly sad." Then, after a moment, I said, "But it would make it easier to leave this place, if we ever decide to leave."

Eventually, after thirty-six years of living in one home and garden, we did decide to leave, taking with us much of the bamboo. It had never bloomed, or if it had, it was before we were acquainted with it, and the event was not fatal. I had already started another clump in another corner, which I decided to take whole, if I could. Since this clump was far too heavy for me to handle, I hired the Green Brothers, who were in the business of moving gardens. At work on my bamboo, one of them asked, "Ma'am, why don't you sell some of this pretty stuff?"

"Sell it!" I cried. "If I had a daughter, would I sell her?" The Green Brothers thought me very amusing.

Today I live in the Napa Valley, where I have close to fifty kinds of bamboo, some established in the ground, some only on the potting table. I cannot overlook the disappointments and failures that have come to me through bamboo, due to my own mismanagement and lack of direction. At the side of a woodland, I have now tried to make a terraced garden featuring various bamboos and the chief ornamentals. It is all very special to me, my own green portion. I dote on it, in an angry way, because I have not done better by it. There are fine bamboos I should have encouraged to dominate, and lesser ones that here are too prominent. Also, the volcanic soil with which we must live and work should have been richer with the right fraction of acid, and the stones, enthusiastically proliferating underground, should have been softer.

I must not feel sorry for myself, yet the salt of depression savors my exotic hunger. Worst of all, does my husband, who now shares in gathering bamboos, think ill of what little I have achieved? Have we not come 500 miles north from an old southern home, guided by the hope of more space for more bamboo? But my husband is a rare, superhuman human species. He never chides.

A sharp disappointment here is that the bory does not perform with its drama of grace and dignity and its array of copious plumes hung out like big flags of green. Still, it puts on an impressive bamboo performance, and each year its culms are larger and its feathery shade stretches further. I would never permit anyone, even the King of Savannah, to speak of it with condescension. I love it. And nearby I have an excellent stand of *Phyllostachys viridis,* which was fortunately planted in a rich spot and flourished, proving that a difference in soil is a difference in a plant's incentive. After twenty-five years it is thirty feet tall with green-striped yellow culms, and a great way of throwing itself about and bending in rain and wind, or a tranquil way of standing utterly still in placid moments. It is a lofty, magisterial, poetic creature.

Recently, I found a pile of shipping tags from the Department of Agriculture giving the names of species sent to me years ago. They did not all prosper, but the warm pleasure of possession by a citizen is with me still. *P. pubescens,* the mighty Moso. *Arundinaria amabilis,* the lovely name and the illustrious culm. I go around our garden wondering whether this clump or that one which I have failed to identify may be one of these most desirable ones, lost but not, I hope, lost forever in the mess of time. Some day it will all be clear, if not to me, then to one whose gaze is keener.

I trust that my grandchildren are going to enjoy the fact of bamboo in their lives. May they learn to watch for the new culms breaking through the soil and quickly rising to the rustling light above, shedding the sheathes with their curious details of dots and dashes and speckles of black and brown, or those that bear no design but are a fashionable chamois color all over, like the best gloves. Also the little whiskery ears and the ribbony blades.

In all of these, I take a child's pleasure, not deserving the pleasures of a scientist. The taxonomy and nomenclature of this tribe are challenges to an able scientist. I am not even remotely of that elevated class. My familiarity with bamboo is simply an honest love affair, and if it is not requited, that's my own business.

Have I begotten any bamboo lovers? I do not know. Today my grandchildren should be using the large culm sheath of *P. viridis* as platters for ripe strawberries, but my Australian cattle dog Anna has eaten all the berries in the bed. Well, the unexpected gains and losses of life are of much interest.

Lacking the actual strawberries I had thought to present to them, I may still attract their imaginations by pointing to the clump of *P. vivax* with its bright green culms four inches broad. "Look at this," I say, "thirteen years ago your grandfather and I gathered the seed and planted it. We grew this bamboo for you, and some day it will be enormous, one of the biggest and strongest. The seed is like oak or wheat, and it is thrilling to feel for it hidden inside the husk, to press with your finger and feel the little hard morsel inside."

I wish I could think of a graphic way to express the bamboo's mysterious command of time, how swiftly it grows tall, and stops forever; how, if it blooms, it blooms with the same tidal fervor everywhere at once. For thousands of years in the Orient, bamboo has been of supreme importance to mankind, providing the means of food, materials for building, the substance of countless artifacts, promptings for religious symbolism, the high stuff of art, even the miraculous scaffolding that holds and bends better than steel and is used in the erection of many-storied buildings. What other plant has provided an omnipresent relation between nature and man? It is reasonable, I feel, to hope that one's family may be aware of this great plant and its influence on men and women, even as poetry, art, and music are civilizing possessions.

May I presume to offer advice to those eagerly beginning their collections? Like most advice it will be unwanted and discarded, giving satisfaction only to myself, for whom it is too late. However, I would say: Be selective. Don't try to get everything you hear of. There is no end to that. Get only the single best for your needs, and cultivate it devoutly. Make everything that you acquire into the most perfect specimen possible. Decide what you want in a certain situation and then fill it with the one inevitable, most precious bamboo.

If your climate permits, have the rather tender *Bambusa beecheyana* or *B. oldhami*, both large and stately, and keep the obnoxious scale off the culms. If you can't grow one of these, then have an impressive *Phyllostachys*, which will soar forty feet or more, resembling the pillars of a temple. And, of course, a clump of exotic *P. nigra*. At the other extreme, don't forget the pretty, dwarf fern leaf, nor the white and green-striped *Sasa variegata*, also *S. veitchii*, for its handsome foliage . . . Already this would give you enough to make a reputable bamboo paradise in a piece of mortal real estate. But it is with barely controllable lust that I turn from others, seductive, amazing, or modest.

My friends, I have not long, it may be, to tarry and see how your bamboos grow. How poignantly I wish I might begin again and explore with you the delights and temptations of these most fascinating plants. In the many years I have lived with bamboo, it has always been a delighter, never a deceiver. Its meaning is the meaning of grace, a grace that drips with rain, the first rain and the second rain as it takes the storm and sluices it into the earth and the wet branches sigh and bend upon each other, as the culms bear the weight of water and foliage, then straighten tall when their burden eases. In the sun bamboo dries quickly and shakes itself for another day, another weather. Small birds, the bushtits, hang their long, knitted nests where no cat can climb. At night the stars sit lightly in the branches.

I lay my tribute down. Oh, yes! I wish I might begin again, now that at the end I know better how to begin.

◇ DAVID HARRIS ◇

My Best Friend

I first laid eyes on JC Crampton October 24, 1969.

It was, as I noted in my journal, "a day that seemed to stumble only slowly to its feet." Our work crew had recently moved lower in the mountains after two straight days of snow flurries at 7,000 feet, but, even at the lesser elevation, it took until well past 10:30 for the morning haze to burn off. At noon, the Lieutenant drove up from the camp in his jeep and took two draft resisters from L.A., Vane and Zack, back with him. By 3:30, when the work day was over, word had gotten around that Vane and Zack had been "shipped out" to La Tuna for "disciplinary reasons." Word then spread that all draft prisoners would meet after dinner on the baseball bleachers to figure out what to do in response.

Back in camp, the mountain crews scattered across the compound, some heading for the Clothing Room to get clean laundry, others to their barracks. Smokey, the camp's inmate barber, was standing in the shade of a roofed-over card-playing area at the laundry end of the compound, and I headed in his direction. Smokey had done ten years for the state of Arizona and was working on another five for the feds, all for the same armed robbery. He had one year left.

"What's happenin?" he greeted me.

"Nothin to it," I answered. "What's happenin down here?"

"They got me workin today," Smokey snickered. He motioned over at the concrete walkway where the guard we called Dick Tracy was leading a group of four new arrivals up to the processing barracks.

◇ *David Harris lives in Mill Valley, California. His most recent book is* The League *(Bantam).*

Each carried a roll of fresh bedding and a stack of Safford-issue khakis. "Old Dick Tracy caught hisself some fresh fish," Smokey laughed.

"County jail?"

"No, they come over in the car that took them two draft dudes back to La Tuna."

The short procession was just about even with us, Tracy in the lead. He had a face like a rat and a walk like a duck. When he saw us watching, he added a little strut to his step. Crampton was next in line.

JC didn't look half-Indian except for around his cheekbones and the slope of his profile. The first thing I noticed about him was how thick his chest and shoulders were. His neck and arms were the same way. His legs were short, wiry, and nimble. As a physical specimen, Crampton resembled a cross between a cat and a tree trunk. Even from twenty feet away it was obvious both that he could handle himself and that he knew it. He didn't swagger, but his confidence was tangible. He looked around with his chin up, his mouth set in a half-grin, showing no hint of the apprehension usual to new arrivals. He seemed convinced that he was on top of the situation, whatever it might prove to be.

Smokey and I followed his approach with automatic curiosity.

When JC saw us watching, he made a little stage wave in our direction and launched into a perfect imitation of Dick Tracy's duck walk.

Smokey and I cracked up.

Our laughter flustered Tracy and he whirled around to see what Crampton was doing, but not quick enough. JC had dropped his imitation.

"You better stop dickin around, Crampton," Tracy warned, "less you want to go right back where you came from."

"What'd I do?" JC answered in mock innocence.

"Just stop dickin around," Tracy ordered. Then he turned and started walking again. JC looked over at us with a grin, flashed a peace sign, and began to skip along in Tracy's footsteps.

This time, Tracy ignored him.

"Who was that?" I asked Smokey as the procession headed off.

"Name JC Crampton. I knowed him at La Tuna," Smokey chuckled. "He be a genuine trip, let me tell ya. He gonna drive these dogs crazy."

◊

Thirty of Safford's Selective Service violators met after dinner that evening on the bleachers near the camp's boundary. Most of us were veterans of the California draft resistance movement and publicly pledged "to carry on the struggle," inside jail as well as out. Everyone was angry about what had happened to Vane and Zack, and many considered it "harassment" that demanded a response. The meeting began by discussing what we knew about why they had been singled out.

Vane's case was the culmination of three run-ins with authorities during the last three weeks. The first was with the camp's medical officer, who brought him up on charges of ignoring an order to get his hair cut. The second involved Vane's asking why, when Baldhack, officer-in-charge of the swing shift, ordered him to change shirts. The third was a conflict with the Lieutenant himself. Vane's hair was by then touching his ears and the Lieutenant wanted it cut again. Two days earlier, he had stopped Vane out on the yard.

"I thought I told you to get a haircut," the Lieutenant fumed.

"I did," Vane had answered, handing the Lieutenant an envelope. Inside the envelope were two locks of Vane's hair.

That explained Vane's case. Zack had apparently been shipped out for raising his voice to the Lieutenant during an argument over the rule that every prisoner had to shave daily.

By then, a number of people had reached decisions. Curly, Fishman, Gould from Denver, Reedy, Pineapple, Emmett the Baker, and Pablo had all made up their minds to refuse to go to work tomorrow. All of them knew they would lose good time, jeopardize their possible paroles, and be shipped out to a heavier security institution if they went through with it. I didn't know whether to join them. Our baby was due in a month and I had promised Joanie not to get into any more trouble until after the birth. It was a promise I was reluctant to break.

After the all clear sounded, Pablo and I walked around the yard, a regular evening ritual among Safford's population.

"I promised Joanie," I told Pablo. "No more strikes until after the baby."

He was sympathetic. "We can all understand that kind of situation, David. You've got to do what you've got to do. Everybody knows that."

"So what does that mean? Am I supposed to go back up that fuckin mountain while you guys are bagged off to La Tuna?"

Pablo shrugged. "Beats me," he said.

At the corner in the walkway next to the camp hospital, we caught up with Curly and had the same conversation all over again. On the next lap after that, the three of us merged with Smokey and JC.

"You gonna be in this strike tomorrow?" he asked.

"I don't know," I told him. "I really don't. My wife's havin a baby next month and I promised her I wouldn't get into anything."

JC said he could understand that. Births were important. His youngest, he said, had been born right before he got locked up this time and he claimed to have copped a plea in order to stay out long enough to be part of it. "You got any other kids?" he asked.

"No, this is the first."

"I've got two others. A boy, seven, and a girl, six."

Then JC asked just what the strike was supposed to be about. I told him about Vane and Zack being shipped out and then told the story of Vane and his envelope of hair. JC burst out laughing so hard his great bull neck turned red.

"And you guys are goin on strike to tell the cops that you ought to be allowed to cut your hair when you want to?" he finally guffawed.

"More or less," I answered.

"Good luck," JC said, slapping me on the shoulder. "Good fuckin luck."

Our conversation was interrupted by the siren and Crampton went back to the Arrival barracks. Lights were out at 10:00. I lay awake for a long time. Half my mind was occupied with becoming a father. The other half, as I wrote to Joanie, was full of "nothing but walls for the next thirty months."

◊

For Safford's normal morning work count, the crews were required to line up around the compound. When the 7:30 siren went off, the crew boss officers called roll. At 7:50, the Lieutenant walked out of the administration building with a clipboard and collected the morning's numbers. The morning of October 25 was different. At 7:30, Fishman announced the strike by occupying one of the card tables in the middle of the yard. He played his banjo at top volume for the next half hour. By the time the Lieutenant emerged, Pineapple had joined Fishman with his guitar and Emmett, Gould, and Reedy had informed their bosses that they weren't going to work. Then Pablo and Curly stepped out of line and told Officer Polack the same thing. Polack ordered everyone else onto the truck.

I stayed right where I was.

"You on strike too, Harris?" Polack asked.

"Looks like it," I said.

When the truck pulled out, Curly and Pablo looked at me with a note of surprise in their faces.

I shrugged. "I always did want to see Leavenworth." We all laughed, but there was a nervous ring to it.

Within five minutes, the yard was empty except for the eight of us who refused to work. We sat out in the morning sun and waited to see what would happen. Nothing did, so I went back to my bunk to write my wife.

> Dearest Joanie,
>   I hate to tell you this but eight of us, myself included, refused to work this morning. We'll be shipped out but I have no idea where yet. I know the promise I made was very important and I feel guilty as hell about breaking it, but I just couldn't go out to work with other people on strike. I couldn't be me and do that. I know you'll understand . . . Please don't worry, just concentrate on having the baby . . . There's nothing they can do that I can't handle.
>
>   I love you,
>   David

Not long after I finished writing, the Lieutenant came looking for me. His face was tight as a drum. "Mr. Kennedy wants to see you," he ordered. "Now."

Kennedy was the camp's chief administrator. He sat behind the desk while I stood.

"What the hell do you guys think you're doing?" he demanded.

"Refusing to work."

"You don't like to work?"

"I like to work," I answered. "I just don't like gettin fucked with. You guys had no call to send Vane and Zack to La Tuna. If that's the way you're gonna be, you'd better ship me out too."

Kennedy snorted. "See the Lieutenant on your way out."

The Lieutenant was waiting in the hallway. He looked pleased. "Pack your shit," he grinned. "And stay on your bunk till I send for you."

I began emptying my locker. According to Bureau of Prisons regulations, I would be allowed to take the clothes on my back, my shaving gear, cigarettes, toothbrush, tennis shoes, the letters I'd saved, any legal papers I might have, and five books plus a Bible. The limit on books posed a problem. I had at least fifty, squirreled into my locker and stored under my bunk in a cardboard box and a brown paper shopping bag. I pulled them all out and picked a collection of Isaac Babel's short stories, *Mr. Johnson* by Joyce Cary, Tolstoy's *Resurrection,* a history of the IWW, and a volume of Lao-tse. The rest I crammed back into their containers. Then I turned in the direction of JC's bunk. He was lying down, killing time. All I could see were his feet and the peace symbol tattooed on his ankle.

"Hey, Crampton."

After a rustle of springs, his head popped above the wall.

"You want these books?"

"What?"

I picked up the box and bag. "Take them," I said. "They're yours."

"You just givin em away?"

"I can't take em with me."

I now doubt if Crampton ever read as many as five books in his entire lifetime, but I didn't know it then and it didn't much matter. He was, I realize, flattered that I considered him someone who could make use of literature. Also, my gesture had come out of nowhere, and gratuitous generosity was, I would learn, a trademark JC prided himself in.

"Thanks," he said. "I'll take good care of them."

For the next two-and-a-half hours, we waited. Each time a new rumor floated in, the four of us awaiting shipment clustered back at my bunk to talk it over. The first rumor was that we were all being shipped to Marion, the federal penitentiary in Illinois, built to replace Alcatraz when it closed in 1963. Another rumor was Lompoc in California, then La Tuna, Texarkana, and then Phoenix. One version had three of us going to Terminal Island, outside of L.A., four to El Reno in Oklahoma, and me to Leavenworth. I had a very tight knot in my stomach. The possibilities seemed endless and universally darker than anything I'd yet encountered. As we discussed them, JC came up and sat in.

"They'll ship you to La Tuna," he soon asserted flatly, "and put you in the hole." He spoke with absolute authority, betraying irritation that anyone might be dumb enough to think otherwise.

"Have you been in the hole there?" I asked.

"Have I?" he chuckled. "Woowee, you're gonna love it." His amusement made it seem both dire and adventurous at the same time.

As the noon count approached, the conversation lapsed into bitching about the uncertainty and the waiting. Finally, Pineapple got up and said he was going up to the office to check for news.

He came running back five minutes later, whooping and jumping in the air. We rushed out to meet him. "We won," Pineapple screamed. "We won."

"What do you mean?"

"Washington called back. They ordered Kennedy to keep us here and bring Vane and Zack back on the next bus from La Tuna. We won."

◇

After celebrating for a bit with the others, I went back to my bunk and wrote a note to Joanie, telling her to ignore the letter I'd mailed two hours earlier. When I had finished, JC walked up, carrying the books I'd given him.

"I guess you'll want these back," he said.

"No, you keep em. I've got too many anyway."

JC appreciated the offer but put the books down on my bunk. "They're yours," he said, shaking his head.

"Keep them," I insisted. "It doesn't matter who has them. I can get em back if I need them."

"Come on, Harris. That's too much. There must be fifty books here."

"OK," I bargained. "I'll split em with you."

Looking back, I can see my insistence about the books as a measure of my impulse to connect with JC. He seemed something of a bull goose in a world where I still felt like a freshman. He cut a romantic figure, and I sensed that he possessed the missing elements to the person whom circumstances now demanded that I become.

For his part, JC recognized my gesture for the connection it was meant to be.

"You're on," he laughed, extending his palm for me to slap.

I slapped it, he sat down on Chimp's bunk next door, and I began to divide up the books. I can still remember JC sitting there, forearms on his knees. There was always something of the blunt instrument in his presence, whatever the posture. His prison-issue T-shirt was tight around the collar and the sleeves short enough to show the rose on his shoulder. He still seemed on top of everything, but was clearly astonished at what had gone on that morning. He said he'd never seen anything like it before.

"I don't believe it," he added, laughing. "They just gave you guys a fucking blank check."

My thirteen-year friendship with Joseph Howard Crampton had begun.

◊

My relationship with JC was unlikely from the beginning. On paper, it seemed as though we had come of age on two different planets. Four-and-a-half years older than me, Crampton was born at home, a converted chicken coop in Mt. Clements, Michigan, because his parents could not afford even the public maternity ward. His father, a former army enlisted man from Texas, never married his mother, an off-the-reservation Cherokee who ended up supporting her five children (by three different husbands) as a waitress and part-time prostitute. His father disappeared before he was two, and, at age six, JC himself ran away from home for the first time. When asked on a 1967 Bureau of Prisons Personal Data Sheet to indicate "Place or places where you spent boyhood and youth," he answered, "All over."

I lived my entire childhood in Fresno. I lived in a three-bedroom stucco house. Both my father and mother were lawyers; my older brother became a surgeon.

When JC was twelve, he came home from a camping trip to find that his mother had taken his brothers and sisters and disappeared. He was left to fend for himself. He was arrested not long after and charged with burglary. At the same age, I was a member of the Bobwhite Patrol, Boy Scout Troop 31. JC ended up in New Mexico, shuffling between orphanages, juvenile courts, and foster homes. At the Catholic institutions, the nuns razor-stropped him for wetting his bed. I won a football letter and was selected Fresno High's Boy of the Year; he stabbed a teacher in a classroom argument and was expelled from the eleventh grade as "incorrigible."

At seventeen, I went to Stanford; he enlisted in the 101st Airborne. At twenty, I was an honors student and Student Body President; he had already been discharged. He had been married and divorced, and was raising two children in Albuquerque, working in a garage. He was also dealing a little weed on the side.

In 1966, I had publicly returned my draft cards to the government, and, by 1968, I had become something of a symbol of resistance. That January, I refused an order to report for induction and in May, I was convicted of a felony violation of the Selective Service Act and sentenced to three years in prison. I had married Joan Baez in 1968 in New York City. While my conviction was being appealed, I travelled around the country, agitating for massive disobedience against the draft.

That phase of my life ended on July 15, 1969, when I was arrested. Joan was four months pregnant.

For JC, having grown up "born to lose," going to prison seemed almost a matter of course. For me, it was a more forbidding journey. I brought an intense agenda to my confinement. I wanted to prove I had what it took to be myself in a world of physical danger and deprivation, stripped of privilege and surrounded with intimidation. I wanted to prove I was my own man, capable of enduring the consequences of my acts without recantation, retreat, or regret. "Backing your action" is what we called it on the yard. Also "holdin your mud," "doin your number," and "gettin your shit down." Whatever the tagline, it seemed, at least in the abstract, an adventurous and inspired task. I was ripe, I can see now, for a best friend to go along with the new life I was leading.

My relationship with JC was just as unlikely when it ended. By then, I was thirty-six, an established journalist, a former Democratic Party candidate for Congress, the author of four books, and the owner of twenty-two credit cards. My wife and I had a penthouse in San Francisco, and a house in the suburbs. JC, forty, wore one diamond in his left ear and another in an incisor. He was an active suspect in simultaneous investigations by U.S. Customs, the Drug Enforcement Agency, the Federal Attorneys for both Los Angeles and

El Paso, the State of Oregon, the Royal Canadian Mounted Police, and the Bell Telephone Company's Security Division. He was reachable only through an answering service under the alias of Bob Brown. The unclaimed messages on the day after his death were from Bobo and Wolfman. Each said he intended to kill "Mr. Brown" if he didn't pay the money he owed. The prime suspect in his homicide told investigators that JC himself had bragged about committing as many as nine killings-for-hire in the last six months.

◇

JC and I spent most of sixteen months in each other's company in prison. After our separate releases, we put together the Peoples Union Coop Farm, a fantasy we had talked a lot about. Located in Raisin City, California, outside of Fresno where I'd grown up, the farm lasted until January 1974. I lived on the farm for its final six months.

◇

On its last legs, the Peoples Union Coop Farm still had to feed sixteen people. JC, Lamb, JC's four kids, my son Gabe, and I were all living in the main house; Pablo, Marvella, Sgt. Rock, Sgt. Rock's girlfriend, Jim Bowie, the Machine Gunner, Rob, and the urchin Bobby were spread between the various outbuildings. For most of December we had eaten on the proceeds of my last *Rolling Stone* assignment, but by Christmas that money was exhausted. There would be more coming when the sale of the farm went through, but just when that was going to happen was not altogether clear. JC worried, and the worry set his ulcer off. He spent the entire day after Christmas lying on his bed, drinking milk, and complaining about his stomach. He did the same thing for the next three days. By December 30, the tractor had been repossessed, PG&E had shut off the irrigation pump, and we were down to our last day's food. That morning, JC finally emerged from his bedroom. "I'm gonna go find some money," he said. He took Jim Bowie and drove off into the tule fog.

Two hours later, JC and Bowie returned to trade the pickup for the flatbed. They came back after dark with a load of railroad switches and twenty-foot lengths of rail. JC said they'd found the stuff piled up along the Santa Fe track outside Carruthers. It had been posted Private Property, but JC had decided it amounted to discarded scrap.

He set the Machine Gunner to work cutting up the rails with his acetylene torch.

The next morning, Bowie hauled everything that had been cut to the scrap dealer in Easton. He returned with $600. JC gave $200 to Lamb for groceries, and then disappeared into Fresno with the rest. There he began a series of small-time marijuana transactions. In three days, he tripled his money. While he was gone, a sheriff's cruiser pulled into the yard.

"Is this 8734 West Manning?" the deputy asked me when I went out to see what he wanted.

I said it was.

"I'm looking for a James Bowie. You know him?"

I said I did. "But he hasn't been around in a while," I lied. "This is a halfway house. We handle ex-convicts, Vietnam veterans, and referrals from the juvenile court in Fresno. Bowie used to live here, but I haven't seen him in a couple weeks."

"You in charge?"

"No," I answered. "A man named Crampton is in charge, but he's not here, either. He went to Fresno and won't be back till late."

"Who are you?"

"David Harris."

My name seemed to touch something in the deputy's memory. He scratched his head and looked around the yard. Most of it was heavily splattered with goose shit. "David Harris," he clicked. "Ain't you that Fresno boy who didn't go into the army and got married to that folk singer?"

"Used to be married to that folk singer," I corrected him.

"Well, what d'ya know. What're you doin out here?" The deputy's arm motioned at the gray landscape running off towards Emma's Feedlot and the Raisin City grocery store.

"I helped raise the money to start this place two years ago," I answered. "I've been livin here for the last six months. What's this all about, anyway?"

"I just want to talk to this Bowie fella about a load of scrap he sold down in Easton this mornin. Seems it belonged to the Santa Fe Railroad."

I felt fear and anger start in the pit of my stomach.

He looked at me. "You know anything about that load of scrap?" he asked.

"No, I don't," I said, furious at JC for putting me in this position and thinking about the uncut rails that were still lying out back. I tried to appear nonchalant.

After looking at me a while longer, the deputy took a card out of his pocket and handed it to me. "If you see this James Bowie, give me a call."

"Sure," I said, "I'll give you a call."

I watched the sheriff's car drive out past the Peoples Union Coop Farm sign and turn toward Kerman. When I was sure it was gone, I went back into the house, slamming the front door behind me, and stomped through the kitchen to the room Gabe and I shared. I was furious. I took a flying kick at one of the boxes of books I kept packed up while waiting for the farm to finally die. "God damn it," I screamed at the empty room. "God fucking damn it." Here I was, two months from twenty-eight years old, spending my time trying to keep from being busted by the sheriff for stealing pig iron from the railroad. This was not what I wanted from my life. It was not even close.

When my fury eased, I knew that when the farm closed down, I wasn't going to move to New Mexico with JC like he wanted.

I felt relieved at that decision, brewing for weeks now, but I still couldn't figure how to tell him our days as partners were over.

When he came back that evening, I casually mentioned the sheriff's visit. I didn't say how angry I'd been. JC immediately sent Bowie to Fresno to hide out for a few days and dispatched Rob, Sgt. Rock, and Little Joe to bury the rest of the stolen rails. They worked by lantern until 3:00 A.M. By then, Crampton had finished off another half gallon of milk and, saying how much better his stomach felt, had fallen asleep.

◊

On January 3, sale of the farm went through. JC cashed the check immediately, paid off most of our creditors, and reserved the rest as "travelling money." We had two weeks to vacate the premises. To honor the occasion, Crampton fried up a stack of round steaks and the last of the summer's onion crop. Afterward, he and I walked out to the alfalfa field together. It was an uncommonly clear night and the moon was almost full. When we reached the end of the field, we turned around and stood looking back at the house.

"Well, Hareese," JC said, "it's all over now." He motioned at the squares of light and vague silhouettes in the distance. "No more Peoples Union Coop Farm."

"No more Peoples Union Coop Farm," I echoed.

JC scuffed at the dirt with his work boots. "We never stood a chance," he said. "It was just a jailhouse fantasy."

That's not so, I said to myself. It could have worked if you hadn't run it with a wad of bills in your pocket. If you'd kept books, planned, and played it close to the vest. It would have worked. When it came down to it, you singlehandedly managed the farm into an economic grave. "It's all history now," is all I said out loud.

"You're not comin with us to New Mexico, are you?" JC asked suddenly.

"No," I answered. "I'm not. I think I'll try my luck with Pablo and Marvella up in San Francisco."

"What're you gonna do?"

I shrugged. "Try and make it with my typewriter."

"I knew it," JC laughed, grabbing my arm with one hand and punching it with the other. To him, such body language was an affectionate tap, but it still sent a jolt through me. "Fuckin Harris," he jibed.

"What?"

"I knew you wouldn't come. From the first time I mentioned New Mexico, I knew."

"How'd you know?" I asked defensively.

He laughed again. "Come on, Harris. How long have we been friends? I know you. You're straight, David. You always have been. Things like the sheriff comin by freak you out."

Embarrassment emerged on my face and JC saw it right away.

"Busted you, didn't I?" he chortled. "That sheriff freaked you out. I knew it did. You wonder what people will think, what will happen to you. You're not gonna wander off to New Mexico. You're different than me. Face it."

"I've done a few weird things over the years."

"I know you have, David. I saw a lot of them myself. But you're still straight, believe me. And you know what's even stranger than that? You're supposed to be. You wouldn't be Harris if you weren't. It's all right. I love you anyway."

I gave in and laughed. I felt my eyes get wet. In the glow of the moon, I could see light reflecting off his as well.

"So we can still be friends?" I asked.

"Come on, Harris. You know that. We're friends till the wheels fall off."

◊

JC and I stayed in touch. After New Mexico, he spent six months wandering up through the Yukon to Alaska. He returned to California and settled with his burgeoning family near Tomales Bay. We did not communicate at all during 1976, even though we were within a two-hour drive of each other. I was running for Congress, and it was agreed that my relationship with JC ought to go underground during the course of the campaign. After losing the election, I returned to journalism and began writing for the New York Times Maga-*zine. Our friendship came out of the woodwork at the same time. At the end of August 1977, I took an assignment to write about marijuana smugglers. It seemed only natural to accompany JC to Oaxaca to watch him do business.*

◊

JC, Carlos, and I spent the siesta hours of September 2 in our room at the Hotel Margarita. It had three beds and orange walls. Carlos slept. JC closed his eyes a couple of times but never nodded off. Mostly, he sat on his bed with his arms folded across his chest. We were waiting. JC had an air of irritation about him that tightened the skin around his cheekbones and drew his eyes into a squint.

When JC went outside "to get some air," I joined him. The giant avocado tree in the courtyard was full of birds fleeing the storm on the way from Tehuantepec. Instinctively, JC and I fell into pacing the courtyard together as if it were a prison compound.

"Well, Harris," he asked when we'd turned under the racket of the avocado tree, "you gettin a good story?"

"It's great stuff."

"You think the *New York Times* will really print all this?"

"They sent me down here," I shrugged.

Though he hated the very idea of New York and had never even seen a copy of the *Times,* the paper's professional interest in him and what he was doing pleased him. He definitely took this interest personally. "If you liked what we've been doin so far," he said, "tonight'll blow your mind. These guys we're meeting are far out."

"This is that Cuban you told me about?"

"He'll be there, with a whole bunch of Indians carryin guns."

My palms started to sweat. This kind of hardcore danger was out of my league and I knew it. "You think there'll be trouble?" I asked.

JC grinned. "No problem, David," he said sarcastically. "You just show the Federales your press pass. Tell em you ran for Congress. They'll understand."

He laughed and I got embarrassed.

◇

We headed for the mountains, JC driving the LTD rented in my name, Carlos following in a rented van. JC was carrying a .38 in his boot, Carlos a .45. I had my notebook on my lap.

JC was grinning and full of energy. "Going out on the edge," I scribbled as we turned onto the dirt one-lane near the *mescal* village. I couldn't see my hand in the darkness so my writing wandered across the page. "JC thrives on it. I, however," I wrote, "am nervous."

"Nervous" was a decided understatement. I held my breath every time we rounded a blind curve. Each time I discovered the Federales weren't waiting on the other side I let out a sigh of relief. Finally, JC pulled the LTD over on the shoulder and killed the lights.

"It's on foot from here," JC said.

I let out another breath.

"You asked for it," he laughed.

"I guess I did."

Suddenly, JC moved his head closer to mine and dropped his humorous tone. "Don't worry," he said in a half-whisper. "I won't let anything happen to you, Harris. This is a piece of cake." He punched my arm and got out of the car.

I stayed close to him as we started along a footpath leading down the slope. Carlos was in the lead with a flashlight. There was a smell of approaching rain in the air. After a few minutes, we reached a clearing in the underbrush and a small adobe hut. Several armed figures stepped out of the darkness. Two had shotguns, the rest just had machetes. They all looked like village Zapotecs. I could feel their eyes.

"Mucho gusto," Carlos opened.

The lead figure took Carlos' offered hand. *"Mucho gusto,"* he answered.

Carlos asked in Spanish if Jesus was around. We were directed into the hut. The darkness inside was broken by several candles stuck to a small table. The Indian Jesus was squatted against the back wall next to another man. JC and Carlos exchanged greetings with Jesus. JC was as relaxed as he was in his own kitchen. Then he tumed to me. I was stooping to avoid the roof beams. "*Sta mi amigo,* David," JC told the Indian. "He's one of us."

Jesus nodded at me and then motioned at the man next to him. "*Sta mi amigo, El Cubano.*" The Cuban was dressed like a Zapotec. His skin was mocha-colored and he had a thick mustache. I nodded, wondering what a Cuban was doing in the Sierra Madre del Sur. JC and Carlos squatted across from Jesus and the Cuban. I squatted behind JC's right shoulder.

"Tell him we're after *sin semilla,*" JC said to Carlos. "No seeds. We want number one leaf, the kind with the red hairs on it."

Carlos did as he was told. Jesus answered that he had fifty kilos left. He wanted $220 American a kilo.

JC said he wanted to see the goods first. The Indian called out an order in Zapotec. A cardboard box was brought in. Jesus opened it for JC. The box was full of marijuana tops, tied into neatly bound bundles. JC extracted one of the tops and held it up to the light, examining it thoroughly. Everyone looked at him. Suddenly, he turned to me; everyone's eyes shifted with him. I cringed. I had been trying to meld into the shadows, but Crampton wanted to give me the full treatment. "What d'ya think?" he asked me. A trace of amusement crossed his face as he passed the marijuana cluster.

I shifted nervously in my squat and took the top. It smelled piney. I studied it in the light, playing my role, and handed it back. I tried to say "looks good," but the words stuck in my dry throat.

I had to repeat myself. I dropped the top when I passed it. Several buds fell off.

The Cuban snickered.

JC swept it up and turned to Jesus, "Two hundred a kilo and I'll take it," he said.

"Two twenty," Jesus insisted. They went back and forth, Carlos translating. I watched the Cuban. His eyes were shifting back and forth between JC and myself. I thought maybe he knew I didn't belong and wondered why I was there. When his eyes met mine, I looked back at the conversation between JC and Jesus.

"Two ten and I'll throw this in," Crampton offered. He pulled the .38 out of his boot. There was a moment of high electricity the second he moved. It evaporated when he extended the weapon, butt first. Jesus held the pistol up to the light, had a rapid-fire conversation in Spanish with the Cuban, and then agreed to the deal.

The Indians from outside brought in five identical boxes. Carlos checked to make sure they were the same goods as the first. JC took a roll of bills out of his other boot and counted out $11,000 in twenties, fifties, and hundreds.

Afterward, there was handshaking all around and I was included.

The Indians led us back to our cars and stashed the boxes in the van. It had started drizzling.

By the time we'd reached the Tehuantepec highway, it had turned into rain.

"The rain's a good sign," JC commented. "The fuckin Mexicans don't run roadblocks in this kinda weather. They don't wanta get wet."

I lit a cigarette and said a silent prayer for continued rain. Carlos' headlights seemed glued to our back window.

Halfway back to Oaxaca, JC pulled off the highway and followed the road shoulder to a one-lane dirt track. Vicencio's house was the first one we came to. While Carlos and JC went inside and paid off Vicencio and loaded out the van, I stayed in the LTD. Vicencio's *mota* was cut into two-foot branches and stashed in burlap sacks. Rain was still thumping on the car's roof. "1:35 A.M.," I scribbled in my notebook. "JC still sailing along. I'm fading. Tension like weight. No sign of Federales."

Our LTD led the van back toward Oaxaca. In the city, we came abreast of a police car stopped at a red light. I froze in my seat. JC, looking every inch the hippie smuggler he was, rolled down his window and waved at the cops.

They waved back.

"What'd I tell ya," he said, "a piece of cake."

I sucked on the joint. "Right," I finally sighed. "A piece of cake."

We were back at the Margarita by 5:00 and asleep five minutes later. My dreams were full of candlelit adobes and mysterious Cubans.

◊

Doing that story together set the context for the rest of our relationship. I became JC's chronicler. He would call me regularly and let me know what he was doing. Every once in a while, I visited his house on Tomales Bay. It was his golden period. He was making lots of money, and everything seemed to be going right. In the spring of 1978, he put together a scam to bring in a ten-ton load from Colombia. Had it come off, it would have catapulted him into the realm of major dealers. Instead, it fell apart and JC seemed to fall apart with it. On February 22, 1982, JC was shot to death in the house of his nineteen-year-old girlfriend. His killer was her sister's boyfriend, a twenty-two-year-old ex-marine. I handled the arrangements after JC's death.

◊

By Wednesday evening, I was reasonably sure that I had compiled a complete list of the assets in his estate. The list was dominated by automobiles. The first was a '71 Pontiac Firebird, up on blocks next to his house. Its engine, hood, front bumper, and all four wheels already had been sold. The second was a '73 Buick convertible on which JC still owed $2,500. It was parked near the Firebird with a cracked engine block and a burnt-out starter. An almost identical '74 Buick convertible, owned free and clear, was at Joe's Performance Towing Yard in Santa Rosa, compromised by a mechanic's lien and the fact that JC had never bothered to register it. The only car that was actually legal *and* running was the fourth one, the '72 wood-paneled Plymouth station wagon he'd driven over to his girlfriend's house late Monday afternoon. He still owed $2,000 on it.

The Sheriff's Department had $300 cash found in JC's wallet, a sandwich bag of marijuana from the Plymouth's glove compartment, and the Nikon camera JC had brought back from Jamaica in January. The rest of his estate included three pedigreed pit bulls, several Zapotec rugs, a .38 Smith and Wesson revolver, a packing crate full of clothes, and a cardboard box of what JC called "antiques." Among the latter were a leatherbound 1897 copy of *Little Journeys to the Homes of Famous Women,* a brass railroad lamp, a piece of fossilized mastodon bone, and several sets of shark jaws. If they could be sold, the whole lot would be worth maybe $200.

When his children called around 9:00 P.M., I ran the list past them to see if there was anything of value that I had left out.

"The diamond."

"The diamond?"

"The one in his tooth."

"Right," I said. "The one in his tooth."

◇

I arrived at the Chapel of the Roses, a pink stucco imitation-Tudor funeral parlor in Santa Rosa at 10:00 A.M. on Thursday. I asked the receptionist to speak with Mr. Weidow, the manager. "The name's Harris," I explained. "I have an appointment regarding the Crampton body."

The receptionist buzzed Weidow on the intercom. He emerged from the door behind her. He was five-and-a-half feet tall, balding, with a brown mustache. He wore a brown-checked coat and a brown-striped bow tie. The bow tie tended to move up and down with his Adam's apple. In the privacy of his paneled office, Mr. Weidow sat behind the imitation French antique desk. I sat on one of the imitation antique chairs across from him. The carpet was beige.

I reminded him that, as I'd mentioned on the phone, I was a reporter with the *New York Times Magazine* and an "old friend of the Crampton family." I claimed to have "lost touch" with Crampton himself "over the last few years." The "lost touch" part was largely a lie, but I hoped that, at least in the mortician's eyes, it would distance me some from JC's growing reputation.

Weidow smiled consolingly. "Of course," he murmured. His profession required him to agree a lot and Weidow seemed well practiced.

The family, I continued, had asked me to represent them in their dealings with the Chapel of the Roses. They also wished me to look at the body before it was sent for cremation.

"You understand," Weidow inquired, "the remains are in a state we consider *unviewable?*"

"I understand."

The mortician's voice dropped to evoke confidentiality. "All our head wounds are that way," he explained.

"I can see where they would be," I said. Nonetheless, "the family did not feel it was right" that the body be destroyed without someone who knew Crampton at least seeing him off. It had been agreed that I ought to be that someone.

"Of course," Weidow agreed. "Of course." His bow tie jerked as he cleared his throat.

At the end of the hall, Weidow unlocked a solid door.

The embalming room had a high ceiling. It was lit with banks of buzzing fluorescent lights. The walls were painted pale green. JC was on the gurney closest to the door. He was laid out on his back in a gray plastic body bag. The top third of the bag was unzipped, revealing his head, shoulders, and upper chest. Weidow retreated several paces.

Looking at my dead friend this way was a scene I'd been imagining almost as long as I'd known him. I had assumed the moment would be emotional, but it wasn't. I only felt a distant visual curiosity and the strong sensation of having been through it before.

JC's "unviewable" aspect was on the left side of his head. The coroner had cut out a crater of hair around the entry wound. The rest of him appeared untouched. A single bullet had apparently shattered into fragments after impact, bouncing back and forth inside his brain cavity. Only three of the fragments had exited, and the marks they left were inconspicuous. Massive bleeding inside his skull had turned his eye sockets purple. His skin had started to go waxy. Other than that, he just looked shrunken and vacant.

I cleared my throat and turned to Weidow.

"I have . . . uh . . . a problem," I hemmed. "I thought perhaps you might be able to . . . help me with it."

"Of course."

"Well," I stammered, turning back to the body, "you see, Mr. Crampton had a diamond in one of his teeth."

Weidow's tie began to move.

I reached my hand over to JC's upper right incisor and used my fingertip to rub off the film of blood. My touch caused the pool of fluid inside JC to slosh. Several bubbles of trapped gas rose to the surface of his mouth. The diamond looked dull, but it was large enough to be worth something. It was a small white stone set in a circle of gold.

"I see," Weidow murmured.

"Crampton called it his insurance," I tried to explain.

The mortician's face went blanker than normal.

A fly landed on JC's forehead. I watched it for a moment, trying to recapture my momentum. "He wasn't quite broke when he died," I finally continued, "but he was close. That jewel would mean a lot in terms of his kids' future."

Weidow's eyes tightened as he sensed the question I was about to ask.

I blurted it out: "Think you guys could pop that tooth for me?"

Weidow's tie froze at the peak of an upstroke. It stayed there until he had re-composed his face. "We don't do that kind of thing here. I'm afraid there are no exceptions."

I looked at the pale green wall, trying to figure out what to do.

"Perhaps you could find a dentist," Weidow suggested.

I ignored his suggestion. "How hot does the oven get," I asked.

"Pardon?"

"The cremation process. How hot is it?"

He said he thought it was several thousand degrees.

"OK," I said. "Send him to the crematorium. The diamond shouldn't burn. I'll find it at the other end."

The mortician cleared his throat several times, visualizing me sifting through the ashes. "Of course," he rasped politely. "As you wish."

◇ JOSHUA FREIWALD ◇

The Secluded Garden

Richard packed up some more dirt yesterday and has most of it in place; some apportioning and compacting remains before planting, but the difficult part — packing those two yards of dirt up the stairs in buckets to level the slope — is done. The little pond even has water in it. Though most of the brick work above the old concrete water trough Mrs. DeMasi built is new, it already has that patina on it that speaks of age and change. The edges have been softened, and old leaves are scattered everywhere. The garden already has the look of an old and faded photograph, like one of Atget's Paris park photographs, like one of those pictures he took at Versailles, or at Saint-Cloud and Sceaux. . . .

There's a similar sense that someone was here in my garden tending to things long before I came and that the garden, like those decaying classical gardens, was made, no, composed a very long time ago, in another era, in a brighter era, out of a wholly different set of values and sensibilities. Now that the work is in disrepair, it has lost much of its vigor and magnificence. But enough splendor remains to cause in the viewer a bit of consternation and a sense of wonder as to who it was who left these marks with such a disarming sense of elegance and style. . . .

My own garden is minuscule, a mere postage stamp, 20-odd paces long by 20-odd paces wide. But it shares with those magnificent old gardens that sense of being present in the past. There's a delicacy to the fabric, a sense of something fading; the air seems to quiver in the sunlight. The garden seems to mirror my soul. It seems to open up the possibility of introspection and understanding. I find it so attrac-

◇ *Joshua Freiwald is a photographer of architecture. He lives in Los Angeles.*

tive, so touching, so sad; it voices for me a galactically silent lament for the man I could have been.

The lovely pond at the center of the garden, not more than five or six feet in diameter, contains my water lilies and reflects the old poplar tree at the edge of my neighbor's property. The poplar gives evidence of time having passed and contributes to the sense I have of a place forlorn and abandoned. . . .

I find myself inclined to wander about like a taster sampling fine wines, feeling then again more like an intruder or a trespasser. I sample the riches of my garden, like a thief, fearful of losing these delicious moments, of upsetting its delicate balance and lovely fragility. When the poplar is seen in the pool, between the lily pads and ripples, it becomes like an old hag shaking in a tattered dress, disfigured but harmless. Late in the day, the sun backlights the old tree and turns its heart-shaped leaves a bright green, and the breeze, which usually comes up about four, causes them to flutter like butterflies.

As the water in the pond becomes murkier and fills with debris and fallen leaves and perhaps with more lily pads, it will take on still another dimension. The stillness, the sadness, and the calm will get richer and more profound. Why I'm so enchanted with these considerations and contradictions I hardly know. Perhaps such a setting is only the setting for a transcendental fiction in the eye of the beholder. It is perhaps only the ancient dream of a gifted storyteller. . . .

◇

It's another of those incredibly beautiful, breezeless mornings. Yesterday I didn't manage to leave: I got caught up with phone calls and busy work and with aimlessly wandering about. It was not that I did anything, I didn't prune or water or weed anything, but by the time I looked it was four o'clock and the breeze was up as usual and the sun was behind the old poplar turning it emerald green. This tiny garden is beginning to obsess me; the obsession seems to be growing, deepening; I continue to find myself fascinated by it, by its mutability, and I can't get used to all its different aspects, how it changes and is changed by the light. Each hour here is different, even each minute. Now, at just after eight, the wisteria and the daisies are spotlighted; the light on the reflecting pool is still soft and the lily pads seem

suspended in black space. The water, though now brackish, is absolutely still. In another hour, as the sun gets higher, the one iris in
flower and the other about to flower will be illuminated; their blue
petals, the blue of promise and of forgiveness, the blue of the Virgin's
mantle, will open like a smile and they'll curtsy to each other and to
me and to the light.

It's these soft, warm mornings that I find so delicious; their beauty
is infectious and disabling. It's like being sucked into a spider's web.
There's an intimacy here, such an infinite pleasure in just *seeing;* it is as
if I had taken a lover. . . .

Denny said the other morning that the garden reminded her of the
Villa d'Este, or the Medici gardens at Fiesole, that what was common
to my garden and the Italian gardens of the hill country was a sense of
intimacy and seclusion. My garden, she said, felt like a private
preserve, a cloister, or a secret grotto. She understood too, she said,
that the pond is crucial to the opacity of the place, indeed everything
in the garden depends on it. It's the female element in an otherwise
masculine world, shaded by those luxurious pepper trees, their
branches hanging down like willow trees, almost touching it. . . .

In a sense it doesn't matter if she's right or not, whether my garden
approaches other finer, more luxurious gardens of the past. It's her
response that counts: it's that desire for a cloister and the cloister itself
that she recognized and responded to and needed to define for
herself. Such a sanctuary, unkempt and paltry as mine unquestionably
is, is perhaps more understandable in these brutal and atavistic times:
The garden, with its myriad of conflicting details all needing attention
and cultivation, seems so much more civilizing in a barbarous age.
Without question it becomes a necessary refuge away from an anony-
mous and restive crowd, which has a difficult time understanding and
appreciating authenticity, and usually doesn't until it's too late. The
gardener, like the modern artist, becomes a medieval monk, the
immemorial recluse, or a seeker like Baudelaire or Monet or like
Walter Benjamin himself, a supplicant willing to acknowledge and
accept entropy but unable to participate in the savagery. . . .

The price the gardener pays for the loveliness of his refuge and for
his desire to garden is high, for in the process of perfecting his garden
he condemns himself to loneliness and irrelevance in an age that
needs his learning and expertise, his ability to see and attend to detail.
Perhaps it was this *slippage away* that most informed Monet's last

works. As his old friend Clemenceau remarked, "A moment came when what he was doing was no longer painting; he had left painting behind. It was a kind of escape. . . . He should have lived another ten years: then we would no longer have understood anything of what he was doing; there might no longer have been anything on his canvases."

The Chinese, however, have always understood that old men make better gardeners than painters.

◇

My neighbor's cypresses, five in all, each about six feet tall and not quite a foot in circumference, are also critical to my sense of seclusion and sanctuary. The cypresses frame the view to the south, towards Bernal Heights, the airport and Mount San Bruno. They seem like statues of Roman centurions standing at an ancient gate. Their martial presence is reassuring and protective. . . .

Between these young cypresses and the southernmost pepper tree next to the lily pond is an old wire fence marking the southern border of the garden. It has some ivy on it and an old bougainvillea vine about to flower, which surely Mrs. DeMasi planted when she planted the rose bushes against the west wall. Yesterday while watering it I came across a single deep red crimson flower and this morning, from where I sit on the brick patio under the deck with my writing pad and coffee, I detect some other deep red flowers all clustered together forming an almost solid patch of vivid hot color and giving my garden yet another dimension.

◇

It isn't necessary for me to venture out anymore except to purchase some more water lilies, which will complete the reflecting pool and provide more shelter for my tiny goldfish, who are vulnerable to the depredations of the raccoons who seem to wander the neighborhood at night and at times stray into my garden, vandalizing it while looking for something to eat. In the dark hours, I've heard them splashing around in the pond trying to catch the goldfish. In the morning I'd find the goldfish still healthy, the lily pads would have been chewed up, no doubt in frustration.

A stranger came by the other day and suggested some papyrus for the pond, Egyptian papyrus I believe she said, not as a foil for the raccoons but to accompany the flowering water lilies. It's a marvelous idea I'll have to look into.

It's another of those lovely, quiet mornings and I'm taking my coffee once again in my garden. The city surrounding me seems unusually quiet; the usual early morning sounds of garbage trucks and buses have for some reason disappeared. It's unbelievably clear: Mount San Bruno to the south is a pastel blue; the Bay to the east sparkles; Mount Diablo is itself a pale blue, and, though a good 40 miles away, seems to tower over the hazy brown East Bay hills, dwarfing them and making them seem mean or inconsequential. . . .

The patch of dichondrea Richard planted only 10 days ago is already coming up like the stubble of a green beard and in a matter of another week or two the patch should be totally green and cover the remaining bare ground. It's all so magical and sensuous. I'm taken with the variety and textures of things and find them satisfying, even delicious. Even the old Chinese red bougainvillea I had given up for lost a year ago is in leaf and in flower: it looks so fragile and perishable that I would hesitate to touch it.

Of course I should have made such a paradise years ago. Ten years ago I planted an acacia at the east edge of the patio. And the pepper tree on the west edge is another testimonial to my early attempts to make a garden. The brick patio itself, put in when I built the deck for the upstairs, is another early effort. But it has not been until now that I could find the time, or the energy and purpose, to put it all together and to apply those necessary final touches.

Much of the garden comes from remnants or relics left to me by the previous owners of the house. The old brick walkway I discarded completely, the potting shed became the bedroom, and the rose bushes against the west wall I replaced with ivy. All these abandoned forms and the various arrangements of flowers and things inherited and borrowed from others, plants and trees, the debris from another's vision of a perfect garden, became fused together when I leveled the existing slope to the back fence, planted the pepper trees, and made the lily pond from the old concrete water trough left me by the DeMasis, who built the house and a garden behind it in 1929, when there wasn't much else on the hill besides a few Irish shanties and Mayor Rolff's cozy Victorian cottage for his mistress way up at the crest of the hill. It was Mrs. DeMasi who was interested in gardening.

She planted the roses against the west wall and the iris bulbs which perennially flower between what is now the patio and the new or, say, rejuvenated lily pond, built and retained perhaps in deference to her. In all likelihood the blazing red bougainvillea is hers too. . . .

Yet with all this planning and accomplishment it's still difficult to understand myself as a gardener. Even in this still early light, surrounded as I am by what is obviously a wonderful garden, it is still difficult to be or to think of myself as a gardener, a tiller of the soil. In fact, of course, I'm not really a gardener at all, or the type of gardener I am is one with a peculiarly monastic or reclusive bent, which quite possibly changes the terms of the gardening and makes of it a means to another end. Quite possibly I am a man who is only secondarily a gardener, a gardener perhaps like Mr. Jefferson — one who gardens not so much for the joy of seeing things grow, but more for the joy of simply *seeing*.

◇

Perhaps it's this combination of things found and things old and new that lends the garden this feeling of wistfulness or poignancy that makes me sad at the prospect of losing it or seeing it change and an uneasiness with being in it at the same time. Perhaps it's an innate uneasiness with tranquillity, an anxiety that's caused by the unfamiliar sounds of birds and trickling water and the wind in the trees. Maybe it's something else which disquiets and worries me, something in me that I find troubling and intrusive and causes me to fear for this tiny piece of paradise and for myself: it's that I may be unworthy of it or unable to appreciate its content or its depth. There are times when I prowl my garden like a caged animal, going round and round the lily pond like a big cat, as if I could by prowling walk off what troubles me. Often I think of myself as not deserving such a place of refinement and I fear that this period of reconciliation and harmony which seems so much a product and so much a part of my garden will come to a sudden end when I'm discovered for what I am — an animal corrupted by luxury and a coward.

I often think of myself as being rather gross or crude, with rough, red prehensile hands, hands shaped more like talons, long and boney, with sharp curved fingernails made for grasping not touching, hands incapable of soothing or stroking. There are moments when it seems I was thrust out into the world without a childhood and without an innocence or with only a small frail innocence which too quickly hardened into stone and was too quickly cast away. It would seem that I was ill-prepared and uneducated in matters of gardening, in matters of finesse or refinement; that I had to make do with what paltry talents I had, and an inhuman and unrelenting drive, which I reluctantly admit has served me well and earned for me this little sliver of paradise I now enjoy. I often regret the baseness of my approach: the harshness and ruthlessness with which I dealt with others, the animal cunning which kept me from danger, the instinct for the kill, my lightness of foot, my deft hands and nimble fingers, the quickness, the agility, the alacrity of a cat, and the raw ugly power of a predator.

I'm sure, no, certain that at the beginning I came equipped with talons and fangs or grew them in early childhood. I would have preferred a great gentleness and a disarming charm. It would have been better if I had had more of a sense of decency and tact, a sensitivity to matters of the heart, an understanding of art and literature and science. Often I've longed for composure and for a reconciliation with my intemperance, and to be finally sated and at peace. I have missed most of all, in the awful monomaniacal climb to perfection and power which has absorbed me, a great love that might have lessened my discontent and cured my narcissism. I would have preferred to see beauty and grace in others and to be able to use terms of affection when dealing with them. I could have been empathic instead of angry. I could have been tender or simply kind instead of selfish and harsh. Instead I was set loose as a rapacious and brutal beast, an animal with the capacity to tear, to rip, to rend, and to let blood with an improbable and sure swiftness.

I understand it may be impossible to sheathe my destructiveness though I no longer need the weapons of the hunter or the skills of the driven. The mantle of gentility I crave is perhaps unassumable. It doesn't matter that I have arranged my garden with sweetness and light, with bird songs, wisteria, and water lilies. I am as Monet was and so many others who couldn't cast off their armor or put down their weapons though they were tired of battle and impatient for something else. Monet's hands were surely like mine, rough, thick, caked with dirt and nicotine. He, too, certainly, had arranged his gardens with an infinite patience and a gentle loving hand only to discover it was too late, the past couldn't be recaptured. His innocence and naïveté were lost forever, and he carried with him to the end the taint of his ambition and the blind passion of his anger and rage.

There are moments when the garden becomes a cage, when it becomes more a bastion or a bunker and when it isolates rather than edifies. At these moments the kind of self-preservation inherent in the act of gardening becomes torture and deprivation. The keeper, the kept, and the gardener seem to become in the course of time the same person: they are all ill at ease with their solitude, impatient with their confinement, resentful of the terms of their internment and unreconciled to their cage and at having to be kept at all. Because the terms of imprisonment are self-imposed, for good reasons, they seem horribly just. I seem to carry under my expensive and stained coat the putrid odor of the jungle I came from just yesterday. There's no concealing the awful stench and no kid gloves can cover my claws.

It's therefore possible at times to misconstrue the signs of the garden, to mistake guilt for melancholia and memory. It's possible to equate the garden with an ancient paradise and with all innocence, when it's not that at all, or only that in part.

Whatever it is, the garden is something profound, perhaps more dream than memory, more desire than satisfaction. It could be that the garden in its essential purity can never be recaptured. Or that it is now being reclaimed, as it should be, from the ugly and restive crowd standing at its gate.

Renewing the Edge

If you start from Los Angeles, there are two ways into Death Valley, like the two gates of Virgil's underworld. The first you enter by heading north from Mojave as if you were ski-bent for Mammoth, then taking a right at Olancha; the other takes you past tiny places with hopeful names like Johannesburg and Randsburg, then up the middle of the Panamint Valley by way of the moonscape mining town of Trona, owned lock, stock, and air pollution by Kerr-McGee. You'll have to decide for yourself which is the ivory gate and which the horn gate, the gate of false dreams and the gate of true.

The turn at Olancha is about 20 miles longer than the way through Trona. It's also about half an hour faster and has a lot more traffic. Along the way, you can see Red Rock Canyon, the Red Hill cinder dome, and Fossil Falls. You can also stop at the Ranch House Café for an Indian Fry-Bread Sandwich with a side of Sheepherder Potatoes and some iced tea. The Trona route lacks native road-food and officially designated natural wonders, but I like it better. It's lonelier, more in keeping with the mysteries of Death Valley, where the lines between the false dreams and the true are fuzzier—like trying to decide whether the desert is empty or full.

In 1960, on my first brief trip to California as a teenager, I could see the desert only as absence. After a visit to Forest Lawn, and a bus ride to Escondido, I wrote a poem about the heat and the emptiness. (Now it would have to be about condos and shopping centers.) The last line was "My name is death and I live in southern California." It was a bit of posturing that suited my teenage sensitivities. But my

◇ Leo Braudy is Leo S. Bing Professor of Literature at the University of Southern California. His collection of essays Native Informant was recently published by Oxford University Press.

mother, I later discovered, took that lugubrious sentiment to heart. In her last years, after I had moved to Los Angeles, she refused even to visit. Death, no respecter of geographic or poetic niceties, found her out in Philadelphia anyway.

While I still lived in the East—first New York and then Baltimore—seven years teaching summer school in Santa Barbara helped me see southern California with more sympathetic eyes. Just as my mother used to tell me the names of the plants and trees as we walked through Valley Forge or Fairmount Park, I dutifully spent time in the Mission Canyon Botanical Garden and learned the names of the indigenous flora. But I forgot them quickly. They weren't the stories I wanted to hear. It was the desert that really drew me, and I began to see it more clearly for itself, not as the absence of a lush eastern greenness built up through time, but as the presence of immense space, in which vegetation was a grace note, accenting shape and holding out the possibility of survival.

Jammed with flora and fauna from all over the world, southern California is quintessentially the *premeditated* landscape, a transparent creation of human desire, and its short history forcibly summarizes a good deal of the "progress" of the last several hundred years: man imposes himself and his needs on nature. Yet there's always a price to pay. Since Greece and Rome, city people have longed for the refreshing otherness of the green world. But the desert represents a different alternative to the City: not the leafy pastoral idyll, but emptiness, barrenness, the Zone Between.

On the way to Death Valley, even before you get to Trona, there are rock-strewn fields with a sense of purpose and inevitability enhanced by the light, as if in this barrenness we can more easily read nature's message. Unlike the shrouding vegetation of the East, which cries for a transcendental interpretation, the clear face of this skeletal earth, streaked with mineral colors, implies that we are close to its secrets. Every passing human speaker seems impelled to lay a name or a story upon the bare rocks and sweeping vistas. Words cling to the niches, notches, cracks, and crevasses like mountain goats, epitaphs and assertions in search of some foothold, some explanation. Already, along the narrow road south of Trona, amid sharp, shaggy rocks delicately painted to suggest sea monsters or dragons crouched on the desert floor, are the petroglyphs of the present—"Shawn Loves Kim,"

"Trona High Class of 87" — trying to absorb some permanence from the earth.

The history of Death Valley is filled with such doomed attempts to make sense of the land. As Mary Austin wrote about a nearby collection of miners' shacks in *The Land of Little Rain*, "Jimville does not know a great deal about the crust of the earth, it prefers a 'hunch'. . . . I have never heard that the failure of any particular hunch disproved the principle. Somehow the rawness of the land favors the sense of personal relation to the supernatural."

The prime secret that drew the first enthusiasts to Death Valley was of course just such a hunch — about the treasures that lurked below the surface. There is something of pure democratic America in gold and silver mining. With luck anyone could go from being nothing to being rich. Unfortunately for the dream, Death Valley had none of the just-stick-your-pan-in-the-stream gold of the Mother Lode. Even when discoveries were made, wood and water and railroads were needed to make even reasonable profits — hardly a romantic proposition. The real mineral money in Death Valley was made from unromantic borax, the household helper. Almost in compensation the stories of "lost" mines kept blossoming: untold riches, if you only knew — or remembered — where to look.

Lighting his cigars with $10 bills and talking of secret gold mines, "Death Valley Scotty," who had once performed in Buffalo Bill Cody's Wild West Show, was the most famous of the con men, speculators, and erstwhile historians who exploited the desire to "know" Death Valley by laying their own names and stories on the landscape. Going far beyond the mixture of hard luck stories and glittering fantasies that raised the stakes in local saloons and in the romantic thoughts of armchair investors, Scotty managed to collect an entourage of admiring reporters who funneled his exploits directly into their big city newspapers. Wyatt Earp had migrated to Hollywood not long before, and silent westerns were filled with cowboy extras who were happy to make a few dollars while the herds were in winter quarters. If "pioneers" like Scotty were still alive and kicking, the reasoning seemed to be, then the Old West wasn't dead after all. Even after he was exposed as a total fraud, his stories still charmed his listeners. His biggest backer was a Chicago mining speculator and insurance executive named Albert M. Johnson, who spent a few million, mostly pre-Depression dollars to build what he called the

Death Valley Ranch, but which everyone else, then and now, calls "Scotty's Castle."

Scotty learned a lot from the early boom-town atmosphere of Los Angeles, and he taught a few lessons as well. But the urge to make your own story out of Death Valley began much earlier, in the often fraudulent guidebooks carried by pioneers; in the U.S. survey maps that misplaced mountain ranges, raised valleys, and found water with cartographic ink rather than dowsing rods. Today's names tell many of the same stories: of natural features (Salt Creek), prospector whimsy (The Devil's Golf Course), personal memorial (Aguereberry Point), and literary pretentiousness (Dante's View).

Even if you can't tell a tufa from a tule, everyone seems to want to tell a story, or be in one, about Death Valley. At best, the anthropologists estimate, Death Valley supported 100 Indians. Now up to 30,000 tourists turn up for the long weekends of the annual forty-niner encampment and the yearly total approaches three-quarters of a million. In the books and pamphlets that fill the shelves in the Death Valley Museum you can find enshrined the naturalist's Death Valley, the geologist's, the ethnologist's, the western historian's, the nostalgia buff's — each adding a few grains to the same experiences, tall tales, facts, and myths. There's even an "archaeology of litter" that allows us to determine when a particular bottle was dropped in the waste — by the nature of the glass, the way the bottle cap was attached, and what material it was made of.

Thinking about the Valley's enigmatic rock formations and its many petroglyphs, I wondered if the Indians might have responded to a similar necessity. Bruce Chatwin in *Songlines* talks about the immense pattern of songs and myths by which the Aboriginals, without any written language, map Australia. Geologists have noticed some places in the Panamints where the rocks have been altered into semi-geometrical forms. Perhaps within the present-day songs and stories of the descendants of the natives of Death Valley there is a similarly hidden map of ancient waterholes and game routes, burial grounds and food stores. Unlike the Greeks, however, who recorded virtually every bit of scenery in the stories of their gods, goddesses, and heroes, the tribes of Death Valley just didn't have the foresight to write it all down.

If you're looking for the desert, there are many places to go. But if you want the Desert with all its emblematic meaning, you have to travel to Death Valley. No one today comes here to make a fortune. But the contrast between its landscape and its pockets of "civilized" comfort offers some sense of adventure and daring, in the face of either nature or the mythic human past. The edge of danger hangs heavily here, despite the domesticating presence of the National Park Service and Cal-Trans signs about loose gravel and how many hours you have to wait to get into Scotty's Castle. A few days before I arrived one October a mere two-tenths of an inch of rain was enough to close out the roads to Scotty's Castle and to Badwater. A few weeks later, a virtually unprecedented sixty-one-hundredths of an inch knocked out virtually everything.

As I drove up the Panamint Valley that fall, I thought about how much the car had helped undermine the total otherness of Death Valley. But when a wagon-train trip of some weeks is reduced to a car ride of a few hours, more modern sorts of isolation, different styles of danger, seep in. My car radio had long since been unable to find anything on AM or FM. The digital numbers went round and round like a wagon train looking for water. A few days later, I walked through the empty Oasis Lounge of the Furnace Creek Inn. Mounted on the wall was a television set on a technological quest as fruitless as my radio's: trying vainly to resolve some human image, only to fall back into patterns of wavy lines that resembled the still-visible mule-team tracks that groove the canyons and the salt beds.

More mobile nature also makes itself known. On the way to Dante's View one evening, I narrowly avoided a few tarantulas crossing the road. The ranger at the museum later told me they were part of the annual migration—the females leave and the males follow; he even had one in a plastic bottle behind the counter to look at close up. It was just another example of the paradoxical purity that Park Service domestication has achieved. There's little here of the Mad-Max debris found in most deserts that civilization has entered. Without one bullet-riddled road sign, most of Death Valley remains close to a nonhuman or at least a precivilized past. The veneer of civilization—of comfortable beds and filling meals—just barely seems to hold off the eruptions still close to the surface: the Ubehebe volcano, the rocks moved by the wind at the Race Course, the swirling dunes, the mudpie hills around Zabriskie Point. They are all reminders of the precariousness of human building on the land, the lack of anything permanent in that space between the minute and the enormous we usually inhabit.

This uncertain edge between civilization and desolation is sharpest at the Furnace Creek Inn, where rooms now go for $165 a night and the food is "continental." The Inn (the word "furnace" refers to a primitive silver-mining operation, not a tribute to the heat) was built by the Union Pacific Railroad in the twenties to capitalize on the delicious contrast between a luxurious present and a devilish past. No doubt: there's still something about a full-course dinner, complete with wine steward and dress code, that effectively summons up gloomy legions of starving forty-niners pressing their noses against the window or perhaps just quietly singing "My Darling Clementine." Just a short walk outside the Inn—200 yards from the swimming pool, less from the tennis courts—stands a bronze marker commemorating the day in 1849 when the Jayhawkers brought their wagons down the Furnace Creek Wash into the Valley.

Ready for a hardy camp-out the night before, I discovered that I'd forgotten to bring a ground pad and had the wrong replacement mantles for my lantern. In the morning, equipped with a set of bruised hipbones and an attack of reading withdrawal, I decided that the price of a room at the Inn was fair enough for the privilege of conquering nature—at least for a night. Like the tourists of the twenties, who were lured by the idea of going to Hell to live in luxury, I wanted to sample the contrast. At the Inn there would be air conditioning to cool me, classico-elevator music to soothe me, and even golden bathroom fixtures.

For the traveler fresh from *nouvelle* Los Angeles or even the fastfood interstates, the cushioned adventure of Death Valley today seems to have a lot to do with eating large quantities of meat. Along with the C&W music on the loudspeaker, the big meals transport you back to the days of physical hardship when you had to eat a lot to survive. The first day I was there, camping out in the Furnace Creek Camp Ground, I had a cafeteria dinner of barbecued chicken, brussels sprouts, and mashed potatoes. I could have had barbecued ribs, kielbasa, brisket, or (the only concession to the low-cholesterol wimp) baked cod. If I had wanted to spend more, I could have gone to the Steak House next door, where a Japanese translation of the menu is also available.

Meals at the Inn were just as substantial, but they had a Mission-style graciousness — heavy furniture, elaborate settings, lace coverings atop deep orange-red tablecloths. Over the fireplace glowered portraits of Fred Harvey, the patron saint of frontier room-and-board entrepreneurs, and William Marion "Borax" Smith, the man who finally made money from Death Valley. I wondered if anyone actually called him "Borax" to his face, or was it just another one of those newspaper inventions? The menu stressed the "timelessness" and "leisurely" quality of life here, first promoted by Union Pacific and Santa Fe package tours along the general lines of "Vacation in luxurious comfort where others have died of hunger, thirst, and exposure." At dinner, I trudged through a hearty stewlike minestrone and then attacked a pair of smoked trout, as leathery as beef jerky from a miner's pack.

There weren't many other people in the dining room at this odd time of year, and so I spent time making up stories about their relationships. The dark-haired young man squinting through his glasses at the next table seemed to have some trouble with his knife and fork, while the bland-faced and heavyset blonde sitting next to him spoke only to point out particularly delicious morsels on his plate. He had the hunched vulture look of someone who had been nearsighted since childhood. I decided that he was a rich semiparalytic who needed the desert air and she was his devoted nurse. Neither said a word during the entire dinner except to chomp and point. Then, after a rerun of the elaborate dessert cart, they abruptly stood up and walked off arm in arm without the hint of disability — just another married couple with nothing to say to each other. Much louder was a table of five: an older man and woman clearly married, a younger woman and two young daughters. Where was the husband? Was this the daughter-in-law, genially taken on an early fall trip while her husband, their son, was on a business trip to Japan? Or was this their daughter, recently divorced from their despicable son-in-law, who needed the comfort of family in the midst of her woe? But she didn't look like she was enjoying herself very much. There was a hint of expectation in the bare arms and scoop neck of her blue-green print dress. While her father (so I had decided) discussed with the waiter the intricate matter of refilling the bread basket, she gazed blankly out at the sunset until one of her children demanded her attention. After that, everyone sat dutifully, speaking in short sentences and cutting their food into precise pieces.

After dessert, I looked unsuccessfully at the stars with a handy Sky Calendar supplied by the desk, and then went back to my room. The night was breezy but warm. Poised uncertainly between the benefits of fan, air conditioner and comforter, I thought about the lure of traveling in comfort to uncomfortable, even unlivable, places. Travel seems to have two modes: the urge for strangeness and the urge for familiarity, neatly synthesized in the chain restaurant that allows you to transport your taste buds and stomach just around the corner from home, no matter where your body happens to be. Then there's the way travel allows you to shed your usual social identity and for a week or two become one of the pampered and privileged, or perhaps the rugged and adventurous — depending on your taste. Thanks to the train and the car, twentieth-century Death Valley makes all these choices stark and simple. Sleep on the ground for $5 a night in the campground; sleep in a bunk or cot for $45 at the Ranch complete with C&W and wood veneer; sleep in a double bed with as many pillows as you'd like for $165 at the Inn. Eat freeze-dried chicken tetrazzini from the sports store; eat brisket with a side of beans at the Ranch; eat cream puffs and drink Cold Duck at the Inn. The landscape promises nothing, and so any menu could apply.

It's hard to stay in Death Valley any length of time without seeing it as a monument to false dreams. Anyone can sell Eden, but the proper selling of Hell requires a little more imagination. The next day I descended along terraced walkways between date palms that marched resolutely toward the Inn pool to the sound of constantly running water. Water is of course the greatest luxury in the desert, and the innumerable green road signs announcing SEA LEVEL never let you forget what the literary critics would call its "structuring absence." There are actually two swimming pools in Death Valley, both at Furnace Creek. The pool at the Ranch is usually crowded with campers. But this October the Inn had opened for the winter season only a week before I arrived. The next day the pool area was virtually empty, perfect for dreams of grandeur. No one else was there except the tennis pro, until the young mother of the night before and her two children appeared. They splashed around while she read a magazine. When I let my imagination wander a bit — an easy thing to do in Death Valley — I could have been in a personal San Simeon. With the splash and trickle and gush of endless water around me, I lay in a deck chair and tried to feel deprived because the snack-and-drink service wouldn't open for another week. But I consoled myself by thinking that in a place famous for blinding heat and bleached bones, you don't actually have to indulge all the available amenities to assume their sacramental power. It's probably cheaper not to. In the economy of the desert, everything gets re-used: mines are reopened; buildings are dragged from one year's ghost town to next year's boom, and even the Furnace Creek Ranch was built from the houses used by the men who built the Inn. Amid all this human reshuffling and recycling, I wondered, not for the first time, where was Death Valley itself?

Crucial to the selling of Death Valley was, of course, its name. Hollywood didn't invent the false-fronted street. That's the way most Western towns really were. If a bunch of forty-niners heading for the Mother Lode hadn't argued with their guide over the best route, Death Valley might never have become the media star it is today. Only one person from that fabled group actually died there, but, as Jimmy Stewart says in *The Man Who Shot Liberty Valance,* when the facts and the legend conflict, print the legend.

And so I couldn't resist a final trip to the Death Valley Museum. When, I asked the ranger on duty, was the last time anyone actually died in Death Valley? Well, she said, there was a swimming-pool drowning not too long ago. No, I said, that's not what I mean. When was the last time someone died because of the Valley itself? The ranger looked more sober than usual. You know, she said, a number of people come out here to commit suicide. They just put on a backpack as if they're going for a hike into the hills. But they don't take along any food or water, and after a while they die.

The lure of imposing one's own rhythms, the desire to make one's own sense of things, is hard to resist, especially at the end. This last story with its solitary deaths brought back the sense of both tenderness and danger in the landscape. As spartan camper and coddled guest, I had felt equally out of place. But now I realized what I shared with the people sitting down to multicourse dinners at the Inn as well as with the RV nomads firing up their Colemans in the campground. We had all come to see the place whose name summoned up the end of things. But we also assumed that when the adventure was over, we would survive, tourists of the edge, ready to tell our tale to family and friends or whoever was still left to listen.

◊ LAWRENCE FERLINGHETTI ◊

A Report on a Happening in North Beach San Francisco

When the lovely bride and groom came out onto the grand front steps of the Catholic church of Saint Peter & Paul at 4:32 in the afternoon a knot of natives was waiting at the bottom of the steps including a bunch of bridesmaids and family friends all of whom were holding onto the straight strings of bright green balloons which were the exact same green as the bridesmaids' dresses And the bride was holding onto a pure white balloon which was naturally the same as her wedding gown and the groom was holding a black balloon that matched his black tailcoat And the newlyweds proceeded to knot the strings of their two balloons together and then with a kind of a whoop let them soar away while at the same instant all the people holding green balloons let theirs go with a little cheer And the beatific bride and her handsome groom laughed and waved as they descended toward the others with never a look up at the balloons that were zooming straight up into blue sky and becoming smaller and smaller every instant while the newlyweds gaily climbed onto the waiting imitation San Francisco Cable Car upon which the bridesmaids were already perched and nobody casting even a glance at the flying balloons that now seemed to be heading South over downtown San Francisco with the black and white balloons keeping close together on their tether while the green balloons started spreading out all over And the groom and bride took their special seats at the front of the cable car which wasn't a real cable car at all since it had rubber wheels not attached to any cable which would have restricted its destiny And the happy couple were still waving and laughing and kissing each

◊ *Lawrence Ferlinghetti is editor and publisher of* City Lights Books *in San Francisco. His most recent novel is* Love in the Days of Rage *(Dutton).*

other and then ringing and ringing the cable car bell while the balloons that nobody looked at were now at least a couple of miles high in the distant sky that now seemed to be growing darker and darker with huge banks of cirrus clouds to the West toward which the tiny balloons now turned like a flock of birds winging seaward with two of them still close together with the others strung out further and further so that they began to look like lost sheep in an alpine landscape of towering white mountains While the cable car of a sudden started up with a great clanging of its bell as everyone cheered and waved without ever a look at the disappearing balloons of their lives so far away now that they looked like very distant mountain climbers scaling the walls of great glaciers in the final working out of their separate fates except for the two climbers still roped together As the cable car zoomed off Westward on Filbert Street and on toward Russian Hill over which in farthest sky still could be seen the tiny black dots of the climbers going higher and higher and disappearing into their destinies in which even the two roped together would in the normal course of life lose their breath and shrivel away and fall to earth out of air

◊ LINDSEY SHERE ◊

Violet Candies

Gardening and cooking are two of my greatest pleasures; I love to use herbs and flowers from the garden in my cooking. I remember my Italian-born Aunt Victoria's zucchini blossom fritters. Later, I discovered that nasturtium blossoms added a peppery accent to a tossed salad. When I began making desserts, it was only natural to use flowers and herbs for flavoring.

At the restaurant we begin in late winter with the first violets. Their perfume brings the promise of spring to desserts. We use fresh violets to garnish citrus sherbets or we make candies with them. By late January or early February the pink flowering plums are in full bloom and the first flower-scented ice creams are being made. The acacias and mimosas quickly follow with their sprays of tiny yellow or white blossoms against gray-green ferny foliage; when they burst into flower, it is time to make crepes with mimosa blossom ice cream and buttered honey. By March we are cooking with scented geraniums, and looking forward to the first roses and jasmine blossoms in April and May. When the first berries arrive, we take our fill of them in tarts and shortcakes and ice creams; but then we begin making rose geranium custards to accompany them. By this time the summer fruits are ripening and we use herbs to accent them. Angelica, basil, cinnamon basil, lavender, and lemon thyme take their places as the seasons advance, to flavor custards and poaching syrups.

I use the petals of old rose varieties to flavor ice creams and to candy for garnishes — they generally have a stronger scent than the

◊ *Lindsey Shere has been the one-and-only pastry chef at Berkeley's Chez Panisse for its first 20 years. This excerpt appeared in* Chez Panisse Desserts, © *1985 Lindsey Remolif Shere, published by Random House.*

newer hybrids. In my front yard I have a hedge of rugosas—a very hardy rose that has a particularly powerful perfume. I like to candy the petals of my climbing Joseph's Coat because they are delicate rather than fleshy, and their variegated sunset colors shine through the sugar beautifully to mark the dinner's and the day's end. Since desserts are made in large quantities at the restaurant and we can get only limited amounts of flowers, we usually make infusions to flavor custards and ice creams. At home you can be more lavish and try many different kinds of flowers—almond-scented broom, clove-scented carnations, hawthorn, orange and lemon blossoms, elder-flowers and their ripe berries, lilacs, orchids, lily of the valley, peach blossoms . . .

Angelica is one of the most versatile herbs. The leaves and stems can be used to flavor custards and the stems can be candied to flavor cakes and cookies, or for a garnish. Commercial candied angelica bears little resemblance in flavor to what can be made at home. The combined herb and spice scent of cinnamon basil suits ripe peaches, pears, and figs beautifully. Rose geranium is meant for ripe blackber-ries or boysenberries—or simply bake the leaves into a pound cake. There are dozens of other scented geraniums to experiment with—some recall citrus fruits, others apples or spices.

Do take care that the plant you decide to use is edible. Sometimes the flowers are edible though other parts of the plant are not. And be sure the plants have not been treated with any poisonous insecticide. Be adventurous—the herbs and flowers around you offer unlimited possibilities.

◇ VIOLET CANDIES ◇

For 2 dozen candies:
24 fresh sweet aromatic violets
Paper bonbon cases measuring 1 inch in diameter
Optional: Tiny pieces of gold leaf
2 ounces white chocolate

Take the violets off their stems and arrange them in the bottoms of the paper cases, face down—if you double the cases they will hold their shape better. Or use chocolate molds if you have them. Tear off little pieces of gold leaf and put them around the violets in the bottoms of the cases or molds. I find three pieces is quite enough.

The gold leaf will tend either to stick to you or to fly away, but if you just tear off pieces with tweezers and drop them directly into the cases, you should have no trouble.

Chop the chocolate into small pieces, put it in the top of a small double boiler, and set it over warm water. Stir the chocolate constantly and don't let it get more than slightly warm. As soon as the melted chocolate is smooth, drop it by half-spoonfuls into the cases. You may also put the chocolate into a pastry bag with a plain round tip and pipe it into the cases. There should be just enough to make a layer 3/16-inch to 1/4-inch thick. If necessary, use a toothpick or the tip of a knife to swirl the chocolate gently into an even layer, taking care not to disturb the violet. There should be just enough chocolate to barely cover the flower. Set the cases in a cool place to firm, or put in the refrigerator or freezer for just a few minutes. Unmold by gently pulling the sides away from the chocolate and turn the violet side up.

Serve within a few hours or the violet will begin to wilt since it is not completely covered with the chocolate. Serve after dinner (but before coffee), or any time you would like a beautiful, simple candy with an unusual taste.

◇ ABOUT THE EDITOR ◇

Photo: Heather Hendrickson

Howard Junker grew up in Chappaqua, New York, the country home of Horace Greeley, who supposedly said, "Go West, young man." Junker graduated from Canterbury School and Amherst College, and, after a stint writing reviews at *Newsweek,* went west to Stanford on a journalism fellowship. He has lived in San Francisco for the past twenty years, working as a television producer, a carpenter (Local 22), a junior high school teacher, a speechwriter, and an art museum public affairs coordinator. He founded *ZYZZYVA* in 1985. He has contributed to many magazines, including *Architectural Digest, Art in America, Esquire, Harper's Bazaar, The Nation,* and *Rolling Stone.*